Bloom's Modern Critical Views

Bloom's Modern Critical Views

Alexander
  Solzhenitsyn
John Steinbeck
Jonathan Swift
Amy Tan
Alfred, Lord Tennyson
Henry David Thoreau
J.R.R. Tolkien
Leo Tolstoy
Ivan Turgenev

Mark Twain
John Updike
Kurt Vonnegut
Derek Walcott
Alice Walker
Robert Penn Warren
H.G. Wells
Eudora Welty
Edith Wharton
Walt Whitman

Oscar Wilde
Tennessee Williams
Tom Wolfe
Virginia Woolf
William Wordsworth
Jay Wright
Richard Wright
William Butler Yeats
Émile Zola

Bloom's Modern Critical Views

JAMES BALDWIN
Updated Edition

Edited and with an introduction by
Harold Bloom
Sterling Professor of the Humanities
Yale University

CHELSEA HOUSE
P U B L I S H E R S
An imprint of Infobase Publishing

Bloom's Modern Critical Views: James Baldwin—Updated Edition

Copyright ©2007 Infobase Publishing

Introduction © 2007 by Harold Bloom

All rights reserved. No part of this publication may be reproduced or utilized in any form or by any means, electronic or mechanical, including photocopying, recording, or by any information storage or retrieval systems, without permission in writing from the publisher. For more information contact:

Bloom's Literary Criticism
An imprint of Infobase Publishing
132 West 31st Street
New York NY 10001

ISBN-10: 0-7910-9365-4
ISBN-13: 978-0-7910-9365-8

Library of Congress Cataloging-in-Publication Data
James Baldwin / Harold Bloom, editor. — Updated ed.
    p. cm. — (Bloom's modern critical views)
  Includes bibliographical references and index.
  ISBN 0-7910-9365-4 (hardcover)
  1. Baldwin, James, 1924-1987—Criticism and interpretation. I. Bloom, Harold.
II. Title. III. Series.
  PS3552.A45Z7235 2007
  818'.5409--dc22   2006031146

Bloom's Literary Criticism books are available at special discounts when purchased in bulk quantities for businesses, associations, institutions, or sales promotions. Please call our Special Sales Department in New York at (212) 967-8800 or (800) 322-8755.

You can find Bloom's Literary Criticism on the World Wide Web at
http://www.chelseahouse.com

Contributing Editor: Gabriel Welsch

Cover designed by Takeshi Takahashi

Cover photo © Getty Images Entertainment / Getty Images

Printed in the United States of America

Bang EJB 10 9 8 7 6 5 4 3 2 1

This book is printed on acid-free paper.

All links and web addresses were checked and verified to be correct at the time of publication. Because of the dynamic nature of the web, some addresses and links may have changed since publication and may no longer be valid.

Contents

Editor's Note

My introduction centers upon James Baldwin's identification of his prophetic stance with Jeremiah's.

The distinguished African-American scholar, Henry Louis Gates, Jr., poignantly traces Baldwin's abdication of a highly individual skepticism in over-reaction to the notorious onslaught of Eldridge Cleaver's ostensibly more revolutionary critique.

Baldwin's career as an essayist is chronicled by Nick Aaron Ford, after which Baldwin's first novel, *Go Tell It on the Mountain*, receives two antithetical interpretations by Shirley S. Allen and by Horace Porter, who then also reflects upon the title-essay of *Notes of a Native Son*.

The homoerotic themes of *Giovanni's Room* and *Another Country* are commended for their honesty in rhetoric by Carolyn Wedin Sylvander, while Trudier Harris emphasizes instead the female dilemma as rendered by *Another Country*.

The late critic Irving Howe reviews *Nobody Knows My Name* with warm approval, rightly praising Baldwin's achievement as a personal essayist, after which Julius Lester offers a more dialectical estimate of *The Price of the Ticket*, observing a moral and political decline in the later essays.

Baldwin's pilgrimage to Africa is seen by his biographer David Leeming as the triumph of *The Fire Next Time*, which chronicles the writer's full emergence into prophetic status.

The short story, "Sonny's Blues," receives complementary analyses by John M. Reilly and Richard N. Albert, while the image of fire in *Going to Meet the Man* is investigated by Arthenia Bates Millican.

No Name in the Street is reviewed by Mel Watkins, who defends the essayist's ability to dramatize his moral stance.

The later novel, *Tell Me How Long the Train's Been Gone*, is praised by Lynn Orilla Scott for its courageous vision of a mature homosexuality, after which Mario Puzo sees in the book only a soap opera.

HAROLD BLOOM

Introduction

I

Whatever the ultimate canonical judgment upon James Baldwin's fiction may prove to be, his nonfictional work clearly has permanent status in American literature. Baldwin seems to me to be among the most considerable moral essayists in the United States, and is comparable to George Orwell as a prose Protestant in stance. The evangelical heritage never has abandoned the author of *Go Tell It on the Mountain*, and Baldwin, like so many American essayists since Emerson, possesses the fervor of a preacher. Unlike Emerson, Baldwin lacks the luxury of detachment, since he speaks, not for a displaced Yankee majority, but for a sexual minority within a racial minority, indeed for an aesthetic minority among black homosexuals.

Ultimately, Baldwin's dilemma as a writer compelled to address social torments and injustices is that he is a minority of one, a solitary voice breaking forth against himself (and all others) from within himself. Like Carlyle (and a single aspect of the perspectivizing Nietzsche), Baldwin is of the authentic lineage of Jeremiah, most inward of prophets. What Baldwin opposes is what might be called, in Jeremiah's language, the injustice of outwardness, which means that Baldwin always must protest, even in the rather unlikely event that his country ever were to turn from selfishness and cruelty to justice and compassion in confronting its underclass of the exploited poor, whether blacks, Hispanics, or others cast out by the Reagan Revolution.

It seems accurate to observe that we remember Jeremiah, unlike Amos or Micah, for his individuation of his own suffering, rather than for his social vision, such as it was. Baldwin might prefer to have been an Amos or a Micah, forerunners of Isaiah, rather than a Jeremiah, but like Jeremiah he is vivid as a rhetorician of his own psychic anguish and perplexities, and most memorable as a visionary of a certain involuntary isolation, an election that requires a dreadful cost of confirmation. As Baldwin puts it, the price of the ticket is to accept the real reasons for the human journey:

> The price the white American paid for his ticket was to become white—: and, in the main, nothing more than that, or, as he was to insist, nothing less. This incredibly limited not to say dimwitted ambition has choked many a human being to death here: and this, I contend, is because the white American has never accepted the real reasons for his journey. I know very well that my ancestors had no desire to come to this place: but neither did the ancestors of the people who became white and who require of my captivity a song. They require of me a song less to celebrate my captivity than to justify their own.

The Biblical text that Baldwin alludes to here, Psalm 137, does begin with the song of the exiles from Zion ("and they that wasted us required of us mirth") but ends with a ferocious prophecy against the wasters, ourselves. No writer—black or white—warns us so urgently of "the fire next time" as Baldwin and Jeremiah do, but I hear always in both prophets the terrible pathos of origins:

> Then the word of the Lord came unto me, saying,
> Before I formed thee in the belly I knew thee; and before thou camest forth out of the womb I sanctified thee, and I ordained thee a prophet unto the nations.
> Then said I, Ah, Lord God! behold, I cannot speak: for I am a child.

> *We*: my family, the living and the dead, and the children coming along behind us. This was a complex matter, for I was not living with my family in Harlem, after all, but "down-town," in the "white world," in alien and mainly hostile territory. On the other hand, for me, then, Harlem was almost as alien and in a yet more

intimidating way and risked being equally hostile, although for very different reasons. This truth cost me something in guilt and confusion, but it was the truth. It had something to do with my being the son of an evangelist and having been a child evangelist, but this is not all there was to it—that is, guilt is not all there was to it.

The fact that this particular child had been born when and where he was born had dictated certain expectations. The child does not really know what these expectations are—does not know how real they are—until he begins to fail, challenge, or defeat them. When it was clear, for example, that the pulpit, where I had made so promising a beginning, would not be my career, it was hoped that I would go on to college. This was never a very realistic hope and—perhaps because I knew this—I don't seem to have felt very strongly about it. In any case, this hope was dashed by the death of my father.

Once I had left the pulpit, I had abandoned or betrayed my role in the community—indeed, my departure from the pulpit and my leaving home were almost simultaneous. (I had abandoned the ministry in order not to betray myself by betraying the ministry.)

Reluctant prophets are in the position of Jonah; they provide texts for the Day of Atonement. Baldwin is always at work reexamining everything, doing his first works over; as he says: "Sing or shout or testify or keep it to yourself: but *know whence you came.*" We came crying hither because we came to this great stage of fools, but Baldwin, like Jeremiah and unlike Shakespeare, demands a theology of origins. He finds it in self-hatred, which he rightly insists is universal, though he seems to reject or just not be interested in the Freudian account of our moral masochism, our need for punishment. The evangelical sense of conscious sin remains strong in Baldwin. Yet, as a moral essayist, he is post-Christian, and persuades us that his prophetic stance is not so much religious as aesthetic. A kind of aesthetic of the moral life governs his vision, even in the turbulence of *The Fire Next Time* and *No Name in the Street*, and helps make them his finest achievements so far.

II

The center of Baldwin's prophecy can be located in one long, powerful paragraph of *The Fire Next Time*:

"The white man's Heaven," sings a Black Muslim minister, "is the black man's Hell." One may object—possibly—that this puts the matter somewhat too simply, but the song is true, and it has been true for as long as white men have ruled the world. The Africans put it another way: When the white man came to Africa, the white man had the Bible and the African had the land, but now it is the white man who is being, reluctantly and bloodily, separated from the land, and the African who is still attempting to digest or to vomit up the Bible. The struggle, therefore, that now begins in the world is extremely complex, involving the historical role of Christianity in the realm of power—that is, politics—and in the realm of morals. In the realm of power, Christianity has operated with an unmitigated arrogance and cruelty—necessarily, since a religion ordinarily imposes on those who have discovered the true faith, the spiritual duty of liberating the infidels. This particular true faith, moreover, is more deeply concerned about the soul than it is about the body, to which fact the flesh (and the corpses) of countless infidels bears witness. It goes without saying, then, that whoever questions the authority of the true faith also contests the right of the nations that hold this faith to rule over him—contests, in short, their title to his land. The spreading of the Gospel, regardless of the motives or the integrity or the heroism of some of the missionaries, was an absolutely indispensable justification for the planting of the flag. Priests and nuns and schoolteachers helped to protect and sanctify the power that was so ruthlessly being used by people who were indeed seeking a city, but not one in the heavens, and one to be made, very definitely, by captive hands. The Christian church itself— again, as distinguished from some of its ministers—sanctified and rejoiced in the conquests of the flag, and encouraged, if it did not formulate, the belief that conquest, with the resulting relative well-being of the Western populations, was proof of the favor of God. God had come a long way from the desert—but then so had Allah, though in a very different direction. God, going north, and rising on the wings of power, had become white, and Allah, out of power, and on the dark side of Heaven, had become—for all practical purposes, anyway—black. Thus, in the realm of morals the role of Christianity has been, at best, ambivalent. Even leaving out of account the remarkable arrogance that assumed that the ways and morals of others were inferior to those of Christians, and that they therefore had every right, and could use any means, to change them, the collision between cultures—and the schizophrenia in the mind of Christendom—had rendered the domain of morals as chartless as the sea once was, and as treacherous as the sea still is. It is not too much to say that whoever wishes to become a truly moral human being (and let us not ask whether or not this is possible; I think we must *believe* that it is possible) must first divorce himself from all the prohibitions, crimes, and hypocrisies of the Christian church. If the concept of God has any validity or any use, it can only be to make us larger, freer, and more loving. If God cannot do this, then it is time we got rid of Him.

This superb instance of Baldwin's stance and style as a moral essayist depends for its rhetorical power upon a judicious blend of excess and restraint. Its crucial sentence achieves prophetic authority:

> It is not too much to say that whoever wishes to become a truly moral human being (and let us not ask whether or not this is possible; I think we must *believe* that it is possible) must first divorce himself from all the prohibitions, crimes, and hypocrisies of the Christian church.

The parenthesis, nobly skeptical, is the trope of a master rhetorician, and placing "believe" in italics nicely puts into question the problematics of faith. "Divorce," denounced by St. Paul as having been introduced because of our hardness of hearts, acquires the antithetical aura of the Church itself, while Christian prohibitions are assimilated (rather wickedly) to Christian crimes and hypocrisies. This is, rhetorically considered, good, unclean fun, but the burden is savage, and steeped in moral high seriousness. The strength of *The Fire Next Time* comes to rest in its final paragraph, with the interplay between two italicized rhetorical questions, an interplay kindled when *"then"* is added to the second question:

> When I was very young, and was dealing with my buddies in those wine- and urine-stained hallways, something in me wondered, *What will happen to all that beauty?* For black people, though I am aware that some of us, black and white, do not know it yet, are very beautiful. And when I sat at Elijah's table and watched the baby, the women, and the men, and we talked about God's—or Allah's—vengeance, I wondered, when that vengeance was achieved, *What will happen to all that beauty then?*

I could also see that the intransigence and ignorance of the white world might make that vengeance inevitable—a vengeance that does not really depend on, and cannot really be executed by, any person or organization, and that cannot be prevented by any police force or army: historical vengeance, a cosmic vengeance, based on the law that we recognize when we say, "Whatever goes up must come down." And here we are, at the center of the arc, trapped in the gaudiest, most valuable, and most improbable water wheel the world has ever seen. Everything now, we must assume, is in our hands; we have no right to assume otherwise. If we—and now I mean the relatively conscious whites and the relatively conscious blacks, who must, like lovers, insist on, or create, the consciousness of the others—do not falter in our duty now, we may be able, handful that we are, to end the racial nightmare, and achieve our country, and change the history of the world. If we do not now dare everything, the fulfillment of that prophecy, recreated from the Bible in song by a slave, is upon us: "God gave Noah the rainbow sign, No more water, the fire next time!"

The shrewd rhetorical movement here is from the waterwheel to the ambivalent divine promise of no second flood, the promise of covenant with its dialectical countersong of the conflagration ensuing from our violation of covenant. That vision of impending fire re-illuminates the poignant question: "*What will happen to all that beauty then?*" All that beauty that is in jeopardy transcends even the beauty of black people, and extends to everything human, and to bird, beast, and flower.

No Name in the Street takes its fierce title from Job 18:16–19, where it is spoken to Job by Bildad the Shuhite, concerning the fate of the wicked:

His roots shall be dried up beneath, and above shall his branch be cut off.

His remembrance shall perish from the earth, and he shall have no name in the street.

He shall be driven from light into darkness, and chased out of the world.

He shall neither have son nor nephew among his people, nor any remaining in his dwellings.

They that come after him shall be astonished at his day, as they that went before were affrighted.

I have to admit, having just read (and re-read) my way through the 690 pages of *The Price of the Ticket*, that frequently I am tempted to reply to Baldwin with Job's response to Bildad:

> How long will ye vex my soul, and break me in pieces with words?
> These ten times have ye reproached me: ye are not ashamed that ye make yourselves strange to me. And be it indeed that I have erred, mine error remaineth with myself.
> If indeed ye will magnify yourselves against me, and plead against me my reproach.

Baldwin's rhetorical authority as prophet would be seriously impaired if he were merely a job's comforter, Bildad rather than Jeremiah. *No Name in the Street* cunningly evades the risk that Baldwin will magnify himself against the reader, partly by the book's adroitness at stationing the author himself in the vulnerable contexts of his own existence, both in New York and in Paris. By not allowing himself (or his readers) to forget how perpetually a black homosexual aesthete and moralist, writer and preacher, must fight for his life, Baldwin earns the pathos of the prophetic predicament:

> I made such motions as I could to understand what was happening, and to keep myself afloat. But I had been away too long. It was not only that I could not readjust myself to life in New York—it was also that I would not: I was never going to be anybody's nigger again. But I was now to discover that the world has more than one way of keeping you a nigger, has evolved more than one way of skinning the cat; if the hand slips here, it tightens there, and now I was offered, gracefully indeed: membership in the club. I had lunch at some elegant bistros, dinner at some exclusive clubs. I tried to be understanding about my countrymen's concern for difficult me, and unruly mine—and I really was trying to be understanding, though not without some bewilderment, and, eventually, some malice. I began to be profoundly uncomfortable. It was a strange kind of discomfort, a terrified apprehension that I had lost my bearings. I did not altogether understand what I was hearing. I did not trust what I heard myself saying. In very little that I heard did I hear anything that reflected anything which I knew, or had endured, of life. My mother and my father, my brothers and my sisters were not present at the tables at which I

sat down, and no one in the company had ever heard of them. My own beginnings, or instincts, began to shift as nervously as the cigarette smoke that wavered around my head. I was not trying to hold on to my wretchedness. On the contrary, if my poverty was coming, at last, to an end, so much the better, and it wasn't happening a moment too soon—and yet, I felt an increasing chill, as though the rest of my life would have to be lived in silence.

The discomfort of having lost bearings is itself a prophetic trope, and comes to its fruition in the book's searing final paragraph:

To be an Afro-American, or an American black, is to be in the situation, intolerably exaggerated, of all those who have ever found themselves part of a civilization which they could in no wise honorably defend—which they were compelled, indeed, endlessly to attack and condemn—and who yet spoke out of the most passionate love, hoping to make the kingdom new, to make it honorable and worthy of life. Whoever is part of whatever civilization helplessly loves some aspects of it, and some of the people in it. A person does not lightly elect to oppose his society. One would much rather be at home among one's compatriots than be mocked and detested by them. And there is a level on which the mockery of the people, even their hatred, is moving because it is so blind: it is terrible to watch people cling to their captivity and insist on their own destruction. I think black people have always felt this about America, and Americans, and have always seen, spinning above the thoughtless American head, the shape of the wrath to come.

Not to be at home among one's compatriots is to avoid the catastrophe of being at ease in the new Zion that is America. A reader, however moved by Baldwin's rhetorical authority, can be disturbed here by the implication that all blacks are prophets, at least in our society. Would to God indeed that all the Lord's people were prophets, but they are not, and cannot be. I recall, fourteen years after the original publication of *No Name in the Street*, being confronted by polls indicating that the President of the United States, enjoying a sixty-eight percent approval rating among all his constituents, also possessed a rather surprising fifty percent endorsement from my black fellow citizens. Whatever the President's place in history may prove to be, time has darkened Baldwin's temporal prophecy that his own people could remain an undivided witness against our civilization.

III

Like every true prophet, Baldwin passionately would prefer the fate of Jonah to that of Jeremiah, but I do not doubt that his authentic descent from Jeremiah will continue to be valid past the end of his life (and mine). The final utterance in *The Price of the Ticket* seems to me Baldwin's most poignant, ever:

> Freaks are called freaks and are treated as they are treated—in the main, abominably—because they are human beings who cause to echo, deep within us, our most profound terrors and desires.
>
> Most of us, however, do not appear to be freaks—though we are rarely what we appear to be. We are, for the most part, visibly male or female, our social roles defined by our sexual equipment.
>
> But we are all androgynous, not only because we are all born of a woman impregnated by the seed of a man but because each of us, helplessly and forever, contains the other—male in female, female in male, white in black and black in white. We are a part of each other. Many of my countrymen appear to find this fact exceedingly inconvenient and even unfair, and so, very often, do I. But none of us can do anything about it.

Baldwin is most prophetic, and most persuasive, when his voice is as subdued as it is here. What gives the rhetorical effect of self-subdual is the precise use of plural pronouns throughout. Moving from his own predicament to the universal, the prophet achieves an effect directly counter to Jeremiah's pervasive trope of individualizing the prophetic alternative. The ultimate tribute that Baldwin has earned is his authentic share in Jeremiah's most terrible utterance:

> O Lord, thou has deceived me, and I was deceived: thou art stronger than I, and hast prevailed: I am in derision daily, every one mocketh me.
>
> For since I spake, I cried out, I cried violence and spoil; because the word of the Lord was made a reproach unto me, and a derision, daily.
>
> Then I said, I will not make mention of him, nor speak any more in his name. But his word was in mine heart as a burning fire shut up in my bones, and I was weary with forbearing, and I could not stay,

HENRY LOUIS GATES, JR.

The Fire Last Time

"I am *not* in paradise," James Baldwin assured readers of the *Black Scholar* in 1973. "It rains down here too." Maybe it did. But it seemed like paradise to me. In 1973 I was 22 years old, an eager young black American journalist doing a story for *Time*, visiting Baldwin at his home just outside the tiny, ancient walled village of St. Paul de Vence, nestled in the alpine foothills that rise from the Mediterranean Sea. The air carried the smells of wild thyme and pine and centuries-old olive trees. The light of the region, prized by painters and vacationers, at once intensifies and subdues the colors, so that the terra-cotta tile roofs of the buildings are by turns rosy pink, rust brown, or deep red.

Baldwin's house was situated among shoulder-high rosemary hedges, grape arbors, acres of peach and almond orchards, and fields of wild asparagus and strawberries; it had been built in the eighteenth century and retained its frescoed walls and rough-hewn beams. And yet he seemed to have made of it his own Greenwich Village café. Always there were guests, an entourage of friends and hangers-on, and always there was drinking and conviviality. The grape arbors sheltered tables, and it was under one such grape arbor, at one of the long harvest tables, that we dined. The line from the old gospel song, a line that Baldwin had quoted toward the end of his then latest novel, suggested itself: "I'm going to feast at the welcome table." And we did—

From *The New Republic*, Vol. 206, No. 22, June 1, 1992, pp. 37–43. © 1992 by *The New Republic*.

Baldwin, and Josephine Baker, well into her 60s but still with a lean dancer's body and the smooth skin that the French called "café-au-lait," and Cecil Brown, author of *The Life and Lovers of Mister Jiveass Nigger* and one of the great hopes of black fiction, my fiancée, Sharon Adams, and I.

At that long welcome table under the arbor, the wine flowed, food was served and taken away, and Baldwin and Baker traded stories, gossiped about everyone they knew and many people they didn't know, and remembered their lives. They had both been hurt and disillusioned by the United States and had chosen to live in France. They never forgot or forgave. At the table that long, warm night they recollected the events that led to their decisions to leave their country of birth, and the consequences of those decisions: the difficulty of living away from home and family, of always feeling apart in their chosen homes; the pleasure of choosing a new life, the possibilities of the untried. A sense of nostalgia pervaded the evening. For all their misgivings, they shared a sense, curiously, of being on the winning side of history.

People said Baldwin was ugly; he himself said so. But he was not ugly to me. There are faces that we cannot see simply as faces because they are so familiar, so iconic, and his face was one of them. And as I sat there, in a growing haze of awe and alcohol, studying his lined visage, I realized that neither the Baldwin I was meeting—mischievous, alert, funny—nor the Baldwin I might come to know could ever mean as much to me as James Baldwin, my own personal oracle, the gimlet-eyed figure who stared at me out of a fuzzy dust jacket photograph when I was 14. For that was when I first met Baldwin, and discovered that black people, too, wrote books.

It was the summer of 1965, and I was attending an Episcopal church camp in eastern West Virginia, high in the Allegheny Mountains. This was no ordinary church camp. Our themes that year were "Is God dead?" and "Can you love two people at once?" (Episcopalians were never ones to let grass grow under their feet.) After a solid week of complete isolation, a delivery man, bringing milk and bread to the camp, told the head counselor that "all hell had broken loose in Los Angeles," and that the "colored people had gone crazy." Then he handed him a Sunday paper, screaming the news that Negroes were rioting in some place called Watts. I, for one, was bewildered. I didn't understand what a riot was. Were colored people being killed by white people, or were they killing white people? Watching myself being watched by all of the white campers—there were only three black kids among the hundreds of campers—I experienced that strange combination of power and powerlessness that you feel when the actions of another black person affect your own life, simply because both of you are black.

Sensing my mixture of pride and discomfiture, an Episcopal priest from New England handed me a book. *Notes of a Native Son*, it was called. Was this man the author, I wondered to myself, this man with a closely cropped "natural," brown skin, splayed nostrils, and wide lips, so very Negro, so comfortable to be so? This was the first time I had heard a voice capturing the terrible exhilaration and anxiety of being a person of African descent in this country. From the book's first few sentences, I was caught up thoroughly in the sensibility of another person, a black person. Coming from a tiny and segregated black community in a white village. I knew that "black culture" had a texture, a logic, of its own, *and* that it was inextricable from "white" culture. That was the paradox that Baldwin identified and negotiated, and that is why I say his prose shaped my identity as an Afro-American, as much by the questions he raised as by the answers he provided.

I could not put the book down. I raced through it, then others, filling my commonplace book with his marvelously long sentences that bristled with commas and qualifications. The biblical cadences spoke to me with a special immediacy, for I, too, was to be a minister, having been "saved" in a small evangelical church at the age of 12. (From this fate the Episcopalians—and also Baldwin—diverted me.) Eventually I began to imitate Baldwin's style of writing, using dependent clauses whenever and wherever I could. Consider a passage from *Nobody Knows My Name*:

> And a really cohesive society, one of the attributes, perhaps, of what is taken to be a "healthy" culture, has, generally, and I suspect, necessarily, a much lower level of tolerance for the maverick, the dissenter, the man who steals the fire, than have societies in which, the common ground of belief having all but vanished, each man, in awful and brutal isolation, is for himself, to flower or to perish.

There are sixteen commas in that sentence. And so in my essays at school I was busy trying to cram as many commas into my sentences as I could, until my high school English teacher forbade me.

Of course, I was not alone in my enthrallment. When Baldwin wrote *The Fire Next Time* in 1963, he was exalted as *the* voice of black America; and it was not long before he was spoken of as a contender for the Nobel Prize. ("Opportunity and duty are sometimes born together," he wrote later.) Perhaps not since Booker T. Washington had one man been taken to embody the voice of "the Negro." By the early '60s his authority seemed nearly unchallengeable. What did the Negro want? Ask James Baldwin.

The puzzle was that his arguments, richly nuanced and self-consciously ambivalent, were far too complex to serve straightforwardly political ends. Thus he would argue in *Notes of a Native Son* that the question of color, especially in this country, operates to hide the graver question of the self. That is precisely why what we like to call "the Negro problem" is so tenacious in American life, and so dangerous. But my own experience proves to me that the connection between American whites and blacks is far deeper and more passionate than any of us like to think.... The questions which one asks oneself begin, at last, to illuminate the world, and become one's key to the experience of others. One can only face in others what one can face in oneself. On this confrontation depends the measure of our wisdom and compassion. This energy is all that one finds in the rubble of vanished civilizations, and the only hope for ours.

One does not read such a passage without a double take. By proclaiming that the color question conceals the graver questions of the self, Baldwin leads you to expect a transcendence of the contingencies of race, in the name of a deeper artistic or psychological truth. But instead, with an abrupt swerve, he returns you precisely to those questions:

In America, the color of my skin had stood between myself and me; in Europe, that barrier was down. Nothing is more desirable than to be released from an affliction, but nothing is more frightening than to be divested of a crutch. It turned out that the question of who I was was not solved because I had removed myself from the social forces which menaced me—anyway, these forces had become interior, and I had dragged them across the ocean with me. The question of who I was had at last become a personal question, and the answer was to be found in me.

I think there is always something frightening about this realization. I know it frightened me.

Again, these words are easily misread. For Baldwin was proposing not that politics is merely a projection of private neuroses, but that our private neuroses are shaped by quite public ones. The retreat to subjectivity, the "graver questions of the self," would lead not to an escape from the "racial drama," but—and this was the alarming prospect that Baldwin wanted to announce—a rediscovery of it.

That traditional liberal dream of a non-racial self, unconstrained by epidermal contingencies, was hopefully entertained and at last, for him, reluctantly dismissed. "There are," he observed, few things on earth more attractive than the idea of the unspeakable liberty which is allowed the unredeemed. When, beneath the black mask, a human being begins to make himself felt one cannot escape a certain awful wonder as to what kind of human being it is. What one's imagination makes of other people is dictated, of course, by the laws of one's own personality and it is one of the ironies of black–white relations that, by means of what the white man imagines the black man to be, the black man is enabled to know who the white man is.

This is not a call for "racial understanding." On the contrary, we understand each other all too well, for we have invented one another, derived our identities from the ghostly projections of our alter egos. If Baldwin had a central political argument, it was that the destinies of black America and white were profoundly and irreversibly intertwined. Each created the other, each defined itself in relation to the other, each could destroy the other.

For Baldwin, America's "interracial drama" had "not only created a new black man, it has created a new white man, too." In that sense, he could argue, "The history of the American Negro problem is not merely shameful, it is also something of an achievement. For even when the worst has been said, it must also be added that the perpetual challenge posed by this problem was always, somehow, perpetually met." These were not words to speed along a cause. They certainly did not mesh with the rhetoric of self-affirmation that liberation movements, including those masquerading as a newly "Afrocentric" science of man, require. Yet couldn't his sense of the vagaries of identity serve the ends of a still broader, braver politics?

As an intellectual, Baldwin was at his best when he explored his own equivocal sympathies and clashing allegiances. He was here to "bear witness," he insisted, not to be a spokesman. And he was right to insist on the distinction. But who had time for such niceties? The spokesman role was assigned him inevitably. The result was to complicate further his curious position as an Afro-American intellectual. In those days, on the populist left, the favored model of the oppositional spokesman was what Gramsci called the "organic intellectual," who participated in, and was part of, the community, which he would not only analyze but also uplift. And yet Baldwin's basic conception of himself was formed by the older but still well-entrenched ideal of the alienated artist or intellectual, whose advanced sensibility entailed his estrangement from the very people he would represent.

Baldwin could dramatize the tension between these two models, especially in his fiction, but he was never to resolve it. A spokesman must have a firm grasp on his role and an unambiguous message to articulate. Baldwin had neither, and when this was discovered a few short years later, he was relieved of his duties, summarily retired, shunted aside as an elder statesman. Indeed, by the time I met him, on that magical afternoon in St. Paul de Vence, he had become (as my own editor subsequently admonished me) passé. Anyone who was aware of the ferment in black America was familiar with the attacks. And nothing ages a young Turk faster than still younger Turks; the cruel irony was that Baldwin may never have fully recovered from this demotion from a status that he had always disavowed.

If Baldwin had once served as a shadow delegate for black America in the congress of culture, his term had expired. Soldiers, not delegates, were what was wanted these days. "Pulling rank," Eldridge Cleaver wrote in his essay on Baldwin, "is a very dangerous business, especially when the troops have mutinied and the basis of one's authority, or rank, is devoid of that interdictive power and has become suspect." He found in Baldwin's work "the most grueling, agonizing, total hatred of the blacks, particularly of himself, and the most shameful, fanatical, fawning, sycophantic love of the whites that one can find in any black American writer of note in our time." According to Amiri Baraka, the new star of the Black Arts Movement, Baldwin was "Joan of Arc of the cocktail party." His "spavined whine and plea" was "sickening beyond belief." In the eyes of the young Ishmael Reed, he was "a hustler who comes on like Job."

Cleaver attacked Baldwin on more than racial grounds. For the heated new apostle of black machismo, Baldwin's sexuality, that is, his homosexuality, also represented treason: "Many Negro homosexuals, acquiescing in this racial death-wish, are outraged because in their sickness they are unable to have a baby by a white man." Baldwin was thus engaged in "a despicable underground guerrilla war, waged on paper, against black masculinity." Young militants referred to Baldwin, unsmilingly, as Martin Luther Queen. Baldwin, of course, was hardly a stranger to the sexual battlefield. "On every street corner," Baldwin would later recall of his early days in the Village, "I was called a faggot." What was different this time was a newly sexualized black nationalism that could stigmatize homosexuality as a capitulation to alien white norms, and in that way accredit homophobia as a progressive political act.

A new generation, so it seemed, was determined to define itself by everything Baldwin was not. By the late '60s Baldwin-bashing was almost a rite of initiation. And yet Baldwin would not return fire, at least not in public. He responded with a pose of wounded passivity. And then, with a kind of capitulation: the shift of political climate forced him to simplify his rhetoric or risk internal exile.

As his old admirers recognized, Baldwin was now chasing, with unseemly alacrity, after a new vanguard, one that esteemed rage, not compassion, as our noblest emotion. "It is not necessary for a black man to hate a white man, or to have particular feelings about him at all, in order to realize that he must kill him," he wrote in *No Name in the Street*, a book he began in 1967 but did not publish until 1972. "Yes, we have come, or are coming, to this, and there is no point in flinching before the prospect of this exceedingly cool species of fratricide." That same year he told *The New York Times* of his belated realization that "our destinies are in our hands, black hands, and no one else's."

It is a stirring sentiment—and a sentiment that the earlier Baldwin would have been the first to see through. How far he had come from the author of *The Fire Next Time*, who had forecast the rise of black power and yet was certain that

> we, the black and the white, deeply need each other here if we are really to become a nation—if we are really, that is, to achieve our identity, our maturity, as men and women. To create one nation has proved to be a hideously difficult task: there is certainly no need now to create two, one black and one white.

All such qualms were irrelevant now. In an offhanded but calculated manner, Baldwin affected to dismiss his earlier positions: "I was, in some way, in those years, without entirely realizing it, the Great Black Hope of the Great White Father." If there was something ominous about this public display of self-criticism, it was because we could not forget that the forced recantation had no value that does not purport to be freely given.

In an impossible gambit, the author of *No Name in the Street* sought to reclaim his lost authority by signaling his willingness to be instructed by those who had inherited it. Contradicting his own greatest achievements, he feebly borrowed the populist slogans of the day, and returned them with the beautiful Baldwinian polish. "The powerless, by definition, can never be 'racists,'" he writes, "for they can never make the world pay for what they feel or fear except by the suicidal endeavor that makes them fanatics or revolutionaries, or both; whereas those in power can be urbane and charming and invite you to those houses which they know you will never own." This view—that blacks cannot be racist—is today a familiar one, a platitude of much of the contemporary debate. The key phrase, of course, is "by definition." For this is not only, or even largely, an empirical claim. It is a rhetorical and psychological move, an unfortunate but unsurprising attempt by the victim to forever exempt himself from guilt.

The term "racism" is here redefined by Baldwin, as it has been redefined by certain prominent Afro-American artists and intellectuals today, to refer to a reified system of power relations, to a social order in which one race is essentially and forever subordinated to another. (A parallel move is common in much feminist theory, where "patriarchy"—naming a social order to which Man and Woman have a fixed and opposed relation—contrasts with "sexism," which characterizes the particular acts of particular people.) To be sure, it does express, in an abstract and extreme manner, a widely accepted truth: that the asymmetries of power mean that not all racial insult is equal. (Not even a Florida jury is much concerned when a black captive calls his arresting officer a "cracker.") Still, it represents a grave political error.

For black America needs allies more than it needs absolution. And the slogan—a definition masquerading as an idea—would all too quickly serve as a blanket amnesty for our own dankest suspicions and bigotries. It is a slogan that Baldwin once would have debunked with his devastating mock-detachment. He would have repudiated it not for the sake of white America— for white America, he would have argued, the display of black prejudice could only provide a reassuring confirmation of its own—but for the sake of black America. The Baldwin who knew that the fates of black and white America were one also knew that if racism was to be deplored, it was to be deplored *tout court*, without exemption clauses for the oppressed.

Wasn't it this conviction, above all, that explained Baldwin's own repudiation of Malcolm X? I should be clear. His reverence for Malcolm was real, but it was posthumous. In a conversation with Kenneth Clark recorded in 1963, a year and a half before Malcolm's assassination, Baldwin ventured that by preaching black supremacy, "what [Malcolm] does is destroy a truth and invent a myth." Compared with King's appeal, he said, Malcolm's appeal was

> much more sinister because it is much more effective. It is much more effective, because it is, after all, comparatively easy to invest a population with false morale by giving them a false sense of superiority, and it will always break down in a crisis. That is the history of Europe simply—it's one of the reasons that we are in this terrible place.

Still, he cautioned, the country "shouldn't be worried about the Muslim movement, that's not the problem. The problem is to eliminate the conditions which breed the Muslim movement." (Five years later, under contract with Columbia Pictures, Baldwin began the task of adapting Malcolm to the screen.)

That ethnic scapegoating was an unaffordable luxury, moreover, had been another of Baldwin's own lessons. "Georgia has the Negro," he once pithily wrote, slicing through the thickets of rationalization, "and Harlem has the Jew." We have grimly seen where the failure of this more truthful vision has led: to the surreal spectacle of urban activists who would rather picket Korean grocery stores than crack houses, on the assumption that sullen shopkeepers with their pricey tomatoes, and not smiley drug dealers with their discount glass vials, are the true threat to black dignity.

As I say, by 1973 the times had changed; and they have stayed changed. That, I suppose, is our problem. But Baldwin wanted to change with them. That was his problem. And so we lost his skepticism, his critical independence. Baldwin's belated public response to Cleaver's charges was heartbreaking, and all too symptomatic. Now he would turn the other cheek and insist, in *No Name in the Street*, that he actually admired Cleaver's book. Cleaver's attack on him was explained away as a regrettable if naive misunderstanding: the revolutionary had simply been misled by Baldwin's public reputation. Beyond that, he wrote,

> I also felt that I was confused in his mind with the unutterable debasement of the male—with all those faggots, punks, and sissies, the sight and sound of whom, in prison, must have made him vomit more than once. Well, I certainly hope I know more about myself, and the intention of my work than that, but I *am* an odd quantity. So is Eldridge, so are we all. It is a pity that we won't, probably, ever have the time to attempt to define once more the relationship of the odd and disreputable artist to odd and disreputable revolutionary.... And I think we need each other, and have much to learn from each other, and, more than ever, now.

It was an exercise in perverse and willed magnanimity, and it was meant, no doubt, to suggest unruffled strength. Instead it showed weakness, the ill-disguised appeasement of the creature whose day had come and gone.

Did Baldwin know what was happening to him? His essays give no clue; increasingly they came to represent his official voice. But his fiction became the refuge of his growing self-doubts. In 1968 he published *Tell Me How Long the Train's Been Gone*. Formally speaking, it was his least successful work, but in its protagonist, Leo Proudhammer, Baldwin created a perfectly Baldwinian alter ego, a celebrated black artist who, in diction that matched the eloquence of Baldwin's essays, could express the quandaries that came increasingly to trouble his creator. "The day came," he reflects at one point, "when I wished to break my silence and found that I could not speak: the actor could no longer be distinguished from his role." Thus did Baldwin, our elder statesman, who knew better than anyone how a mask could deform the face beneath, chafe beneath his own.

Called to speak before a civil rights rally. Proudhammer ruminates on the contradictions of his position:

> I did not want others to endure my estrangement, that was why I was on the platform; yet was it not, at the least, paradoxical that it was only my estrangement which had placed me there? ... It was our privilege, to say nothing of our hope, to attempt to make the world a human dwelling place for us all; and yet—yet—was it not possible that the mighty gentlemen, my honorable and invaluable confreres, by being unable to imagine such a journey as my own, were leaving something of the utmost importance out of their aspirations?

These are not unpolitical reflections, but they are not the reflections of a politician. Contrast Leroi Jones's unflappable conviction, in an essay called "Reflections of Two Hotshots" published in 1963, that "a writer must have a point of view, or he cannot be a good writer. He must be standing somewhere in the world, or else he is not one of *us*, and his commentary then is of little value." It was a carefully aimed arrow, and it would pierce Baldwin's heart.

The threat of being deemed obsolete, or "not one of *us*," is a fearful thing. *Tell Me How Long* depicts a black artist's growing sense that (in a recurrent phrase) he no longer belongs to himself, that his public role may have depleted the rest of him. Of course, "the burden of representation," as Baldwin once called it, is a common affliction in Afro-American literature, an unfair condition of hardship that black writers frequently face; but few black writers have measured its costs—the price of this particular ticket to ride—as trenchantly as Baldwin. He risked the fate, and in some ways finally succumbed to the fate, that Leo Proudhammer most feared, which was to be "a Jeremiah without convictions."

Desperate to be "one of us," to be loved by his own, Baldwin allowed himself to mouth a script that was not his own. The connoisseur of complexity tried his hand at being an ideologue. To be sure, he could still do anything he wanted with the English essay. The problem was that he no longer knew quite what he wanted, and he cared too much about what others wanted from him. For a generation had arrived that didn't want anything from him—except, perhaps, that he lie down and die. And this, too, has been a consistent dynamic of race and representation in Afro-America. If someone has anointed a black intellectual, be assured that someone else is busily constructing his tumbril.

We stayed in touch, on and off, through the intervening years, often dining at the Ginger Man when he was in New York. Sometimes he would introduce me to his current lover, or speak of his upcoming projects. I did not return to St. Paul de Vence until shortly after his death four-and-a-half years ago at the age of 63. This time I came to meet his brother David. The place had changed remarkably in the twenty or so years since Baldwin settled there. The grape arbors are now strung with electric lights. Luxury homes dot the landscape on quarter-acre plots, and in the midst of this congestion stands Baldwin's ten-acre oasis, the only undivided farm acreage left in St. Paul.

When I recounted for David Baldwin the circumstances of my meeting his brother for the first time, his wide eyes grew wider. He rose from the table, went downstairs into the study—where a wall of works by and about Henry James faces you as you enter—and emerged with a manuscript in hand. "This is for you," he said. He handed me a play. It was the last work that James Baldwin completed as he suffered through his final illness, and it was called "The Welcome Table." It was set in the Riviera, at a house much like his own, and among the principal characters were "Edith, an actress-singer/star: Creole, from New Orleans," "Daniel, ex-Black Panther, fledgling playwright" with more than a passing resemblance to Cecil Brown, and "Peter Davis, Black American journalist." Peter Davis—who has come to interview a famous star, and whose prodding questions lead to the play's revelations—was, I should say, a far better and more aggressive interviewer than I was; Baldwin, being Baldwin, had transmuted the occasion into a searching drama of revelation and crisis.

Narratives of decline have the appeal of simplicity, but Baldwin's career will not fit that mold. "Unless a writer is extremely old when he dies, in which case he has probably become a neglected institution, his death must always seem untimely," he wrote in 1961, giving us fair warning. "This is because a real writer is always shifting and changing and searching." Reading his late essays, I would like to imagine him embarking on a period of intellectual resurgence. Despite the unfortunate pronouncements of his later years, I believe that he was finding his course again, and exploring the instability of all the categories that divide us. As he wrote in "Here Be Monsters," an essay published two years before his death, and with which he chose to conclude *The Price of the Ticket*, his collected nonfiction: "Each of us, helplessly and forever, contains the other—male in female, female in male, white in black, and black in white. We are part of each other. Many of my countrymen appear to find this fact exceedingly inconvenient and even unfair, and so, very often, do I. But none of us can do anything about it." We needed to hear those words two decades ago, and we especially need to hear them now.

Now we are struggling in this country to fathom the rage in Los Angeles; and slowly we are realizing how intertwined, as Baldwin insisted, are the destinies of black and white America, and how easily one can lay waste to the other in the fury of interracial fratricide. Thirty years ago, Baldwin believed that an effort by the handful of "relatively conscious" blacks and whites might be able to avert the prophecy of the old spiritual: "God gave Noah the rainbow sign, No more water, the fire next time!" The belief proved difficult to sustain. Good intentions—increasingly scarce these days—seem easily defeated by the cycles of poverty, the structural as well as the cultural determinants of urban decay, alienation, and hopelessness. Today, as black intellectuals try to sort outrage from opportunism, political protest from simple criminality, they may wonder if the sense of mutuality that Baldwin promoted can long survive, or if his "elegant despair" alone will endure.

But perhaps times are due to change again. An influential black intellectual avant-garde in Britain has resurrected Baldwin as a patron saint, and a new generation of readers has come to value just those qualities of ambivalence and equivocality, just that sense of the contingency of identity, that made him useless to the ideologues of liberation and anathema to so many black nationalists. Even Baldwin's fiercest antagonists seem now to have welcomed him back to the fold. Like everyone else, I guess, we like our heroes dead.

NICK AARON FORD

The Evolution of James Baldwin as Essayist

I

James Baldwin is one of the most talented American essayists since Ralph Waldo Emerson (1803–1882). His first three volumes—*Notes of a Native Son* (1955), *Nobody Knows My Name* (1961), and *The Fire Next Time* (1963)—won a popularity hardly equaled by any other essayist in modern times. His most recent volume, *No Name in the Street* (1972), has neither received nor deserved the attention merited by its predecessors. His four novels, with the exception of *Go Tell It on the Mountain* (1953), his one volume of short stories, and his two published plays are distinctly inferior to his best essays in style and substance. It appears, therefore, that his talents demonstrated thus far lie in the general area of unstructured, instinctive, and emotional utterance often unsupported by rational safeguards. Like his nineteenth-century counterpart, his most valuable contributions are in the realms of pragmatism and prophecy rather than logic and rationality. Like Emerson, too, his major thrust is not to impart abstract or concrete knowledge, but to provoke humane thought and announce eternal truths intended to elevate the consciousness of the reader from animal passion to spiritual or philosophical contemplation.

In this discussion I shall examine Baldwin's four volumes of essays for the purpose of offering critical comments on style, content, and method characteristic of the most representative examples. It is hoped that such an

From *James Baldwin: A Critical Evaluation*, Therman O'Daniel, ed., pp. 85–104. © 1977 by Howard University Press.

examination will stimulate the kind of further study that the most significant works of Baldwin deserve.

In "Autobiographical Notes," which serves as an introduction to the first volume, the author tells of his birth in Harlem, in 1924, and of his beginning to plot "novels" at about the time he learned to read. His first story, written at the age of twelve, was published in a church newspaper. Later he received a letter of congratulations from Mayor LaGuardia of New York City for one of his pieces of creative writing. Pressured by his semi-illiterate stepfather, who was a storefront preacher, he became an active preacher at the age of fourteen but ended his religious commitment three years later. At twenty-four, after having used up two writing fellowships during the previous three-year period, he left the United States for a nine-year sojourn in France and other European countries, where he discovered what it means to be an American. He confides:

> I know, in any case, that the most crucial time in my own development came when I was forced to recognize that I was a kind of bastard of the West; when I followed the line of my past I did not find myself in Europe but in Africa. And this meant in some subtle way, in a really profound way, I brought to Shakespeare, Bach, Rembrandt, to the stones of Paris, to the cathedral at Chartres, and to the Empire State Building, a special attitude. These were not really my creations, they did not contain my history; I might search in them in vain forever for any reflection of myself. I was an interloper; this was not my heritage. At the same time I had no other heritage which I could possibly hope to use—I had certainly been unfitted for the jungle or the tribe. I would have to appropriate these white centuries, I would have to make them mine—I would have to accept my special attitude, my special place in this scheme—otherwise I would have no place in any scheme. What was most difficult was the fact that I was forced to admit something I had always hidden from myself, which the American Negro has had to hide from himself as the price of his public progress; that I hated and feared white people. This did not mean that I loved black people; on the contrary, I despised them, possibly because they failed to produce Rembrandt.1

The first two essays in this volume are devoted to literary criticism. "Everybody's Protest Novel" condemns protest fiction as a serious literary activity by castigating the motives and achievements of Harriet Beecher

Stowe's *Uncle Tom's Cabin* and the unreality of Richard Wright's *Native Son.* Baldwin denies that such writing can be justified on the basis that it serves "the 'good' of society." He argues that "since literature and sociology are not one and the same; it is impossible to discuss them as if they were." (P. 19) Evidently it never occurred to him that, like whiskey and water, they could possibly be combined for the improvement of both. In 1955 the thirty-one-year-old author was under the illusion, as many of his fellow blacks were then, that in order to be recognized by the international literary establishment or any legitimate faction thereof he "would have to accept ... [his] special place in this scheme—otherwise ... [he] would have no place in *any* scheme." He declares, as if he believes Wright overlooked the fact entirely, "... Bigger's tragedy is not that he is cold or black or hungry ... but that he has accepted a theology that denies him life, that he admits the possibility of his being subhuman and feels constrained, therefore, to battle for his humanity according to those brutal criteria bequeathed him at his birth." (PP. 22–23) This criticism fails to recognize the fact that Bigger's tragedy is in reality twofold; on the lower level it is indeed the fact that he is cold and black and hungry, while on the higher level it is what Baldwin suggests it is. That Bigger does not understand the deeper or higher meaning of his tragedy makes the whole impact of the novel the more poignant.

Baldwin's attempt to prove in this essay that *Uncle Tom's Cabin* made no worthy contribution to the abolition of slavery because "The virtuous rage of Mrs. Stowe is motivated by nothing so temporal as a concern for the relationship of men to one another—or, even; as she would have claimed, by a concern for their relationship to God," (P. 17) is to confuse results with intentions and therefore to succumb to the discredited "intentional fallacy." Enlightened criticism assesses praise or blame on the basis of the pragmatic results of what an author actually achieved rather than on what he or she intended to do. There is ample evidence available to prove that Mrs. Stowe's friends and foes agree that her masterpiece was a powerful force in helping to inflict the mortal wound to the slavery ethic in the United States.

In "Many Thousands Gone" Baldwin concentrates all of his rhetorical power in a massive attack on the validity of Wright's purpose in the creation of *Native Son* with its monster protagonist Bigger Thomas. Although he admits that "the most powerful and celebrated statement we have yet had of what it means to be a Negro in America is unquestionably Richard Wright's *Native Son*," (P. 30) he unfairly contends that at the end of the novel we know no more about the black protagonist than we did at the beginning and, likewise, we know scarcely any more about the social situation in America which is supposed to have created him. On the contrary, the entire novel, including the court scene, is a graphic unraveling of incidents and attitudes that molded

Bigger's private and public selves and that characterized the social milieu in which such a monstrous creature was spawned and nourished. It is true, as Baldwin suggests, that an important dimension of black life is omitted, namely, the relationship that Negroes bear to one another and the "depth of involvement and unspoken recognition of shared" (P. 35) community experience, but often rigid isolation is absolutely necessary in the interest of most meaningful diagnosis. In this essay, which seems to be a reinforcement of the previous arguments against the effectiveness of the protest novel, Baldwin unwittingly manufactures arguments for later critics to use against him in his own "protest" novels, *Another Country* (1962) and *Tell Me How Long the Train's Been Gone* (1968), both of which are more violently propagandistic and much less artistic than Wright's *Native Son*.

Further evidence of the author's greater concern for startling rhetoric than for solid fact is his unfortunate hyperbolic statement previously noted in the excerpt quoted above: "This did not mean that I loved black people; on the contrary, I despised them, possibly because they failed to produce Rembrandt." In my opinion Baldwin did not intend for his statement to be taken literally. He was anxious to impress upon the reader's mind the monstrous crime that had been perpetrated against black Americans by the white world in its glorification of European culture and complete denial or denigration of the value of anything that blacks anywhere had ever accomplished. In the given context it seems reasonable to assume that there was no more real hate in Baldwin's heart for fellow blacks than there was doubt in the agonized cry of Jesus on the cross: "My God, my God, why hast thou forsaken me?" But because of Baldwin's failure to distinguish sufficiently fact from fable or rhetoric from rationality Eldridge Cleaver could say in *Soul on Ice*, without fear of contradiction:

> I am not interested in denying anything to Baldwin. I, like the entire nation, owe a great debt to him. But throughout the range of his work, from *Go Tell It on the Mountain*, through *Notes of a Native Son*, *Nobody Knows My Name*, *Another Country*, to *The Fire Next Time*, all of which I treasure, there is a decisive quirk in Baldwin's vision which corresponds to his relationship to black people and to masculinity. It was this same quirk, in my opinion, that compelled Baldwin to slander Rufus Scott in *Another Country*, venerate André Gide, repudiate *The White Negro*, and drive the blade of Brutus into the corpse of Richard Wright.[2]

In "The Harlem Ghetto" Baldwin considers analytically the major problems that confront blacks in the largest and most representative ghetto in the United States. He concludes that in searching for a scapegoat upon which to place the blame for all his frustrations—his social ostracism, his economic exploitation, his lack of professional recognition and acceptance—the Harlemite has chosen the Jew. The author argues, "It is not the Jewish tradition by which he has been betrayed but the tradition of his native land. But just as a society must have a scapegoat, so hatred must have a symbol. Georgia has the Negro and Harlem has the Jew." (P. 72) It now seems ironic that since the publication of this essay less than two decades ago, Georgia has elected, with the aid of a considerable number of white votes, the first black congressman from the confederate states, and Baldwin has been condemned by the distinguished black novelist-poet Ishmael Reed as the writer of "Jewish books" whom nobody takes seriously anymore except "Jewish liberals."

With the exception of "Carmen Jones: The Dark Is Light Enough," which is an unfavorable appraisal of a 1955 film by Twentieth Century-Fox with an all-black cast, five of the remaining six essays in *Notes of a Native Son* are commentaries on and interpretations of personal experiences that are covered in a general way by other discussions in later volumes. The sixth essay, however, "Stranger in the Village," deserves comment. The virtually unknown village is located in the mountains of Switzerland four hours from Milan and three hours from Lausanne. The stranger is Baldwin. The six hundred inhabitants are Catholics, and most of the tourists are cripples or semi-cripples who come from other parts of Switzerland to seek relief by bathing in the hot spring water. The essayist's observations and interpretations are made at the end of a prolonged visit. The villagers, who had never seen a Negro before, would often approach the lonely visitor in jocular friendliness and touch his hair with their fingers as though they were afraid of an electric shock and touch his hands as though they expected the color to rub off. Although he admits there was no hint of intentional unkindness, their actions excited within him a feeling that he was considered not quite human. The ambivalence of the situation was most striking when the little children who shouted *Neger!* as he passed glowed with pride whenever he stopped to speak to them.

Baldwin's explanation and interpretation of the interrelations between his historical background and contemporary situation and those of his hosts present the most meaningful understanding of the black–white dilemma that appear in American literature. The following quotations contain the essence of the author's reasoning:

> The idea of white supremacy rests simply on the fact that
> white men are the creators of civilization (the present civilization,
> which is the only one that matters; all previous civilizations are

simply "contributions" to our own) and are therefore civilization's guardians and defenders.

At the root of the American Negro problem is the necessity of the American white man to find a way of living with the Negro in order to be able to live with himself.

The Cathedral of Chartres, I have said, says something to the people of this village which it cannot say to me; but it is important to understand that this cathedral says something to me which it cannot say to them. Perhaps they are struck by the power of the spires, the glory of the windows ... and I am terrified by the slippery bottomless well to be found in the crypt, down which heretics were hurled to death, and the obscene, inescapable gargoyles jutting out of the stone and seeming to say that god and the devil can never be divorced.

No road whatever will lead Americans back to the simplicity of this European village where white men still have the luxury of looking on me as a stranger. I am not, really, a stranger any longer for any American alive. One of the things that distinguishes Americans from other people is that no other people has ever been so deeply involved in the lives of black men, and vice versa. (PP. 172–75)

This first volume reveals certain aspects of style and method that have become the hallmarks of Baldwin's essays. One characteristic is the use of the first person. When the narration is completely personal in its application, the pronoun is "I," but when the assertion is intended to represent or be applied to white-American society, the pronoun is "we" or "our." For instance, in "Everybody's Protest Novel" the following statement is intended to apply to white-oriented society: "Society is held together by *our* need; *we* bind it together with legend, myth, coercion, fearing that without it *we* will be hurled into that void, within which, like the earth before the Word was spoken, the foundations of society are hidden" [italics mine]. Another characteristic is its lack of inhibitions in describing what the author considers to be the awful truth. Like the prophets of the Old Testament, he never allows politeness or the fear of offending to interfere with prophecy or eternal truth. A third distinguishing feature is the use of imagery to create a sense of vividness and emotional involvement. A fourth attribute is the employment of personally related examples to illustrate or enhance the meaning of general or universal truths. As we examine later volumes, we will discover that the foregoing characteristics occur with greater frequency and effect.

II

The thirteen essays in *Nobody Knows My Name* were written during the period between 1954 and 1961. Baldwin explains in the introduction that much of the discussion is centered in or revolves around the question of color, a problem that he suggests "operates to hide the graver questions of the self."[3] In the previous volume he sought to justify his preoccupation with matters pertaining to race on the ground that it was "the gate" he had to unlock before he could hope to write about anything else. Evidently, he later found the gate more difficult to unlock than he had anticipated, for only three of these essays eschew the problems of color.

In "The Discovery of What It Means to Be an American" Baldwin declares, concerning his nine years in Europe, that he was compelled to leave America because he felt he could not survive the abnormal strain of the color problem as it existed in his native land. He felt the necessity of a new setting which would enable him to experience relationships that would reveal his kinship with other people of different colors and races rather than those that always emphasized his division, his separation. In short, he wanted to prevent himself "from becoming merely a Negro; or, even, merely a Negro writer." (P. 3) In one sense, at least, his wish was realized, for the book of which this essay is a part appeared on *The New York Times'* best-seller list for many weeks, a success seldom achieved by writing in this genre. Furthermore, Mark Schorer, distinguished scholar-critic, was quoted in *The New York Times Book Review*, December 3, 1961, as saying:

> Were I to find myself in the role of an unofficial or an official ambassador to another country, especially an Asian or an African country, I would carry with me as many copies of James Baldwin's *Nobody Knows My Name* as I could afford. I would do this in part from a motive of pride in the esthetic accomplishments of a countryman, for we have hardly a more accomplished prose stylist in the United States today. But perhaps more important, I would urge this book upon people in other countries to persuade them that we are by no means without our deep cultural scars and conflicts, and by no means without the capacity for the most searching self-criticism.

In another sense Baldwin's sojourn in Europe produced positive effects upon himself, for he declares in this essay, "In my necessity to find the terms on which my experience could be related to that of others, Negroes and whites, writers and non-writers, I proved, to my astonishment, to be as American as any Texas G.I.," (P. 4) although it required two years or more as a visitor in Paris for him to realize that fact. It was not until he had accepted his "role—as distinguished ... from ... 'place'—in the extraordinary drama which is America" that he "was released from the illusion that I hated America." (P. 5) It is in this context that he dares to define for *all* American writers what Europe can contribute to them and what they can contribute to the indigenous European, namely, a sense of tragedy for the former and a new sense of life's possibilities for the latter. "In this endeavor to wed the vision of the Old World with that of the New, it is the writer, not the statesman, who is our strongest arm." (P. 12) It seems clear at this point in Baldwin's development that he considers himself to be an *American* writer rather than a *Negro* writer and that his vision must embrace and interpret the universal. Yet in four of the essays that follow—"Fifth Avenue, Uptown: A Letter from Harlem," "East River, Downtown: Postscript to a Letter from Harlem," "A Fly in Buttermilk," and "Nobody Knows My Name: A Letter from the South"—the subject matter is devoted entirely to the evils of segregation, the hypocrisy of whites in their relations with blacks in the North and South, and the indifference of middle-class blacks to the plight of their poorer and weaker brethren. In addressing these evils, he finds it necessary to abandon the pose of universality adopted in his earlier references to the American writer's contribution of "a new sense of life's possibilities" for the European. He apparently discovered that there was greater need for the black writer to expose the unlimited possibilities of exploitation of blacks in America than to contemplate the new sense of life's possibilities for the European.

One of the most meaningful essays, "Princes and Powers," in this volume is Baldwin's interpretive report on the Conference of Negro-African Writers and Artists (Le Congrès des Ecrivains et Artistes Noirs), September 19–22, 1956, in the Sorbonne's Amphithéâtre Descartes, in Paris. The leaders included Richard Wright, who had left the United States in 1946 for permanent residence in France; Alioune Diop, editor of *Présence Africaine*; Léopold Senghor, Senegal; Aimé Césaire, Martinique; and Jacques Alexis and Dr. Price-Mars, Haiti. The five official delegates from the United States were John Davis, Mercer Cook, William Fontaine, Horace Mann Bond, and James Ivy. The purpose of the conference, according to one of the principal organizers, was to afford an opportunity unlike any previous experience for representative black intellectuals from widely divergent areas to meet together under favorable circumstances to define and accept their responsibilities, to assess the riches and the promise of their culture, and to open, in effect, a dialogue with Europe.

Baldwin briefly summarizes each major speech and at the same time interweaves his own critical evaluation of it. One of the highlights was the presentation of Césaire, whose central theme was stated as follows: "Wherever colonization is a fact the indigenous culture begins to rot. And among these ruins, something begins to be born which is not a culture but a kind of subculture, a subculture which is condemned to exist on the margin allowed it by European culture!" (P. 34) Baldwin declares that he was stirred in a strange and disagreeable way, for the speaker had very skillfully played on the emotions and hopes of the audience but had not dealt with the most pertinent central question, which was, in Baldwin's opinion, "What *had* this colonial experience made of them [the black colonials] and what were they now to do with it? For they were all, now, whether they liked it or not, related to Europe, stained by European visions and standards, and their relation to themselves, and to each other, and to their past had changed." (P. 36) It was agreed, however, that a culture is not something given to a people but something that they make themselves. Later it was decided to appoint a committee to formulate an acceptable definition of Negro-African culture and to suggest reasons why that culture should be saved.

To Baldwin the question *What is Black-African culture?* cannot be easily or completely answered, but he is satisfied that there is something that all blacks hold in common, even though it may not correctly be defined as *cultural*. This *something* is their precarious and unutterably painful relation to the white world. It is the burning desire to remake the world in their own image, to impose that image on the white world, and to be no longer controlled by the vision of themselves and the world held by other people. The report of the Committee on Culture did little to clarify the main question that it had been appointed to adjudicate, but it did emphasize the fact that there can be no *one* definition of Black-African culture: there are now and will continue to be many such cultures with different characteristics and different emphases. It did, however, insist on the necessity of a continuing effort to compile and evaluate the cultural inventory begun by the committee in relation to the various black cultures that have been systematically misunderstood, underestimated, and sometimes destroyed, and it did enlist the "active aid of writers, artists, theologians, thinkers, scientists, and technicians" in efforts to revive, rehabilitate, and develop these cultures as "the first step toward their integration in the active cultural life of the world." (P. 50)

One of the most significant revelations in Baldwin's report on the address of Léopold Senghor, the poet-statesman from Senegal, is the explanation of the difference between European and African reasoning as illustrated by means of the bloodstream in which all things mingle and flow to and through the heart. He points out "that the difference between the function of the arts in Europe and their function in Africa lay in the fact that, in Africa, the function of the arts is more present and pervasive, is infinitely less special, 'is done by all, for all.' ... Art itself is taken to be perishable, to be made again each time it disappears or is destroyed. What is clung to is the spirit which makes art possible .... European art attempts to imitate nature. African art is concerned with reaching beyond and beneath nature, to contact, and itself become a part of *la force vitale*." (P. 24)

Baldwin's comment on Richard Wright's role in the conference is caustic. He takes exception to the older man's pronouncement that Europe had brought the Enlightenment to Africa and that "what was good for Europe was good for all mankind." He expresses even greater shock at Wright's apparent approval of the dictatorial methods of the new African leaders, who felt it necessary to adopt such tactics temporarily in order to break for their subjects the spell of Western ways of thought and action. (PP. 46–47)

In a three-part discourse entitled "Alas, Poor Richard," the essayist elaborates further on his differences with Wright, who had earlier been an inspiration and adviser to him and many other youthful writers of the period, including Ralph Ellison. With the exception of a few paragraphs concerning his former mentor's sudden death in Paris and the effect of his work upon blacks in America and abroad, he devotes the first section of this essay to a critical review of *Eight Men*, Wright's second book of short stories, published immediately after his death. His personal reaction to the expatriated American's life and death can be summarized as follows: Wright was a great inspiration to him, although he had found it necessary to fight his benefactor occasionally. America, Europe, and Africa had failed his dead friend, but despite this failure the fallen hero had survived long enough to begin to tell the tale of his struggles and achievements. In fact, as he unknowingly approached death he appeared on the threshold of a new beginning. Baldwin's criticism of the eight stories as a group was that they emphasized the fact that Wright's bleak landscape was not merely that of Chicago, as revealed in *Native Son*, or the deep South, as revealed in *Uncle Tom's Children*, but that of his entire world and of the human heart. "Even the most good-natured performance this book contains, good-natured by comparison only, 'Big Black Good Man,' takes place in Copenhagen in the winter, and in the vastly more chilling confines of a Danish hotel-keeper's fears." (P. 186)

Rather than comment on Baldwin's criticism, I submit my own critical summary of the book as it appeared in my annual critical survey of significant books by and about Negroes:

In each of the eight stories in *Eight Men* Richard Wright presents a situation in which a colored man is a victim of the white man's inhumanity. In half of them the white man or the white man's cause suffers because of this inhumanity. In all of them the reader is made aware that the Negro characters are the sensitive ones, the knowing ones, the superior ones, that the strong are never right, and that the prejudiced whites are to be pitied as much as the wronged Negroes.[4]

The second section is described by Baldwin as a memoir, and was first published in *Le Preuve* two months after Wright's death. It tells of his great admiration for the deceased, whom he describes as his "ally and my witness, and, alas! my father," (P. 191) although he declares in the same paragraph that they were as unlike as any two writers could possibly be. They had met in 1944, two years before Wright left his native America for self-chosen European exile. He admits, however, that the relationship between them was not one of equality, since he was always conscious of a tinge of condescension in the older man's attitude toward him. Finally, the open break came after four years, when he arrived in Paris intent on repudiating his American citizenship, which Wright never did, and wrote for *Zero* magazine "Everybody's Protest Novel" attacking *Native Son* and assigning it to the same "discredited" category as he had assigned Harriet Beecher Stowe's *Uncle Tom's Cabin*, concluding with the pronouncement: "The failure of the protest novel lies in its rejection of life, the human being, the denial of his beauty, dread, power, in its insistence that it is his categorization alone which is real and which cannot be transcended."[5] It is noteworthy that at this time the publication of Baldwin's first novel, *Go Tell It on the Mountain*, which was not in the protest tradition, was four years in the future, and his third and fourth, which contained protest no less acrimonious than that of *Native Son*, were thirteen and nineteen years away. It is conceivable that the twenty-six-year-old essayist was unaware at that time of the necessity for various kinds of protest, as a socially concerned writer struggles to bring to life the compelling vision that his personal and social experiences presage. Recently, as I watched a television colloquy between Baldwin and Nikki Giovanni, the young black poet, I was not surprised to hear the essayist, in reply to a query from his interlocutor, acknowledge that if he were writing "Everybody's Protest Novel" today his point of view would be different.

The third section of "Alas, Poor Richard" is Baldwin's assessment of the effect of Wright's self-imposed exile upon the older writer's life, on his relationships with other black Americans, Africans, and Algerians in Paris, and on his writing career. His commentary might be appropriately entitled "The Decline and Fall of Richard Wright." His major conclusion is: "Richard was able, at last, to live in Paris exactly as he would have lived, had he been a white man, here, in America.... Richard paid the price such an illusion of safety demands. The price is a turning away from, an ignorance of, all of the powers of darkness." (PP. 213–14) He accuses his former idol of arrogance and condescension toward American and African blacks, of hypocrisy in pretending to organize a Franco-American Club for the purpose of forcing American businesses in Paris and American government offices to hire American Negroes on a proportional basis, of really not wanting to know the problems of his black countrymen in Paris because "his real impulse toward American Negroes, individually, was to despise them." (P. 212) He fails to point out the continual harassment of Wright by the American Secret Service during his later years, the seeming conspiracy among American and European publishers not to publish new works by Wright during his last years, the unexplainable cooling of the ardor of white friends, and the financial difficulties that plagued the beleaguered expatriate. In sum, this essay seems to support Wright's belief as reported by the essayist earlier: "I know that I liked him [Wright], then, and later, and all the time. But I also know that, later on, he did not believe this." (P. 193)

In "The Male Prison" Baldwin praises André Gide for the manner in which the famous French writer managed his problem of homosexuality in relation to his wife Madeleine, a problem that inhibited in him "all carnal desire" and "meant that some corresponding inhibition in her prevented her from seeking carnal satisfaction elsewhere." (P. 158) Eldridge Cleaver, like Robert Bone, assumes that Baldwin's writings on homosexuality, including all of his novels except the first, are reflections of his own preferences and that these preferences are fair game for critical judgments of his work.[6] Bone declares:

> One senses that Baldwin in his portrait of Eric [in *Another Country*], has desired above all to be faithful to his own experience. He will neither falsify nor go beyond it. Central to that experience is a rebellion against the prevailing sexual, as well as racial mores. But on either plane of experience, Baldwin faces an emotional dilemma. Like Satan and the fallen angels, it is as painful to persist in his rebellion as to give it up. Total defiance is unthinkable, total reconciliation only less so. These are the poles of Baldwin's psychic life, and the novel vacillates helplessly between them.[7]

If indeed Baldwin is a victim of the sexual dilemma to which Cleaver and Bone have assigned him, his thoughts on "The Male Prison" as expressed in this essay deserve much better than the shabby treatment by these critics.

I recommend the following passage as a typical example of the sympathetic understanding Baldwin has brought to the discussion of this much abused facet of the human condition:

> ... It is one of the facts of life that there are two sexes, which fact has given the world most of its beauty, cost it not a little of its anguish, and contains the hope and glory of the world. And it is with this fact, which might better perhaps be called a mystery, that every human being born must find some way to live. For, no matter what demons drive them, men cannot live without women and women cannot live without men. And this is what is most clearly conveyed in the agony of Gide's last journal. However little he was able to understand it, or, more important perhaps, take upon himself the responsibility for it, Madeleine kept open for him a kind of door of hope, of possibility, the possibility of entering into communion with another sex. This door, which is the door to life and air and freedom from the tyranny of one's own personality, must be kept open, and none feel this more keenly than those on whom the door is perpetually threatening or has already seemed to close. (P. 161)

I must, however, agree with Cleaver's condemnation of Baldwin's verdict on Norman Mailer's "The White Negro," although for different reasons. In his essay "The Black Boy Looks at the White Boy" Baldwin devotes twenty-five pages to a discussion of his impressions of Mailer, one of the most talented and distinguished contemporary writers, whose major contribution to the literature of black–white relations in America is the essay under examination. In his rather lengthy consideration of Mailer, the essayist chooses to concentrate on several frivolous, self-serving, insipid encounters with his white counterpart, relegating his two-page monologue on the greatly misunderstood essay largely to commonplace chitchat, of which the following summary is the most meaningful: "I could not, with the best will in the world, make any sense out of *The White Negro* and, in fact, it was hard for me to imagine that this essay had been written by the same man who wrote the novels." (P. 228) Nevertheless, he admits that a black musician talking to him about Mailer—the context seems to imply that Mailer's essay was the subject—said, "'Man ... the only trouble with that cat is that he's white.'" (P. 231) Baldwin adds, "What my friend meant was that to become a Negro man, let alone a Negro artist, one had to make oneself up as one went along.... Now, this is true for everyone, but, in the case of a Negro, this truth is absolutely naked: if he deludes himself about it, he will die. This is not the way this truth presents itself to white men, who believe the world is theirs and who, albeit unconsciously, expect the world to help them in the achievement of their identity." (P. 232)

In fact, Mailer's thesis, which Baldwin does not choose to explain, is that "in certain cities in America ... this particular part of a generation was attracted to what the Negro had to offer. In such places as Greenwich Village, a menage à trois was completed—the bohemian and juvenile delinquent came face to face with the Negro, and the hipster was a fact in American life.... And in this wedding of the white and black it was the Negro who brought the cultural dowry."[8] The *white* Negro, therefore, is the non-black hipster who has accepted the urban non-middle-class Negro's philosophy of existence, including living in the present, substituting the pleasures of the body for the pleasures of the mind, and voicing in his music the character and quality of existence. Mailer suggests that since the Negro has been living on the margin between totalitarianism and democracy for two centuries, it is natural for him to be the source of Hip—both a special language and a way of life. "Sharing a collective disbelief in the words of men who had too much money and controlled too many things," hipster disbelieves in "the socially monolithic ideas of the single mate, the solid family and respectable love life."[9]

According to Mailer, Hip is a language of energy. The words and/or expressions he chose for discussion are *man, go, put down, make, beat, cool, swing, with it, crazy, dig, hip, flip, creep,* and *square.* As to the future, he believes that the most central fact "is that the organic growth of Hip depends on whether the Negro emerges as a dominating force in American life. Since the Negro knows more about the ugliness and danger of life than the white, it is probable that if the Negro can win his equality, he will possess a potential superiority, a superiority so feared that the fear itself has become the underground drama of domestic politics."[10]

It seems to this writer that Baldwin's appraisal of the basic philosophy expressed in "The White Negro" would have made an infinitely greater contribution to an understanding of Mailer's thought and attitude toward black–white relations than his superficial treatment of the author's personal dealings with him.

III

The Fire Next Time is a book of only two essays, one entitled "My Dungeon Shook" and the other "Down at the Cross: Letter from a Region in My Mind." The first, consisting of seven pages, advises the author's fifteen-year old nephew how to avoid the death his white fellowmen have prepared for him and at the same time to remake America so that he and his would-be executioners will survive together. It is a remarkable exercise in eloquence, hyperbole, sleight-of-hand, romanticism, and naiveté—in other words, a delightful exercise in the creation of what could be the pure poetry Carl Sanburg described in his famous paradox "hyacinth and biscuits." He assures his nephew that, with sufficient stamina, wariness, and love, he can save himself from the diabolical schemes of his white brothers, who intend

> ... that you should perish in the ghetto, perish by never being allowed to go behind the white man's definitions, by never being allowed to spell your proper name.... But these men are your brothers—your lost younger brothers. And if the word *integration* means anything, this is what it means: that we, with love, shall force our brothers to see themselves as they are, to cease fleeing from reality and begin to change it.[11]

He suggests that there is no reason for Negroes to become like whites, and that there is no basis for the assumption by whites that they must accept Negroes. Rather, Negroes must accept white people in order to save them from self-destruction. Negroes must be their saviors, for "We cannot be free until they are free." (P. 24)

The second essay, consisting of ninety-one pages, provides the background experiences responsible for generating the advice he gave his nephew. It begins with capsule descriptions of his childhood, adolescence, and young adulthood, including the influence on his development of such powerful forces as the Christian religion, dope, prostitution, and other crimes characteristic of the Harlem ghetto, the counterforce of the Black Muslim movement, and the ever-present threat of white power in its varied manifestations. Although at the early age of seventeen he had rejected the Christian church (the storefront variety) and its basic practices, after having been a practicing preacher for more than three years, he admits that its early influences had, in all probability, saved him from the corrupting power of the worst elements of his environment and from a sordid life worse than death. He admits that during his early ministerial experiences "I have never seen anything to equal the fire and excitement that sometimes, without warning, fill a church, causing the church ... to 'rock'." (P. 47) Nothing that has happened to him since, he confesses "equals the power and the glory" (P. 47) that he sometimes felt when, in the middle of a sermon he knew that he and the church were one. But he was finally convinced that there was no love in the church. Hatred and despair were the constant companions of those who surrendered to the temporary visitations of the Holy Ghost during the services. The admonition to love everybody applied neither to white people nor to blacks whose beliefs were different from theirs. But Baldwin could see no value in salvation that did not permit him to behave with love toward others regardless of their behavior toward him.

Later he discovered in the Black Muslim religion a superiority over Christianity as practiced by the so-called Christian churches. He found that Elijah Muhammad, national leader of the Muslims, "had been able to do what generations of welfare workers and committees and resolutions and reports and housing projects and playgrounds had failed to do: to heal and redeem drunkards and junkies, to convert people who have come out of prison and make men chaste and women virtuous, and to invest both the male and the female with a pride and a serenity that hang about them like an unfailing light." (P. 64–65) In all these things, according to Baldwin, the Christian church has been a spectacular failure. But, despite these successes, the essayist found the Muslims blameworthy in one major respect: their religion forbids the concept of integration among whites and blacks; therefore, he could not accept their doctrine as the best guide to the promotion of acceptable human relations. He made it clear to Elijah Muhammad that he had many white friends and did not object to intermarriage between whites and blacks. He emphasized that if it ever became necessary to die with his friends rather than seek survival at their expense, he would have no choice but to die with the white and the black. He thought to himself as he lectured the Muslim leader: "I love a few people and they love me and some of them are white, and isn't love more important than color?" (P. 85)

It is clear from the tenor of the discussion in both essays that at this period in his life Baldwin is committed to two courses of conduct, *love* and *integration*, for he uses both as fulcrums in each of the two essays. He commits himself, and urges a commitment upon his nephew, to these two modes of conduct despite his admission that in practice neither has been accepted by his white fellowmen. He suggests, in respect to integration, "We, the black and white, deeply need each other here if we are really to become a nation." (P. 111) But he concludes, "To create one nation has proved to be a hideously difficult task; there is certainly no need now to create two, one black and one white. But white men ... have been advocating exactly this, in effect, for generations." (P. 111) In the conclusion of his letter to his nephew, he links both concepts as the two major poles of his creed: "And if the word *integration* means anything, this is what it means: that we, with love, shall force our brothers to see themselves as they are, to cease fleeing from reality and begin to change it." (PP. 23–24) This is indeed the substance of the gospel of Martin Luther King and the evidence that at this point in his life Baldwin is King's devoted disciple.

In this volume Baldwin offers new definitions for old ideas. He defines love "as a state of being, or a state of grace—not in the infantile American sense of being made happy but in the tough and universal sense of quest and daring and growth." (P. 109) He suggests a new definition of beauty when he says, "And black has *become* a beautiful color—not because it is loved but because it is feared." (P. 91) He pays loving tribute to the "Uncle Toms" of the past who have been maligned and reviled by the new breed of black militants for the necessary compromises they had to make to gain educational advantages for their children. "I have great respect for that unsung army of black men and women who trudged down back lanes and entered back doors," he declares, "saying 'Yes, Sir' and 'No, Ma'am' in order to acquire a new roof for the schoolhouse, new books, a chemistry lab, more beds for the dormitories, more dormitories." (P. 114)

This is a beautiful book, a challenging book, a powerful book. It is a profoundly philosophical book. It is the best of Baldwin's writings, but it offers no new solutions to the problem of race relations in America. Indeed, its basic solution is as old as the Holy Bible and as simple as the Sermon on the Mount.

IV

No Name in the Street, Baldwin's fourth book of essays, reveals a sadder but hardly wiser writer than has come to light in the three previous volumes. It is a more hardboiled, pessimistic, disillusioned view of his country and its people. It bids farewell to idealism, to positive and unselfish love, to the belief in integration, and to a viable future for the United States of America. It accepts as a valid prophecy the curse of Job's friend Bildad, who pronounces this doom upon the wicked of his generation: "His remembrance shall perish from the earth and he shall have *No Name in the Street*. He shall be driven from light into darkness, and chased out of the world."

In this book Baldwin has selected for dramatic exposure a *potpourri* of exasperating and tragic incidents of black life in America and abroad and has formulated frightening conclusions based on the reactions of blacks to these incidents. He has rehashed with new insights and emphases experiences in his life from childhood to the present which are responsible for his changing attitudes toward life in general and white Americans in particular. He interweaves in the tapestry of events, moving back and forth in time intimate experiences and associations with Martin Luther King, Medgar Evers, Malcolm X—all charismatic black leaders who were associated because of their forthright determination to secure equal rights for black people—and a young black man named William A. Maynard, Jr., who had served as his bodyguard and chauffeur several years previously and who had been arrested later for a murder he did not commit and who subsequently fled to Hamburg, Germany, while awaiting trial in New York. The Maynard case, including the brutal and inhuman plight of black prisoners in general, is given more space than any other single subject.

Other bitter grievances that influenced Baldwin's repudiation of God, of European culture, which he previously adored, of a belief in the possibility of American justice, and even of the taboo against murder are, among a multitude of others, "the storm of fire and blood which the Black Panthers have been forced to undergo merely for declaring themselves as men,"[12] the genocidal treatment of black Algerians by the French, and the determination by the American press and the movie industry to prevent the exposure of worthy achievements of black people. "All of the Western nations have been caught in a lie," he declares, "the lie of their pretended humanism: this means that their history has no moral justification, and that the West has no moral authority." (P. 85) Evidently, he no longer worships at the shrine of the Cathedral at Chartres as he so boldly proclaimed in his first book of essays, *Notes of a Native Son*. In reference to the repudiation of his past attitudes, he says with sarcasm, "It must be remembered that in those great days I was considered to be an 'integrationist'." (P. 93)

In the closing pages of this volume he summarizes his break with his past in the following dramatic terms:

> ... whereas white men have killed black men for sport, or out of terror or out of the intolerable excess of terror called hatred, or out of the necessity of affirming their identity as white men, none of these motives appear necessarily to obtain for black men: it is not necessary for a black man to hate a white man, or to have any particular feelings about him at all, in order to realize that he must kill him. Yes, we have come, or are coming to this, and there is no point in flinching before the prospect of this exceedingly cool species of fratricide—which prospect white people, after all, have brought on themselves. (P. 191)

Finally, one of the most sensitive writers in the Western world, in the middle of a brilliant career that has earned him respect and honor at home and abroad, whose early vision was rooted in love and brotherhood and whose faith in the integration of the races was genuine and compulsive, has come to this.

V

A comparative and/or contrasting examination of Baldwin's four volumes of essays in respect to theme, style, and philosophy reveals interesting information. They were published during a span of seventeen years. Some individual essays were written as early as twenty-five years ago and others as late as two years ago. The quarter of a century represented covers the period between the author's twenty-fourth and forty-eighth birthdays, a period in which youthful idealism had to make room for mature realism and possible pragmatism. Certainly *Notes of a Native Son*, containing the first fruits of his authorship, is characterized by exuberance, cockiness, self-assurance, and idealism. The style is fresh and at times eloquent, with the fervor, personal involvement, and conviction of the apostles of the New Testament, which he had learned to emulate in his youthful sermons. On the other hand, *No Name in the Street*, his latest, is sober, somber, pessimistic, and pragmatic. It is steeped in gloom and hopelessness. The New Testament philosophy of forgiveness has given way to the Old Testament's pronouncements of doom. The intermediate volumes fluctuate in style and tone between the two extremes.

In theme, the last two volumes rely heavily upon quotations from the Old Testament to furnish texts for the sermons they preach. *The Fire Next Time* announces the threat "God gave Noah the rainbow sign, No more water the fire next time" but stresses the twin virtues of love and brotherhood as foils for the impending holocaust. *No Name in the Street* flaunts the curse of destruction and holds out no shred of hope for salvation. The only question is how long the imminent catastrophe can be postponed: "There will be bloody holding actions all over the world, for years to come: but the Western party is over, and the white man's sun has set. Period." (P. 197)

In what respect does Baldwin differ from other American essayists? Probably the most unique feature of his style is his tendency to tie in his personal life and experiences with whatever commentary he offers on social and philosophical questions. In other words, his caustic criticisms of local, national, and world conditions result directly or indirectly from his personal experiences. He, therefore, speaks with an authority that most essayists reject as not sufficiently objective. He has accepted as the major theme in all of his writings the horrendous task of exposing with candor and acerbity what it means to be black in a nation and a world dominated by "white" power in social, political, religious, artistic, and ethical matters. He has publicly announced: "We are the generation that must throw everything into the endeavor to remake America into what we say we want it to be. Without this endeavor we will perish. However immoral or subversive this may sound to some, it is the writer who must always remember that morality, if it is to remain or become morality, must be perpetually examined, cracked, changed, made new."[13]

To those who say that a writer who expects to be accepted and respected by his generation must approach his task objectively, taking his subject matter from the past and disguising his criticism by means of metaphor or other types of figurative language, Baldwin replies: "Not everything that is faced can be changed; but nothing can be changed until it is faced."

NOTES

1. James Baldwin, *Notes of a Native Son* (Boston: Beacon Press, 1955), pp. 6–7. All subsequent references to this work will appear in parentheses in the text.

2. Eldridge Cleaver, *Soul on Ice* (New York: McGraw-Hill, 1968), p. 105.

3. James Baldwin, *Nobody Knows My Name* (New York: Dial Press, 1961), p. xiii. All subsequent references to this work will appear in parentheses in the text.

4. Nick Aaron Ford, "Battle of the Books," *Phylon* 22 (Second Quarter, 1961): 119–20.

5. Baldwin, "Everybody's Protest Novel," *Notes of a Native Son*, p. 23.

6. Cleaver, *Soul on Ice*, pp. 97–111.

7. Robert A. Bone, *The Negro Novel in America*, rev. ed. (New Haven: Yale University Press, 1965), p. 235.

8. Norman Mailer, "The White Negro," in *Advertisements for Myself* (New York: G. P. Putnam's Sons, Berkley Medallion Editions, 1966), p. 314.

9. Mailer, "The White Negro," pp. 313–14.

10. *Ibid.*, p. 329.

11. James Baldwin, *The Fire Next Time* (New York: Dial Press, 1963), pp. 23–24. All subsequent references to this work will appear in parentheses in the text.

12. James Baldwin, *No Name in the Street* (New York: Dial Press, 1972), p. 167. All subsequent references to this work will appear in parentheses in the text.

13. James Baldwin, "As Much Truth as One Can Bear," *New York Times Book Review*, January 14, 1962.

SHIRLEY S. ALLEN

The Ironic Voice in Baldwin's
Go Tell It on the Mountain

A number of questions raised in critical interpretations of James Baldwin's first novel, *Go Tell It on the Mountain*, can be answered by studying his use of irony. Such questions include Baldwin's artistic distance from the characters, his attitude toward their religious beliefs, the identity of the ironic voice in Part Three, and the meaning of the novel's denouement. Although there are at least three different kinds of irony in the novel, they are closely related because they result from the narrative technique Baldwin employs, an internal and subjective point of view limited to the thoughts, feelings, and perceptions of the main character. In order to transcend the limitations of this point of view, Baldwin uses irony in the narrator's diction, irony of statement and event in the action, and an ironic voice as a character.

In the major action of the novel, which is the struggle of young John Grimes to leave childhood and achieve maturity with a sense of his own identity, the narrator is limited to John's internal point of view. Although he speaks in the third person, this point of view is strictly maintained, so that even the physical appearance of the hero is described subjectively through comments he hears from others and the images he sees in the mirror.

The point of view is further limited by confinement in time. Although the narrator uses the past tense, he recounts events as they happen, unedited by the perspective of time. We follow John Grimes through the course of his

From *James Baldwin: A Critical Evaluation*, Therman O'Daniel, ed., pp. 30–37. © 1977 by Howard University Press.

fourteenth birthday as if we were experiencing the events with him. Careful use of adverbs denoting present time, such as "now" and "still," maintain this sense of contemporary action. So does a scrupulous use of tenses, particularly the past-perfect for every event occurring even recently before the moment of the present action and frequent use of "would" to express future time in the past tense. A few sentences taken from the episode of Roy's injury illustrate Baldwin's use of tenses:

> His mother leaned over and looked into Roy's face with a sad, sympathetic murmur. Yet, John felt, she had seen instantly the extent of the danger to Roy's eye and to his life, and was beyond that worry now. Now she was merely marking time, as it were, and preparing herself against the moment when her husband's anger would turn, full force, against her.[1]

The effect of this narrative style is immediacy and directness like the first-person, present tense point of view, but it avoids the literary awkwardness of that form. Although such a narrator is not uncommon in modern fiction, Baldwin's use is remarkable for consistency and suppleness. He also exploits fully the freedom of a third-person narrator to use whatever diction the author chooses without limitation to language characteristic of the protagonist. Baldwin's excellent command of language (improved over his earliest short stories) and his talent for almost poetic expression are used to present the thoughts of a Harlem schoolboy without restriction to his grammar and vocabulary.

In fact, the contrast between the narrator's diction and the dialogue of the characters emphasizes both the universality of their inner conflicts and the particular circumstances of their lives as Negroes in America. Baldwin's ear for language and his skill at representing it in print are nowhere better displayed than in the dialogue of *Go Tell It on the Mountain* where the dialect is conveyed with such subtlety and economy that the rhythms, accent, and colloquialisms of Harlem speech do not blur the individuality and dignity of the speakers. Contrasted with the dialogue is the educated and highly literate voice of the internal narrator, compelling the reader's understanding and sympathy beyond suggestions of race or class.

The separation between the subjective narrator and the character that is implied by use of the third-person form is also useful in this novel because in Part Two, "The Prayers of the Saints," the narrator enters the minds of three other characters serially, maintaining the same point of view in relation to each as his relation to John in Part One and Part Three. The narrator becomes in thoughts, feelings, and perceptions John's aunt, then his stepfather, then his mother; but his diction remains his own. This device is important for preserving the continuity of the novel, which has few external indications of continuity.

Having set up this type of narrator, with immediate and intimate knowledge of the character, Baldwin partially overcomes his limitation to a single, internal point of view by introducing verbal irony into his diction. Sometimes he merely uses a word with connotations opposite to the values assumed by the character, as when he describes the great preaching mission that Gabriel regards as the most important of his career as "a monster revival meeting" and his more venerable colleagues as "war horses." Sometimes he simply lifts out of its churchly context a word used with religious conviction by the characters, as when he speaks of the saints doing their housecleaning or refers to Praying Mother Washington as "the praying mother." Several times he describes obviously human motives in terms of divine providence with such naivete^ that the statement becomes ironic:

> Tarry service officially began at eight, but it could begin at any time, whenever the Lord moved one of the saints to enter the church and pray. It was seldom, however, that anyone arrived before eight thirty, the Spirit of the Lord being sufficiently tolerant to allow the saints time to do their Saturday-night shopping, clean their houses, and put their children to bed. (P. 49)

He also uses biblical language to describe an action contrary to the spirit of biblical precept and thus reveals hypocrisy in the pious:

> The ministers were being served alone in the upper room of the lodge hall—the less-specialized workers in Christ's vineyard were being fed at a table downstairs. (P. 107)

Although much of the irony is related to the religious views and practices of the characters, some is purely secular:

> Elizabeth found herself in an ugly back room in Harlem in the home of her aunt's relative, a woman whose respectability was immediately evident from the incense she burned in her rooms and the spiritualist seances she held every Saturday night. (P. 162)

The ironic detachment of the narrator is subtly suggested by Baldwin's careful use of the past tense to express a timeless conviction: "For the rebirth of the soul was perpetual; only rebirth every hour could stay the hand of Satan."

Such irony in the narrator's voice runs the risk of leading the reader's sympathy away from the characters and breaking the illusion of intimacy. Indeed, Wallace Graves has charged Baldwin with "literary cuteness" and lack of "moral energy" (honesty) in his treatment of John's mother and natural father, Elizabeth and Richard, because of the narrator's verbal irony in "Elizabeth's Prayer," where he finds a "shift in technique" from the "highly serious narrator elsewhere in the book."[2] The narrator's irony, however, is not limited to one section of the novel, and it avoids literary cuteness by its subtlety and sparseness. The ironic voice that speaks occasionally through the narrator's diction merely reminds us that there are other points of view from which the ideas and actions might be regarded. Moreover, in many cases the character whose thoughts are being presented may actually share this double view, consciously or unconsciously. A good example is the description of Sister McCandless, seen through John's mind but infused with the narrator's irony:

> There were times—whenever, in fact, the Lord had shown His favor by working through her—when whatever Sister McCandless said sounded like a threat. Tonight she was still very much under the influence of the sermon she had preached the night before. She was an enormous woman, one of the biggest and blackest God had ever made, and He had blessed her with a mighty voice with which to sing and preach. (P. 57)

Similar ambiguity is found in Elizabeth's view of her aunt's threat to move heaven and earth:

> Without, however, so much as looking at Heaven, and without troubling any more of the earth than that part of it which held the court house, she won the day. (P. 155)

Since both John and Elizabeth have serious reservations about the accepted view of the character being described, the irony may reflect their own feelings expressed in the more sophisticated language of the narrator.

The narrator's sophistication and detachment are balanced by his serious tone and poetic intensity of expression in describing important events or psychological perceptions in the lives of his major characters, so that his occasional irony is more like a wry smile than ridicule. The touch of humor in an otherwise passionately serious work relieves tension and gives the complexity of view needed to avoid sentimentality in so closely autobiographical a novel.

Baldwin also uses other kinds of irony to escape from the limitations of the subjective narrator in *Go Tell It on the Mountain*. Most obvious is the dramatic irony made possible by the three long flashbacks, which give the reader information unknown to other characters. For example, when Gabriel is thinking over the events in his life, the reader already knows, because of Florence's revelations, that Gabriel's wife is aware of his infidelity; and therefore the reader finds much irony in his account of scenes between them. Baldwin also uses irony of event to give the reader a corrective viewpoint. So Gabriel's two chance meetings with his bastard son occur under circumstances that emphasize sexual potency and thus contradict the purely paternal relationship Gabriel assumes.

But the most important and pervasive kind of irony in this novel is developed through the use of biblical texts and Christian doctrine to comment upon the attitudes and actions of the characters. Critics disagree about Baldwin's attitude toward the religious faith he ascribes to the characters in *Go Tell It on the Mountain*, often citing statements from Baldwin's subsequent essays to bolster their arguments.[3] The question is important for understanding the novel, since its main action is the conversion of the hero to that faith and the reader must know whether this resolution is tragic or victorious.[4] Aside from other evidence, unrelated to the subject of irony, which I believe points to the latter interpretation, a cogent argument can be found in Baldwin's use of this religious faith to pronounce judgment on his characters by irony of statement.

For example, Gabriel is ironically judged by his own quotations from the Bible and doctrines of the church. Under the title "Gabriel's Prayer" is an epigraph taken from a Negro spiritual, which asserts, "I ain't no stranger now." This expresses Gabriel's conviction that he is "saved," the fundamental tenet of his religious faith and the basis for his holier-than-thou attitude. If this assumption were allowed to stand uncorrected, the reader would condemn that faith as illusory and deplore John's conversion to it, since Gabriel is revealed as more devilish than saintly. But Baldwin carefully shows the irony of Gabriel's assumption by contrasting it with his own preaching. We learn early in the novel that he has taught his sons that they are in more danger of damnation than African savages precisely because they are not strangers to the gospel. In one of his sermons, he stresses the need for humility and consciousness of sin before God: "When we cease to tremble before him we have turned out of the way." In his thoughts about the tarry service, he remembers that "the rebirth of the soul is perpetual." Gabriel, the preacher and expositor of the faith, thus passes ironic judgment on his own self-righteousness.

Baldwin makes ironic Gabriel's favorite text, which is Isaiah's message to Hezekiah: "Set thine house in order, for thou shalt die and not live"—

a quotation Gabriel uses both to terrify his children and to assert his own righteousness. The first mention of this text is ironically placed just after the breakfast scene, which has shown how disordered Gabriel's house is in its family relationships. A second mention during Florence's prayer suggests the further irony that Gabriel is unaware of his own approaching death, or at least of the inevitability of death. But more significantly, the text is used to make ironic Gabriel's unshakeable confidence in the "sign" he believes he received from God. He seizes upon the advent of Elizabeth and her bastard as the sign that God has forgiven him after he has ignored a sign that the reader recognizes as similar to that given Hezekiah the moment after Esther told him of her pregnancy, when the sun stood still and the earth was startled beneath his feet.

In another instance Gabriel's belief that God speaks aloud to men, sometimes through thunder, is turned ironically against his assumption of righteousness. First mentioned early in the novel, this belief becomes important during Deborah's confrontation of Gabriel with his mistreatment of Esther. He justifies his action as God's will: "'The Lord He held me back,' he said, hearing the thunder, watching the lightning. 'He put out His hand and held me back.'" To make certain that the reader sees the irony, Baldwin has Gabriel repeat his belief about the thunder: "Listen. God is talking." Gabriel is thus contradicted by the voice of his own God. The final irony on this theme occurs in the conversation between Gabriel and Florence at the end of the novel:

> "I been listening many a nighttime long," said Florence, then, "and He ain't never spoke to me."
> "He ain't never spoke," said Gabriel, "because you ain't never wanted to hear You just wanted Him to tell you your way was right." (P. 214)

Although Gabriel is the character most often ironically judged by his own religious convictions, Florence and Elizabeth also unwittingly pronounce judgment on themselves. Florence recites the conditions for successful prayer and then fails to meet them in her cry for salvation. Elizabeth tells herself that she is on her way up the steep side of the mountain, and then contracts a loveless marriage as "a hiding-place hewn in the side of the mountain."

By using the tenets of their faith for ironic comment upon the characters' actions and attitudes, Baldwin transcends the limitations of his subjective narrator and at the same time establishes as trustworthy the religious faith they profess, even when they misinterpret it. Within the novel the universe works according to the principles of the Hebrew-Christian tradition, and therefore John's conversion is the opening of his eyes to truth—a giant step on his way up the mountain.

In Part Three, "The Threshing Floor," Baldwin introduces an ironic voice that speaks to John during the early stages of his internal struggle. Critics disagree about the identity of this anonymous internal speaker. David Noble asserts that it is the voice of Gabriel, because it expresses Gabriel's wish that John would get up off the threshing floor.[5] In order to accept this identification the reader must see Gabriel as a conscious hypocrite who could encourage John to rebel against his authority to prevent John's salvation, but Baldwin carefully shows Gabriel as an unconscious hypocrite, never capable of overt double-dealing. Other critics have taken the ironic voice as John's own common sense, fighting a losing battle against his weakness for hysterical religion.[6] If the voice is common sense, then John's conversion is a tragedy and his joyful faith an illusion; and this interpretation is contradicted by the tone of the last few pages, by the meaning of the book's title and supporting epigraph, and by the serious attitude toward religious faith implied by Baldwin's use of it for ironic comment. Moreover, John's struggle on the threshing floor is described in terms of birth imagery, and the accomplished delivery sets him free from the womb of childhood. After his conversion he stands up to his father on the equal footing of adulthood, refuting Gabriel's scornful doubts, openly recognizing the enmity between them, and refusing to obey his command. Obedience to the urging of the ironic voice would have prevented this deliverance and left John in his state of childish rebellion, a prisoner to his longing for parental love and his feeling of sexual guilt.

In terms of the novel, we see the ironic voice as an enemy who presses John to do what Gabriel secretly hopes he will do, what Florence did when she rejected her brother's church and her brother's God. The narrator describes it as malicious: "He wanted to rise—a malicious, ironic voice insisted that he rise—and, at once, to leave this temple and go out into the world." The voice comes from within John, expressing his own wishes, and its main attack is against any belief in this religion, which it attempts to discredit by associating it with "niggers" and by ridiculing the Bible's story of Noah's curse on Ham. The voice, then, is the voice of unbelief within John, which Baldwin describes as predominant in his state of mind before his conversion. At the beginning of the tarry service he is scornful of the praying women and replies to a kindly, though pious, remark by Sister Price with "a smile that, despite the shy gratitude it was meant to convey, did not escape being ironic, or even malicious." Like Florence, who prays, "Lord, help my unbelief," he is not a believer. His unbelief and hidden scorn are expressed by the ironic voice in the first stages of his struggle on the threshing floor.

The voice also expresses his rebellion against his father, his father's religion, and his father's social status. It labels the tarry service as a practice of "niggers," with the implication that John is above that level, and its spurs him to resist his father's authority:

> Then the ironic voice spoke again, saying: "Get up, John Get up, boy. Don't let him keep you here. You got everything your daddy got." (P. 196)

This explicit connection of his sexual maturity with his father's enmity brings him to the brink of understanding, but it is not until the ironic voice leaves him that John is able to penetrate the mystery:

> But now he knew, for irony had left him, that he was searching something, hidden in the darkness, that must be found. He would die if it was not found. (P. 199)

When he has rid himself of malice, he is free to search the subconscious depths of his mind until he grasps the true relationship of father and son—the Oedipal situation common to all human experience or, in Baldwin's interpretation, original sin.

Ridding oneself of malice is a necessary condition to salvation. Florence, unable to escape her hatred of Gabriel, founders on this rock, just as Gabriel's pride prevents him from reaching true understanding of the Oedipal situation. When John's malicious irony is swept away, he faces the psychic realities of his subconscious, and then only fear is left—the fear of being an adult, unprotected by parental love and responsible for his own life. Overcoming this fear is the final step—the step Elizabeth has not yet been able to take, and John makes it with Elisha's help. The ironic voice of unbelief, of the devil, of childish rebellion is replaced with the humble voice of faith, of God's angel, of mature self-acceptance, saying, "Yes, go through."

Perhaps Baldwin is suggesting that all irony is in a sense malicious, that human problems cannot be solved by sophisticated detachment or even common sense reasonableness. Certainly the ironic voice of the narrator is lost in the passionate seriousness of John's religious experience, which is the climax and resolution of his conflict.

NOTES

1. James Baldwin, *Go Tell It on the Mountain* (New York: Dell Publishing Company, 1953), p. 44. Further references to the novel, given in the text, are to this paperback

edition, since the original Dial Press edition is hard to find and differs in pagination from the 1963 Dial edition.

2. "The Question of Moral Energy in James Baldwin's *Go Tell It on the Mountain*," *CLA Journal* 7 (March, 1964): 219, 221, 223. Much of Graves's argument rests on his contention that the rest of the novel is "absent of this sort of irony." He infers that Baldwin is too deeply involved with these two characters to give them objective life.

3. A majority argue that the conversion is a trap into which John falls because of "the unsubduable propensity for religious hysteria implanted in him by his nurture," in the words of Nathan A. Scott, "Judgment Marked by a Cellar: The American Negro and the Dialectic of Despair," in *The Shapeless God*, ed. H. J. Mooney and T. F. Staley (Pittsburgh: University of Pittsburgh Press, 1968), p. 160. See also D. E. Foster, "'Cause my House Fell Down'; the Theme of the Fall in Baldwin's Novels," *Critique: Studies in Modern Fiction* 13, No. 2 (1971): 51; H. M. Harper, *Desperate Faith* (Chapel Hill: University of North Carolina Press, 1967), pp. 144–45; George E. Kent, "Baldwin and the Problem of Being," *CLA Journal* 7 (March, 1964): 204; Robert A. Bone, "The Novels of James Baldwin," *Tri-Quarterly* No. 2 (Winter, 1965): 7; Colin MacInnes, "Dark Angel: The Writings of James Baldwin," *Encounter*, August, 1963, pp. 22–23; Marcus Klein, "James Baldwin: A Question of Identity," in *After Alienation: American Novels in Mid-Century* (Cleveland: World Publishing Company, 1962), pp. 180–82.

4. One of the first reviewers, J. H. Raleigh, *New Republic*, June, 1953, p. 121, complained that "the final impact of the novel is somewhat muffled." Many subsequent critics have shared this view including Michel Fabre, who calls it an "impossible dénouement" in "Pères et Fils dans *Go Tell It on the Mountain* de James Baldwin," *Etudes Anglaises*, 23 (January–March, 1970): 54.

5. David Noble, *The Eternal Adam and the New World Garden* (New York: George Braziller, 1968), p. 211.

6. Scott, "Judgment Marked by a Cellar," pp. 160–161.

.

HORACE PORTER

The South in Go Tell It on the Mountain: *Baldwin's Personal Confrontation*

James Baldwin's *Go Tell It on the Mountain* has been appropriately designated an autobiographical or semiautobiographical work. I have previously tried to suggest how it would be useful to read the novel with a more comprehensive definition of autobiography in mind.[1] I concluded:

> One could persuasively read passages [from his stories and novels] as fictional counterparts of Baldwin's comments in *Notes of a Native Son*, in *The Devil Finds Work*, and in other autobiographical essays. But this direct referential approach, in which the "facts" of John Grimes's life are correctly perceived as mirroring Baldwin's, amounts to only a useful interpretive beginning, not a critical end. The point of view from which one scrutinizes the facts of a writer's life as a writer is also crucial. Thus, the literal facts of Baldwin's boyhood ... pale in significance beside the secrets" of his literary life embedded in the text of *Go Tell It on the Mountain*.[2]

A writer writes a novel at a particular time in a specific place and at a certain moment in her or his career. Such significant factors, in addition to the fidelity of the plot and characters to the biographical details of a writer's life, are important considerations. For instance, *Go Tell It on the Mountain* is

From *New Essays on Go Tell It on the Mountain*, Trudier Harris, ed., pp. 59–75. © 1996 by Cambridge University Press.

53

Baldwin's first novel rather than his sixth. That fact is at least as important as the similarity between Gabriel Grimes, John Grimes's dogmatic and bitter stepfather, and David Baldwin, Baldwin's own stepfather.

Consequently, I refer to *Go Tell It on the Mountain* as a "proving ground" to underscore its weighty psychological and emotional significance in Baldwin's. literary career. The "autobiography" that seems of crucial significance is the story of the writer's attempt to achieve a coherent evocation of a difficult subject no less than an initial realization of his talent.

The challenge Baldwin faced partly involved the portrayal of Gabriel Grimes, a bitter black Southerner who had, like his own stepfather, come north to New York. Having never even visited, let alone lived in the South, Baldwin, in writing his first novel was wholly dependent on vicarious experience— reading, observation, and imagination—in his portrayal of Gabriel Grimes's complex and bewildering fate. We should bear in mind, as previously noted by various critics and Baldwin himself, that the gestation period of *Go Tell It on the Mountain* was long and painful. Responding to Wolfgang Binder in an interview conducted in 1980, Baldwin commented:

> I finished my first novel, *Go Tell It on the Mountain* ... and it was a turning point in my life, because it proved to me, not so much to the world but to me and my baby sister that at least I was serious. A black writer in the world that I had grown up in was not so much wicked, he was insane. So when *Mountain* finally came out in 1953, at least I had proved something to people. And then the real battle began. But nothing happened to me afterwards that was quite as terrifying as the very beginning. I knew that if I could not finish *Mountain* I would never be able to finish anything after that. But that was my ticket to something else. I finally had gotten it. At least I was a writer.[3]

The autobiographical fact that is of primary interest has less to do with the terrifying presence of David Baldwin and Gabriel Grimes in the lives of their respective sons as Baldwin's "terrifying" beginning as a writer.

Furthermore, long before a series of biographical works began to appear shortly after the writer's death, Baldwin had become (partly through his own eloquent autobiography) legendary. His was a literary Cinderella story involving his flight from the Harlem ghetto to Paris, London, Hollywood, Istanbul, and St. Paul de Vence. He became a best-selling author. He was invited to the White House by President John Kennedy. And after the publication of *The Fire Next Time* in 1963, he was featured on the cover of *Time*. Excluding Baldwin's final years when he lived and taught in the United

States (calling himself a "commuter") he spent most of his writing life in France—Paris and St. Paul de Vence.

After his initial long stay in Paris (1948–1957), Baldwin returned to the United States. He spent a few weeks at home with his family in New York and then headed south for the first time. He had been commissioned by *Harper's Magazine* and *Partisan Review* to write essays on the various strategies and programs for bringing an end to racial discrimination and separation. For a month or so during September and October of 1957, Baldwin traveled through a number of southern cities—Charlotte, Atlanta, Birmingham, Montgomery, and Tuskegee. During his stay in Atlanta, he met and interviewed Dr. Martin Luther King, Jr. And while in Birmingham, he met with Rev. Fred Shuttlesworth, a stalwart leader and defender of the rights of African-Americans.[4]

After his return to New York, Baldwin wrote two essays—"The Hard Kind of Courage" which was published in *Harper's Magazine* and would be included in his second collection of essays, *Nobody Knows My Name* (1961) as "A Fly in the Buttermilk." He called the essay he wrote for *Partisan Review* "A Letter From the South: Nobody Knows My Name." It became the title piece of the writer's second volume of essays. These eloquent articles reveal the writer's complex attitudes toward the South. They were also clearly designed to educate, provoke, and inspire a liberal white audience, to awaken the audience from its slumber of moral denial and evasiveness on racial discrimination. In this regard, the essays are a rehearsal for *The Fire Next Time*, his most famous essay, which appeared in its original form in *The New Yorker*.

Thus, Baldwin could neither get around the demands of his own literary design, his conscious and unconscious professional or vocational desire, nor could he avoid entirely a temporary form of blinding northern and cosmopolitan prejudice. He was victimized partly by the mythology of the South. He viewed the South rather reductively as a slow, backward, and brutal land, trapped perpetually in the nightmare of its racial history. In "Nobody Knows My Name" he recalls his thoughts as his plane landed in the South for the first time:

[M]y plane hovered over the rust-red earth of Georgia. I was past thirty, and I had never seen this land before. I pressed my face against the window, watching the earth come closer; soon we were just above the tops of the trees. I could not suppress the thought that this earth had acquired its color from the blood that had dripped down from these trees. My mind now filled with the image of a black man, younger than I, perhaps, or my own age,

hanging from a tree, while white men watched him and cut his
sex from him with a knife.[5]

Baldwin concludes, directly after the preceding passage: "My father must
have seen such sights—he was very old when he died—or heard of them, or
had this danger touch him."[6] This quotation demonstrates how preoccupied
Baldwin was with a sense of the South's emasculating, murderous, and bloody
past, a picture of the region paradoxically as mythological as it was real.

Almost two decades after the publication of *Go Tell It on the Mountain*,
Baldwin, the most famous African-American writer alive at that time,
published *No Name in the Street* (1972), recalling images of the South highly
similar to those passing through his mind as his plane landed for the first
time:

> There was more than enough to fascinate. In the Deep South—
> Florida, Georgia, Alabama, Mississippi, for example—there is
> the great, vast, brooding, welcoming, and bloodstained land,
> beautiful enough to astonish and break the heart. The land seems
> nearly to weep beneath the burden of this civilization's unnamable
> excrescence. The people and the children wander blindly through
> the forest of billboards, antennae, Coca-Cola bottles, gas stations,
> drive-ins, motels, beer cans, music of a strident and invincible
> melancholy, stilted wooden porches, snapping fans, aggressively
> blue-jeaned buttocks, strutting crotches, pint bottles, condoms,
> in the weeds, rotting automobile corpses, brown as beetles,
> earrings flashing in the gloom of bus stops: over all there seems to
> hang a miasma of lust and longing and rage. Every southern city
> seemed to me to have been but lately rescued from the swamps,
> which were patiently waiting to reclaim it. The people all seemed
> to remember their time under water, and to be both dreading
> and anticipating their return to that freedom from responsibility.
> Every black man, whatever, his style, had been scarred, as in some
> tribal rite; and every white man, though white men, mostly, had
> no style, had been maimed. And, everywhere, the women, the
> most fearfully mistreated creatures of this region, with narrowed
> eyes and pursed lips—lips turned inward on a foul aftertaste—
> watched and rocked and waited.[7]

The preceding passage, marked at once by the best and worst of
Baldwin's imagination, captures a certain mythological sense of the South.
Baldwin uses a hard-edged documentary style: "billboards, antennae, Coca-

Cola bottles, gas stations, drive-ins, motels, beer cans." This Whitmanian catalogue of images is presented fleetingly as though a montage viewed rapidly from the window of a moving automobile. And while he speaks of "the Deep South" as a land "beautiful enough to astonish and break the heart" he squeezes "Florida, Georgia, Alabama, Mississippi" together as monolithic "bloodstained land."

To be sure, he succeeds at evoking a physical sense of the southern scene. There are indeed "rotting automobile corpses, brown as beetles," all over the South. But some may also be rotting in New Jersey and New York. What is more significant is the obvious outsider's contempt Baldwin displays. His contempt is betrayed by his dispassionate bitterness. "The land," as he labels it in a superior tone, is vastly removed from New York, let alone Paris, his beloved city of light. "The land," which is "the Deep South" "seems nearly to weep beneath the burden of this civilization's unnamable excrescences." This image of the South haunts Baldwin and is a recurrent theme in his work. It is hardly accidental that Baldwin's initial thought of the South as his plane landed is a vivid scene of lynching, a deeply internalized and bloody scene of castration and death.

He knows that "this land" inspired his stepfather's lifelong hatred of whites. Thus, his sense of the place terrorizes him even as he arrives. Shortly thereafter, as though the gods had arranged a ritualistic scene of initiation and instruction, Baldwin walked through the front door of a cafeteria in Montgomery. It was as though he had stumbled back in time to a revelatory moment that explained what his stepfather had so painfully endured.

The writer captures this memorable incident in *No Name in the Street*:

> I will never forget it, I don't know if I can describe it. Everything abruptly froze into what, even at that moment, struck me as a kind of Marx Brothers parody of horror. Every white face turned to stone: the arrival of the messenger of death could not have had a more devastating effect than the appearance in the restaurant doorway of a small, unarmed, utterly astounded black man. I had realized my error as soon as I opened the door: but the absolute terror on all these white faces—I swear that not a soul moved—paralyzed me. They stared at me, I stared at them.[8]

When he is "barked" at by a waitress who yells "What you want boy? What you want in here?" Baldwin backs out. A white man suddenly appears and advises him to go to the back: "Right around there, boy. Right around there." When Baldwin arrives at the "colored entrance," he concludes: "And this was a dreadful moment—as brief as lightning and far more illuminating.

I realized that this man thought that he was being kind, and he was, indeed, being as kind as expected from a guide in hell."[9]

After Baldwin goes through the "colored entrance" and orders a hamburger, he highly respects the blacks who have been able to adjust and adapt to the southern situation while still maintaining their dignity. He considered himself incapable of such patience and forbearance. As he watched a black man eat a hamburger in apparent aimless abandon, he concluded: "I was far from certain that I was equipped to get through a single day down here.... They had been undergoing and overcoming for a very long time without me ... my role was to do a story and avoid becoming one. I watched the patient man as he ate; watched him with both wonder and respect."[10]

As previously noted, during the period that Baldwin spent writing *Go Tell It on the Mountain*, he had not yet gone to the "old country," as he calls it. Thus, he was entirely at the mercy of his imagination, reading, and whatever conclusions he drew about the region based on the limitations and strengths—real and imagined—of his stepfather's personality. This autobiographical situation partly explains the writer's portrait of Gabriel Grimes, no less than John's response to him in the novel.

Two themes inextricably linked in *Go Tell It on the Mountain* involve the perpetual existence of black rage and the manner in which such rage can either be self-destructive or transformative. These two themes are connected to the image of the South in *Go Tell It on the Mountain* because, as Baldwin sees it, the incipient black rage is partly the legacy of the South playing itself out in the individual as weft as collective lives of blacks in the North. For instance, Elizabeth and Richard, John Grimes's biological parents, flee the South in order to marry and fulfill their dreams in the North. Richard eventually commits suicide, leaving Elizabeth with John and the memory of his love and self-destructive bitterness.

Baldwin explores the sources and consequences of such complex emotional dynamics in *Go Tell It on the Mountain*. And precisely because he was able to begin fulfilling his own dream of becoming a writer by completing his first novel he was later able to clarify and name in "Notes of a Native Son" the rage and avenging will he felt in his teens and early twenties.

A telling moment of truth arises in *Notes of a Native Son* when Baldwin's father asks him whether he would rather write or preach. The memory of, or indeed remembering, this incident is an inspired moment. As the minister delivers the eulogy at his father's funeral Baldwin, having celebrated his nineteenth birthday earlier that day, unexpectedly remembers the singular incident: "I remembered the one time in all our life together when we had really spoken to each other. It was on a Sunday and it must have been shortly before I left home. We were walking, just the two of us, in our usual silence, to or from church. I was in high school and had been doing a lot of writing and I was, at about this time, the editor of the high school magazine. But I had also been a young minister and had been preaching from the pulpit.... my father asked me abruptly, 'you'd rather write than preach, wouldn't you?' That was all we said. It was awful to remember that that was all we had *ever* said."[11]

This passage represents a highly revelatory autobiographical moment whether one considers it in light of *Notes of a Native Son* or in relation to *Go Tell It on the Mountain*. When Baldwin says he would rather write than preach, he is asserting so much more than the straightforward statement apparently indicates. The statement takes us considerably beyond a mere choice of vocation. Writing represents a comprehensive way of seeing and a habit of being in the world.

To write or preach is the figurative question on Baldwin's mind as he creates John Grimes and his brooding stepfather, the Reverend Gabriel Grimes, in *Go Tell it on the Mountain*. The opening paragraph of the novel, no less than Part One, "The Seventh Day," addresses the matter of John Grimes's potential fate relative to that of his stepfather: "Everyone had always said that John would be a preacher when he grew up, just like his father. It had been said so often that John, without ever thinking about it, had come to believe it himself. Not until the morning of his fourteenth birthday did he really begin to think about it, and by then it was too late."[12]

The opening lines of the novel suggest the literal and figurative weight of paternal authority in the work. The narrator also foregrounds the issue in an implicitly antagonistic or indeed oedipal way: "Not until the morning of his fourteenth birthday did he really begin to think about it and by then it was too late." The passage clearly suggests John's apparent, if adolescent, ambivalence about life as a minister. And as the first section of the novel develops, we discover that John finds the attractions outside the church equally and perhaps even more alluring. The narrator alludes to John's sense of "the darkness of his father's house."[13]

Furthermore, we learn that John's response to the assertion that one day he would be a "Great Leader of His People" is negative and defiant: "John was not much interested in his people and still less in leading them anywhere."[14] John has dreams of another kind of public role. He envisions himself as "a poet, or college president, or a movie star; he drank expensive whiskey, and he smoked Lucky Strike cigarettes in the green package."[15]

Baldwin takes considerable care in the novel's opening section to provide the reader with a sharply sketched portrait of John. We know, for instance, that he is singularly intelligent. And given his precocious nature, he discovers that he can use his intelligence as a source of pride and protection. He makes this discovery when a principal singles him out in the first grade. She refers to him as "a very bright boy" after noticing work with the alphabet that he had done at the blackboard. This moment of recognition becomes a scene of extraordinary empowerment: "That moment gave him from that time on, if not a weapon at least a shield; he apprehended totally, without belief or understanding, that he had in himself a power that other people lacked; that he could use this to save himself, to raise himself; and that, perhaps, with this power he might one day win that love which he so longed for."[16]

John's yearning for power is expressed most dramatically in the passage often quoted in which he stands on top of a hill in Central Park and imagines his future as a "giant" or "tyrant":

> At a point that he knew by instinct and by the shape of the buildings surrounding the park, he struck out on a steep path over-grown with trees, and climbed a short distance until he reached the clearing that led to the hill. Before him, then, the slope stretched upward, and above it the brilliant sky, and beyond it, cloudy, and far away, he saw the skyline of New York. He did not know why, but there arose in him an exultation and a sense of power, and he ran up the hill like an engine, or a madman, willing to throw himself headlong into the city that glowed before him.
>
> But when he reached the summit he paused; he stood on the crest of the hill, hands clasped beneath his chin, looking down. Then he, John, felt like a giant who might crumble this city with his anger; he felt like a tyrant who might crush this city beneath his heel; he felt like a long-awaited conqueror at whose feet flowers would be strewn, and before whom multitudes cried, Hosanna! He would be, of all, the mightiest, the most beloved, the Lord's anointed; and he would live in this shining city which his ancestors had seen with longing from far away. For it was his; the inhabitants of the city had told him it was his; he had but to run down, crying, and they would take him to their hearts and show him wonders his eyes had never seen.[17]

Since John Grimes knows the point in Central Park "by instinct" and since he "struck out" for it, Baldwin suggests that John's is a recurrent fantasy that he is driven to act out. "He did not know why, but there arose in him an exultation and a sense of power, and he ran up the hill like an engine, or a madman." The setting, Central Park, is a noted public space in America's largest and most influential city. Thus, John's fantasy also betrays genuine ambition and a personality marked by a need for consummate self-expression.

John's adolescent self gives way to a raging spirit within him, which the narrator likens to that of a "madman," but the metaphorical resonance of the passage does not suggest madness so much as profoundly troubling ambivalence. John's adolescent fantasy is symptomatic of his struggle with "the darkness of his father's house" and "Jesus in the darkness of his father's church" but it also represents Baldwin's early and figurative meditation on his complex and bewildering fate as an artist. The immediate scene is superimposed on a more significant aspect almost hidden in John's avenging imagination, the portrait of an ambitious young artist with a confident and raging will to public expression and power.[18]

Even here where the South has no ostensible relation to the moment, there are significant connections. The Manhattan skyline represents the antithesis of his father's house. Gabriel Grimes has brought the emotional baggage of the South north with him. It is this legacy that threatens to limit John's possibilities.

Furthermore, Gabriel Grimes is a man victimized and burdened by the sins of his past. The South—"the blood stained land"—is the scene of his personal fall from the glory of God as well as the space in which his embattled black manhood has been so ruthlessly socialized. Thus, his rage, his hatred, suspicion, and contempt for whites periodically erupt. The "rage in his blood," to borrow from Baldwin's *Notes of a Native Son*, is essentially a southern rage. And it is this rage that is literally John Grimes's legacy, the nightmarish history with which he must contend and which he must overcome.

Consequently, it is hardly an accident that a bloody image of a murdered and castrated black man should also appear in *Go Tell It on the Mountain* and that such a moment would directly involve Gabriel Grimes. The moment comes in "Gabriel's Prayer" as the Reverend worries about his favorite son Royal. As he walks through town threatened by the hostility of the white men who watch him, he muses:

> There were no black men on the streets at all, save him. There had been found that morning, just outside of town, the dead body of a soldier, his uniform shredded where he had been flogged, and, turned upward through the black skin, raw, red meat. He lay face downward at the base of a tree, his fingernails digging into the scuffed earth. When he was turned over, his eyeballs stared upward in amazement and horror, his mouth was locked open wide; his trousers, soaked with blood, were torn open, and exposed to the cold, white air of morning the thick hairs of his groin, matted together, black and rust-red, and the wound

that seemed to be throbbing still. He had been carried home in silence and lay now behind locked doors, with his living kinsmen, who sat, weeping, and praying, and dreaming of vengeance, and waiting for the next visitation. Now, someone spat on the sidewalk at Gabriel's feet, and he walked on, his face not changing, and he heard it reprovingly whispered behind him that he was a good nigger, surely up to no trouble.[19]

The recurrent image of a lynched black man in Baldwin's work is a telling detail. In *Go Tell It on the Mountain*, the castrated and dead body of the black man simultaneously signifies powerlessness and avenging rage. In many instances black men were lynched on the basis of mere suspicion and false claims about their sexual involvement with white women. They found themselves trapped in a web of psychosexual circumstances which often led to death. Their legacy was the anger of their bereaved kin—fathers and mothers, sisters and brothers. It is no wonder that directly after Gabriel Grimes merely hears about the dead black soldier, he responds vicariously in a deep psychological and visceral way. He is surrounded by white men watching him in a threatening manner: "While he walked, held by his caution more rigid than an arrow, he prayed, as his mother had taught him to pray, for loving kindness; yet he dreamed of the feel of a white man's forehead against his shoe; again and again, until the head wobbled on the broken neck and his foot encountered nothing but the rushing blood."[20] It is significant to note here, however, that the preceding scene does not involve so much a ritual as a horrible *fait accompli*. The man had already been killed and castrated, leaving "the wound that seemed to be throbbing still."[21] Furthermore, the scene shows Gabriel Grimes worrying about the apple of his eye, his son Royal, whom he briefly encounters and warns to be careful.

The figure of the lynched black man who first appears in Baldwin's fiction in *Go Tell It on the Mountain* surfaces again in *Nobody Knows My Name* and is fully explored in *Going to Meet the Man*. Here is the lynching scene from that story:

The man with the knife walked toward the crowd, smiling slightly; as though this were a signal, silence fell, he heard his mother cough. Then the man with the knife walked up to the hanging body. He turned and smiled again. Now there was a silence all over the field. The hanging head looked up. It seemed fully conscious now, as though the fire had burned out terror and pain. The man with the knife took the nigger's privates in his hand, one hand, still smiling, as though he were weighing them.

> In the cradle of the one white hand, the nigger's privates seemed as remote as meat being weighed in the scales; but seemed heavier, too, much heavier, and Jesse felt his scrotum tighten; and huge, huge, much bigger than his father's, flaccid, hairless, the largest thing he had ever seen till then, and the blackest. The white hand stretched them, cradled them, caressed them. Then the dying man's eyes looked straight into Jesse's eyes—it could not have been as long as a second, but it seemed longer than a year. Then Jesse screamed, and the crowd screamed as the knife flashed, first up, then down, cutting the dreadful thing away, and the blood came roaring down.[22]

This bloody image partly represents Baldwin's ongoing effort to make articulate the significance and consequences of his stepfather's life in his own. It represents a memory of the South apparently deep-seated in a region of his mind.

In *Exorcising Blackness: Historical and Literary Lynching and Burning Rituals*, Trudier Harris provides a heart-wrenching picture of the lynching ritual. She describes how it encapsulates for the white onlookers—men, women, and children—elements of theater of the grotesque, sport, and entertainment.[23]

I referred earlier to Baldwin's sense of the South on his first visit there in 1957 as being paradoxically as mythological as it was real. Apparently, this sense of the South persisted. In *Going to Meet the Man* (1965), Baldwin provides a *tableau vivant* of the lynching ritual from its start to its bloody end. David Leeming has commented that Baldwin (during 1965) wrote the story more easily, he said, than he had written anything."[24] Leeming sums up the significance of the story in the following manner:

> The story "Going to Meet the Man" was a fictional articulation of ideas that its author had also treated in his essays; like all of Baldwin's fiction, it can best be seen as a parable, in this case a parable on the relationship between racism and sexuality, in which the white sheriff, from whose point of view the story of a lynching is told, becomes a representative of the long-held Baldwin belief that the race problem—the so-called Negro problem—was really a white problem. The "man" in "Going to Meet the Man" is the white man, as was "Mister Charlie" in *Blues for Mister Charlie*. The black man who is lynched during the sheriff's childhood is, like so many earlier fictional creations of Baldwin's mind, a scapegoat for the facing of the race problem. Hanging on the

tree, deprived of his masculinity in a violent ritual of castration rooted in the white man's myth of black sexuality, he provides the white man—represented by the sheriff—with the sexual power he otherwise lacks.

We can speculate and extrapolate and use some of Baldwin's own words ("My father must have seen such sights ... or heard of them, or had this danger touch him") in order to conclude that. Baldwin's stepfather actually told the young writer such horror stories about the South. We certainly know that David Baldwin was extremely suspicious of, and disapproved of Baldwin's association with, whites on the grounds that they could not be trusted. However, to whatever degree the horror of the South lived on in Baldwin's mind—as demonstrated over time by his stories and essays—the direct autobiographical influence of his father through tales of southern lynchings is finally less significant than the comprehensive and indirect threat the South posed to his literary ambition.

David Baldwin's bitter perspective on the world, no less than his embattled pride and sense of manly dignity, is what he tried, with patriarchal authority and studied vengeance, to pass on to his young stepson. And in his instinctive, inchoate writer's way Baldwin, like John Grimes, began to covet and protect his intelligence, his developing literary sensibility, as a barrier of protection between him and the stepfather he feared. This particular oedipal dynamic leads him to tell his stepfather one fateful Sunday morning that he would rather write than preach.

The various lynching scenes highlighting Baldwin's preoccupation with images of powerlessness and emasculation, the ultimate rooting out of manhood and authority, along with John Grimes's dreams of a world beyond "the darkness of his father's house" surface repeatedly. We have already discussed his fantasy on the hill in Central Park. A similar moment and perhaps of equal significance occurs when he travels defiantly downtown and watches a movie alone. The movie is set in London.

The image of a woman John Grimes sees in a movie becomes an appropriate metonym of his rage, defiance, and artistic desire. I readily concede that any direct connection to John Grimes's (read James Baldwin's) views about the South is not readily apparent. But here I return to my initial suggestion of a more comprehensive and perhaps more significant definition of autobiography. The woman appears as a fleeting image on the silver screen as John Grimes's mind is wavering to and fro between the pleasure this dark and forbidden (by Gabriel Grimes) palace of illusion affords his inchoate artistic or literary sensibility and the intense anguish it inspires about the damnation that awaits him for his defiance and sinful indulgence.

Against Gabriel Grimes's expressed wishes, John finds himself wandering down 42nd Street past "the stone lions that guarded the great main building of the Public Library, a building filled with books and unimaginably vast."[25] He imagines a future life of glamour and power. He eventually finds himself in front of the movie houses. He enters one and watches a movie about a woman who lived in London: "She had a great many boyfriends, and she smoked cigarettes and drank."[26] John Grimes identifies with her for the following reasons:

> Nothing tamed or broke her, nothing touched her, neither kindness, nor scorn, nor hatred, nor love. She had never thought of prayer. It was unimaginable that she would ever bend her knees and come crawling along the dusty floor to anybody's altar, weeping for forgiveness. Perhaps her sin was so extreme that it could not be forgiven; perhaps her pride was so great that she did not need forgiveness. She had fallen from that high estate which God had intended for men and women, and she made her fall glorious because it was so complete. John could not have found in his heart, had he dared to search it any wish for her redemption. He wanted to be like her, only more powerful, more thorough, and more cruel; to make those around him, all who hurt him, suffer as she made the student suffer, and laugh in their faces when they asked pity for their pain. *He* would have asked no pity, and his pain was greater than theirs. Go on, girl, he whispered, as the student, facing her implacable ill will, sighed and wept. Go on, girl. One day he would talk like that, he would face them and tell them how much he hated them, how they had made him suffer, how he would pay them back!

How, one must surely wonder, does this image relate to Baldwin's personal confrontation with the South, no less than with the specific and recurrent images of lynchings previously addressed? First, the intensity and instinctive knowingness of John's identification with a defiant and fallen woman begs a simple question. Why her? Her pride is the courageous pride of those individuals who, against all odds and obstacles, fight back and say, to recall Melville, in the midst of the "personified impersonal," a personality stands here. The woman's point of view represents the serious artist's point of view by which he or she will prosper or fail, live or perish. And in John's instance, like Baldwin's and those of numerous others, this point of view must be embraced with vitality and vigilance. Thus, John empathizes and appropriates the woman's vision. Disregarding her ugly and troubling circumstances, he cheers her on: "Go on, girl. One day he would talk like that, he would face them and tell them how much he hated them, how they made him suffer, how he would pay them back!"[27]

John Grimes, with such power, could free himself from the nightmare of history represented by his father's house, the nightmare of history that includes the southern threat and horror of emasculation and death. He could thereby become the master of his fate, a principal actor in the creation of his own reality.

Like John, Baldwin began early on to negate the power of his southern stepfather and later that of another powerful Southerner and surrogate father, Richard Wright. He would allow neither to compromise his attempt to create an original literary space for himself. It is useful to bear in mind some of Baldwin's own comments on escaping the nightmare of history. It may even prove an exercise in futility, he warns us. Why? We are fatally "trapped in history," no less than "history is trapped in us." Nevertheless, the writer must always make an attempt to free himself or herself through periodic gestures of eloquence. And Baldwin brilliantly succeeded. Writing became the agency, the holy spirit, by which Baldwin transformed history. And by this same agency and spirit, he was released from the tyranny of his father's house. He built a castle of his own and imagined a world and a point of view that took him far beyond the confines of his father's dogmatically religious view of the world and the limitations imposed by peculiarly American dilemmas involving race and sexuality. He translated his choice of vocation and his concomitant search for a new form of empowerment and fulfillment into Art. To borrow a phrase from his mentor Henry James, his life involved *par excellence* "the madness of art." And through the mad agency of Art, he perpetually attempted to create another culture, another country, another world. He tried, to use his own words, "to end the racial nightmare, achieve our country and change the history of the world."[28]

NOTES

1. Horace Porter, *Stealing the Fire: The Art and Protest of James Baldwin* (Middletown, CT: Wesleyan University Press, 1989).

2. Ibid., p. 16.

3. Fred L. Standley and Lewis H. Pratt, eds., *Conversations with James Baldwin* (Jackson: University of Mississippi Press, 1989), p. 202.

4. David Leeming, *James Baldwin* (New York: Alfred A. Knopf, 1994), pp. 137–141.

5. James Baldwin, *The Price of the Ticket* (New York: St. Martin's, 1985), p. 184.

6. Ibid., p. 184.

7. Ibid., p. 485.

8. Ibid., p. 487.

9. Ibid., p. 487.

10. Ibid., p. 488.

11. Ibid., p. 142.

12. James Baldwin, *Go Tell It on the Mountain* (New York: The Dial Press, 1953), p. 9.

13. Ibid., p. 19.

14. Ibid., p. 19.

15. Ibid., p. 19.

16. Ibid., p. 20.

17. Ibid., p. 35.

18. For a thorough discussion of this, see Porter, *Stealing the Fire*, pp. 15–20.

19. James Baldwin, *Go Tell It on the Mountain*, p. 161.

20. Ibid., p. 161.

21. Ibid., p. 161.

22. James Baldwin, *Going to Meet the Man* (New York: Dell Publishing, 1966), p. 216.

23. Trudier Harris, *Exorcising Blackness: Historical and Literary Lynching and Burning Rituals* (Bloomington: University of Indiana Press, 1984), p. xi.

24. David Leeming, *James Baldwin*, p. 248.

25. Baldwin, *Go Tell It on the Mountain*, p. 39.

26. Ibid., p. 41.

27. Ibid., p. 42.

28. Baldwin, *The Price of the Ticket*, p. 379.

HORACE PORTER

The Significance of "Notes of a Native Son"

Baldwin's title essay in *Notes of a Native Son* is an autobiographical tour de force.[1] Its title, while seeming to exploit or appropriate in an obvious way the title of Richard Wright's *Native Son* and Henry James's *Notes of a Son and Brother*, is not as simple as that.[2] First, "notes" suggests something provisional, temporary, or inconclusive; in that light, it is synonymous with "outline." But "notes" tells us something more meaningful in what it suggests about the essay's symbolic significance for the writer's literary career. In that context the word can be read as "prologue." Baldwin had published only one book before *Notes of a Native Son*. He had just turned thirty. *Notes of a Native Son* constitutes Baldwin's first decisive efforts as a professional writer. The individual essays had actually appeared in various magazines before the publication, in 1953, of his first novel, *Go Tell It on the Mountain*. Essays like "The Harlem Ghetto," "Everybody's Protest Novel," and "Many Thousands Gone" were quite literally his debut as a writer. He wrote them when he was in his twenties. So the word "notes" suggests a kind of prelude—the dramatic opening chords proclaiming a literary event of public note.

"Notes of a Native Son" also suggests the idea of family. Baldwin's status as "son" will be in the foreground. But even if we are unfamiliar with the details of his life—the fact, for instance, that he had been a child evangelist—the essay promptly tells us that through the intimation of the

From *Stealing the Fire: The Art and Protest of James Baldwin*, pp. 23–37. © 1989 by Horace A. Porter.

biblical parable of the prodigal son. Thus, Baldwin becomes considerably more than the stepson of a Negro minister in the Harlem ghetto. He is a son of God and a citizen of the world. The family in question is the human family with its multifarious range of terrors and wonders.

Baldwin begins his essay on a universal note, connecting his life and his family's life to all mankind. A man dies; a child is born. He tells us in his opening sentences: "On the 29th of July, in 1943, my father died. On the same day, a few hours later his last child was born." The essay is divided into three sections, paralleling the three sections—"Fear," "Flight," and "Fate"—of Wright's *Native Son*. Baldwin devotes the first to a description and candid examination of what he calls "the intolerable bitterness of spirit" in which his father (actually his stepfather) lived and died. He shows dramatically how his father's bitterness and fanatical asceticism deeply affected the fives of his nine children; so much, in fact, that they resent his very presence. And their father in turn believes, Baldwin says, that his children "had betrayed him by ... reaching towards" the world which had despised him." Baldwin is chief among the traitors. He is utterly contemptuous of his father's world view. His father warns him of the poisonous effects of white prejudice and hatred. He tells his son that even those white classmates he considers his best friends are not to be trusted. Baldwin rejects this warning. This, among other disagreements, compels him to leave his father's house, and after he has graduated from high school, he leaves Harlem for Trenton, New Jersey, to take a job in a defense plant. His co-workers are mostly black and white Southerners. He is rudely awakened by their hostile responses to him. He is fired after a while, and on his last night in Trenton, when he is refused service at a fashionable restaurant, he explodes in an unexpected fit of murderous rage.

In the second section of the essay, Baldwin, the prodigal son, returns home. He knows his father is dying and that his mother is about to give birth to another child. Baldwin's description of Harlem and its somber wartime mood leads to the essay's final section, a poignant recapitulation, complete with cinematic effects, of his father's funeral. Through a stunning series of deftly arranged flashbacks, we witness Baldwin responding to his father, first as an angry son approaching manhood, then as a rebellious adolescent, and finally as a small boy. Baldwin carefully prepares the reader for his revelations. His central theme is the complex legacy his father left him. The son—reflective and troubled—must ponder perpetually the self-destructive black rage and bitterness fueled in his father and then in himself by the prejudice of white Americans. Baldwin examines the capricious nature of the black rage he feels, an anger simultaneously personal and collective. His experience is, of course, specific but it is hardly unique; every black American is somehow victimized by racial prejudice. Thus, Baldwin's essay, even in the most literal way, reminds one of Wright's *Native Son*.

This link is established in the essay's first section, in which Baldwin is a victim of overt racial discrimination. Using a telling form of symbolic suggestion, he recounts the story of that last night in Trenton. He and a white friend go out on the town and see a movie titled *This Land Is Mine*. That ironical and suggestive title is highlighted when the reader discovers that the diner they go to after the movie is called the American Diner. Baldwin asks for a hamburger and a cup of coffee, and is rebuffed by the counterman. He is told, "'We don't serve Negroes here.'" After a brief, sharp reply, Baldwin and his white friend walk out into the street: "People were moving in every direction but it seemed to me, in that instant, that all of the people I could see, and many more than that, were moving toward me, against me, and that everyone was white.... I wanted to do something to crush these white faces which were crushing me." As in a trance, Baldwin then comes to the door of an "enormous, glittering, and fashionable restaurant," where, he knows, "not even the intercession of the virgin" will allow him to be served. He enters the restaurant, nevertheless, sits at a table for two, and waits. When the young white waitress, with "great, astounded, frightened eyes," comes over and predictably announces, "'We don't serve Negroes here,'" Baldwin loses control. He throws a water mug at her with all his strength. It misses and shatters against the mirror behind the bar. Suddenly he comes to his senses: "I saw, for the first time, the restaurant, the people with their mouths open, already as it seemed to me, rising as one man.... I rose and began running for the door." Baldwin's friend misdirects his pursuers and the police, and after Baldwin is alone and safe, he ponders the event over and over and arrives at two shocking and alarming conclusions: "I could not get over two facts, both equally difficult for the imagination to grasp, and one was that I could have been murdered. But the other was that I had been ready to commit murder. I saw ... that my life, my real life, was in danger, and not from anything other people might do but from the hatred I carried in my own heart." The murderous rage Baldwin feels is clearly reminiscent of Bigger Thomas's blind hatred and anger. But Baldwin hopes the love he has in his heart will serve as an antidote, mitigating the effects of his poisonous, self-destructive bitterness. The essential emotional drama of the essay arises from his dilemma: How can a native son whose democratic American dreams must seemingly be perpetually deferred strike the necessary balance between love and hate? All of his work thereafter would elaborate that theme.

In the second section, when Baldwin visits his father in the hospital, the sight of his father as he lies dying awakens Baldwin's compassion: "The great, gleaming apparatus which fed him and would have compelled him to be still even if he had been able to move brought to mind, not beneficence, but torture; the tubes entering his arm made me think of pictures I had seen when a child of Gulliver, tied down by the pygmies on that island."

In the final section Baldwin explores the significance of his father's life and death. And, through that process, he discovers something about the nature of the hatred and bitterness he carries in his own heart. He reminds the reader that the day of his father's funeral had also been his own nineteenth birthday. He had spent most of the day downtown at the apartment of a girl he knew. They celebrated by drinking and tried to focus on Baldwin's birthday rather than on the funeral that night. This particular detail is telling in a special way. The birthday celebration, such as it was, was a pretext for Baldwin's temporary and what became, eventually, in a special way, a permanent departure from his father's house and his father's world. Thus, even on the day of his father's funeral, Baldwin appears to be headed in the direction of another country, another culture.

Baldwin's father saw downtown Manhattan as a city of sin and corruption rivaled only by Sodom and Gomorrah. Baldwin is attempting to escape the overwhelming power of his religious tradition, and his success in escaping will remain in question. Even on the most superficial level, he worries about the appropriateness of his behavior. A "nagging problem" has oppressed him "all day long"—the fact that he has nothing black to wear to the funeral. Baldwin understands that a funeral ritual is a necessary and proper ending in human affairs. As he says, "Every man in the chapel hoped that when his hour came he, too, would be eulogized, which is to say forgiven, and that all of his lapses, greeds, errors, and strayings from the truth would be invested with coherence and looked upon with charity." Baldwin certainly knows, even at nineteen, that his religious convictions are not universally shared downtown. But he will share the cultural assumptions of the mourners who will come. The girl who is drinking and celebrating his birthday with him finds him a black shirt for the occasion, and, as Baldwin remembers, "dressed in the darkest pants and jacket I owned, and slightly drunk, I made my way to my father's funeral."

"It seemed to me, of course, that it was a very long funeral," Baldwin writes. "But it was, if anything, a rather shorter funeral than most, nor, since there were no overwhelming, uncontrollable expressions of grief, could it be called—if I dare to use the word—successful." Baldwin reaches a kind of autobiographical stasis at the funeral. He recovers a memory that heightens the intensity and sharpens the tone of the moment. We see and hear the young writer moving slightly away from his theme like an accomplished musician guided by a magical spell of improvisation. "While the preacher talked ... my mind was busily breaking out with a rash of disconnected impressions.

Snatches of popular songs, indecent jokes, bits of books I had read, movie sequences, faces, voices, political issues—I thought I was going mad." Even as Baldwin breaks away from his straightforward description of the funeral and describes his own intense interiority, even as he concentrates on what appears to be a predictable emotional reaction of loss and incipient grief occasioned by his father's death, the real focus is on the young writer himself. The things that are rising up, perhaps out of the deep blue of repressed memory, are not, at first, specific, or at least he does not report them as such. They are essentially abstract agents of narrative association—"snatches of popular songs," "bits of books," "movie sequences." What one might call the writer's characteristic disposition toward extraordinary mental association surges up and is played upon. Thus, we arrive at the moment where Baldwin, like Proust's Marcel, relives his own past:

> Then someone began singing one of my father's favorite songs and, abruptly, I was with him, sitting on his knee, in the hot, enormous crowded church which was the first church we attended. It was the Abyssinian Baptist Church on 138th Street.... With this image, a host of others came. I had forgotten, in the rage of my growing up, how proud my father had been of me when I was little. Apparently, I had had a voice and my father had liked to show me off before the members of the church. I had forgotten what he looked like when he was pleased but now I remembered that he had always been grinning with pleasure when my solos ended. I even remembered certain expressions on his face when he teased my mother.... I remembered being taken for a haircut and scraping my knee on the footrest of the barber's chair and I remembered my father's face as he soothed my crying and applied the stinging iodine.
> ("Notes of a Native Son," P. 107)

Some readers may have experienced an analogous, vicarious, moment. Pulled into the swirling vortex of the essay's central theme, the legacy of the death of the father, the reader connects Baldwin's memory to his or her own sense, actual or potential, of loss and grief. The song each reader hears in his or her mind's ear is not the song Baldwin hears, but a song of personal identification and a note of counterpoint. Baldwin plays a universal note and touches a familiar nerve. Even more significant is the precise nature of the memory. Baldwin captures the "forgotten" moments of the past as they surface on the wave of memory induced by the sound of one of his father's "favorite songs." He is recalled, through song, to his original relationship to his father. Now there is no cacophonous collage of "popular songs," "bits of books," and "movie sequences," but rather memories that are specific and somewhat separate. With each repetition, indeed each playing of the word "remembered," a new scene unfolds. Now we see the little boy on his father's knee, now the smiling face of the proud father at the end of his son's solo, now we see the little son summoning forth his father's consoling hand.

Baldwin's emphasis on music is telling, whether it is his unexpected memory of popular songs, his recalling of the singing of his father's favorite songs, or the shocking recognition and remembrance of his own youthful church solos; all of the music is connected to the theme of the dead father. The theme of music looms large in the essay because "Notes of a Native Son" is, essentially, the solo Baldwin could not sing for his father at his father's final hour. It is the best that Baldwin can do, now that his father is dead and, no matter the intensity and power of memory, irrecoverable. And the solo is part and parcel of the moving picture we see of Baldwin's father. Viewed from one angle, his father is a brutal and bitter man; from another he is the victim, like many anonymous thousands, of racial prejudice and discrimination; from yet another he is a religious fanatic with a tempestuous personality; and finally, he is the smiling, proud, protective, and loving father of Baldwin's youth.

The memorable passage reflects the essay's multifaceted design. On a superficial, as well as a more profound, level, "Notes of a Native Son" is a classic instance of protest. Its message is clear. It is the story of a son who tries relentlessly to escape the crippling environment of his father's house. Along the way, the religious father views the son as a prodigal ingrate. But the willful son's extraordinary insistence upon his own vision of American life, his choice of writing over preaching, eventually provides the means by which he moves beyond the circumscribed limits of his father's house. Using his narrative resourcefulness, Baldwin rescues his essay from the banality of a predictable, if justifiable, Afro-American cry of racial prejudice and discrimination to a universal story of potential liberation of the self.

Baldwin's narrative ingenuity is complicated by his use of devices that are suggestive of certain cinematic techniques—including the use of voice-overs, collages, and flashbacks spliced seamlessly into the ongoing autobiographical narrative. Take, for example, the recurrent theme of the death of the father. When Baldwin brings the reader out of the flashback that leads the essay back to sweet memories of his childhood, he rolls his narrative abruptly away from the "forgotten" but now "remembered" world of his childhood and adolescence back into the enormous present of the church and the ongoing funeral. We see him staring at his father's open casket as the mourners, including his aunt and younger brothers and sisters, are led "one by one" to the bier. Then it is Baldwin's momentous turn:

> One of the deacons led me up and I looked on my father's face. I
> cannot say that, it looked like him at all. His blackness had been
> equivocated by powder and there was no suggestion in that casket
> of what his power had or could have been. He was simply an
> old man dead, and it was hard to believe that he had ever given
> anyone either joy or pain. Yet, his life filled that room. Further up
> the avenue his wife was holding his newborn child. Life and death
> so close together, and love and hatred, and right and wrong, said
> something to me which I did not want to hear concerning man,
> concerning the life of man.
>
> ("Notes of a Native Son," p. 109)

The technique appropriated from the cinema is tried and true. He shows
the audience a close-up of a dead man's face and body. At first glance it
appears to be a cheap shot, pandering, via sensationalism and sentimentality,
to stock emotions. But Baldwin presents emotions far more complicated.
He focuses on the reaction of the mourner. We are reminded that the son
is seeing his father for the last time. And the son observes his father's face
"equivocated by powder." It is as though the undertaker, realizing some
hidden aspect of personality, had tried to protect the dead man's face from
the cold scrutiny of the living. But Baldwin's use of "equivocate" suggests
that what the undertaker had intended to be a charitable, face-saving device
has failed. Baldwin recognizes the hopeless ethnic phenomenon of applying
white powder to black skin. The white powder, designed to save the face by
softening its features and presumably setting them free, actually imprisons. It
reminds the son of his father's self-hatred and bitterness and the white hatred
that had helped to destroy him.

By playing upon this moment of finality, Baldwin reminds us of the
universal nature of the scene. Standing before his father's casket, he becomes
the disembodied and timeless voice of mankind by way of his evocative
rhetoric about the implacable forces and facts of the human condition. His is
a chorus-like and representative voice, reminding us of the eternal recurrence
of "life and death," "love and hatred," "right and wrong."

After the funeral, Baldwin goes back downtown to continue celebrating
his birthday, and, while his father lies in state in the undertaker's chapel, a riot
breaks out in Harlem. Baldwin connects his father's funeral to the chaos and
violence in the Harlem streets and exploits the riot's symbolic significance: "As
we drove him to the graveyard, the spoils of injustice, anarchy, discontent, and
hatred were all around us. It seemed to me that God himself had devised, to
mark my father's end, the most sustained and brutally dissonant of codas." By
setting his father's death and funeral in the context of a race riot, he suggests

that his father's death is a matter of far-reaching public, not only private, significance. But beyond that, and moving directly from one of the connotations of "notes" in his title, he uses "coda," which signifies the formal ending of a musical composition. But the harmonious closure that characterizes a coda is nonexistent. The symbolic notes surrounding his father's death are troubling and discordant. Baldwin writes with poignancy about the death and funeral of his father eleven years after the fact in order to understand his own. Baldwin, just shy of thirty, is still, in effect, starting out as a writer. Thus, in crucial ways, "Notes of a Native Son" can be read as an autobiographical position paper. As we shall see, it is an implicit extension of his earlier comments in "Everybody's Protest Novel" and "Many Thousands Gone."

In the essays in *Notes of a Native Son*, Baldwin is attempting to create order out of the disorder of his own life. Indeed "Everybody's Protest Novel" and "Many Thousands Gone," though ostensibly literary criticism, are as vital and profoundly autobiographical as "Notes of a Native Son." Writing, for Baldwin, is a matter of life and death. And that essential exercise in personal and vocational clarification requires an extended examination of self, society, and history. It requires an analysis of how the three simultaneously conspire against and corroborate one's fate. In this context, the death of Baldwin's father cries out for interpretation. Thus, when the son, the aspiring writer, takes his last look at his father's face, he yearns for definitive answers. But the only authoritative answer his father, like any dead father, can give is symbolic. On one level the son is finally free. He is released from his father's house, if not entirely from his influence, in order to cultivate his own garden. Baldwin ponders the future as his father is driven "through a wilderness of smashed plate glass" to the graveyard. Focusing on the street, Baldwin uses another device appropriated from cinematic narration, this time, cinema verité. The camera, which is the "I" of Baldwin, the participant observer, simply follows the riotous *tableau vivant* as it unfolds on the Harlem street:

> ... bars, stores, pawn shops, restaurants, even little luncheonettes had been smashed open and entered and looted.... The shelves really looked as though a bomb had struck them. Cans of beans and soup and dog food, along with toilet paper, corn flakes, sardines and milk tumbled every which way, and abandoned cash registers, cases of beer leaned crazily out of the splintered windows and were strewn along the avenues. Sheets, blankets, and clothing of every description formed a kind of path, as though people had dropped them while running. I truly had not realized that Harlem *had* so many stores until I saw them all smashed open.
>
> ("Notes of a Native Son," p. 111)

Although, at the essay's beginning, Baldwin has described the riot as "the most sustained and brutally dissonant of codas," arranged by God to signal his father's end, he discovers, as his father is being driven to the graveyard, that the cacophony of the streets is also unmistakably his own. It reminds him of the rage and bitterness within him that may erupt suddenly and uncontrollably. The riot is also Harlem's collective black rage monstrously personified. On a more profound and perhaps even prophetic level, the riot is an intimation of what is in store for America. This scene anticipates the precautionary exhortations of *The Fire Next Time*, which would be written just before another time of turmoil and death.

The description of the riot, coming as it does near the essay's end, affords a narrative opportunity of dramatic poetic closure. Orchestrating a form of counterpoint in which the narrator observes Harlem disintegrating, the writer makes us privy to his interior monologue as he struggles to salvage personal and symbolic meaning out of the wreckage around him. We are shown the final flashback, which is not so much a scene in the sense of an actual place or incident as it is a private region in Baldwin's mind. He recalls his father's favorite biblical text, what Baldwin calls "the golden text":

> And if it seem evil unto you to serve the Lord, choose you this day whom you will serve; whether the gods which your fathers served that were on the other side of the flood, or the gods of the Amorites, in whose land ye dwell: but as for me and my house, we will serve the Lord.
> ("Notes of a Native Son," p. 113)

By remembering his father's "golden text," characterized by an either–or scenario, Baldwin underscores the fact that he will be forced to reflect upon his failure to follow in his father's footsteps and "serve the Lord." A consideration of his father's text takes him back to his own days of adolescent evangelical fervor, back to that momentous occasion when his father rebuked him: "You'd rather write than preach, wouldn't you?" The young evangelist's answer that fateful Sunday afternoon was "Yes." But his was hardly a simple answer. By replying "Yes," he was saying "No" to his father's whole way of life.

The rage Baldwin felt when he was nineteen, the riot he witnessed, and the memories he recalled during his father's funeral would only later achieve their full significance. Thus, reflecting on his father's death as the hearse rolls through the "wilderness of smashed plate glass," Baldwin concludes, "All of my father's texts and songs, which I had decided were meaningless, were arranged before me at his death like empty bottles, waiting to hold the meaning which life would give them for me. This was his legacy: nothing is ever escaped." Baldwin's use of the phrases "texts and songs ... arranged ... like empty bottles," though oddly mixed, derives crucial significance through the agency of subconscious or subliminal metaphorical suggestion. The songs and texts are "arranged." And since they are like "empty bottles," they can be viewed as a form of musical notation to be played out or played upon by the son. Since the "arranged" composition is inescapable, the son can, of course, willfully misread the composition or he can improvise. But the composition will always remain the point of departure. And the degree to which the son succeeds or fails will, at least in part, depend on his ability to translate or transpose the composition and arrangement of the songs and texts for his own purposes. Moreover, the empty bottles Baldwin refers to as his father's "legacy" might be compared to a series of precious burial urns. Viewed in this light, the bottles become the final resting place of his dead father's spirit. And Baldwin's memory becomes a mantel on which the bottles will remain forever "arranged." Of course, from time to time, the "golden text" will surface unexpectedly with genie-like fidelity: "Now the whole thing came back to me as though my father and I were on our way to Sunday school." Baldwin's memory of and response to his father's golden text underscores Kafka's observation that all profound writing is a kind of prayer. Baldwin's prayer simultaneously seeks the wisdom of his dead father and that of the living God the Father to whom his dead father was faithful to the end.

During this period of his life, Baldwin is compelled to interpret the meaning of his father's death in order to get on with his own life. He addressed this question in an introduction, written in 1984, to a new edition of *Notes of a Native Son*. Baldwin defines the words "inheritance" and "birthright"; he views inheritance as "particular, specifically limited and limiting." One's "birthright" is another matter; it connects him "to all that lives, and to everyone, forever." Calling the "conundrum of color" the inheritance of all Americans and asserting that "one cannot claim the birthright without accepting the inheritance," Baldwin concludes:

> I was trying to locate myself within a specific inheritance, precisely, to claim the birthright from which the inheritance had so brutally and specifically excluded me. It is not pleasant to be forced to recognize, more than thirty years later, that neither this dynamic nor this necessity has changed.
> ("Notes of a Native Son," p. xii)

Baldwin's rather intense concern with his birthright drives him to distill that which is universal out of the "limited and limiting" disorder of the particular in "Notes of a Native Son." "The dead man mattered, the new life mattered; blackness and whiteness did not matter; to believe that they did was to acquiesce in one's own destruction."

"Notes of a Native Son" is a brilliant example of Baldwin's efforts to arrive at or claim his birthright by focusing on his inheritance. Yet his separation of "inheritance" from "birthright" is an academic dichotomy. What, we might be inclined to ask, would the term birthright mean to him if American life were not racially rigged? The idealistic democratic rhetoric describing certain "inalienable" rights—life, liberty, and the pursuit of happiness—is comprehensive. Perhaps Baldwin has in mind a subtle spiritual realization. Whatever the case, Baldwin dramatizes in "Notes of a Native Son" how inheritance can cripple and eventually destroy, particularly if that inheritance is defined by bitterness and rage. Such was the nature of his father's legacy. At the essay's end, we hear a note of compromise and deference in Baldwin's voice: "Now that my father was irrecoverable, I wished that he had been beside me so that I could have searched his face for the answers which only the future would give me now."

Baldwin's tone is also apprehensive. During that year in Trenton, when he was so often rebuffed, he felt as though he had contracted a "chronic disease":

> ... the unfailing symptom of which is a kind of blind fever, a pounding in the skull and fire in the bowels. Once this disease is contracted, one can never really be carefree again, for the fever, without an instant's warning can recur at any moment.... There is not a Negro alive who does not have this rage in his blood—one has the choice, merely, of living with it consciously or surrendering to it. As for me, this fever has recurred in me, and does, and will until the day I die.
>
> ("Notes of a Native Son," p. 94)

This is indicative of Baldwin's recognition of the rage in his own heart, a rage symbolized by the riot-torn streets of Harlem. Thus, Baldwin takes care to push the essay in the direction of the future. His father's death was certainly momentous, but, as he reminds us at the essay's end, the birth of his baby sister was also a significant event. "The new life mattered." He suggests that each time a child is born, regardless of the parents or life circumstances, the extraordinary potentiality of the human race is born again.

Baldwin's struggle to clarify the significance of his father's fife and death in the context of his own is deeply related to his literary ambition. After he is released from the tyranny of his father's house, he discovers two literary parents—Harriet Beecher Stowe and Richard Wright—standing in his path.

NOTES

1. James Baldwin, *Notes of a Native Son* (Boston: Beacon Press, 1955, 1984).
2. Richard Wright, *Native Son* (New York: Harper & Row, 1940, 1966).

CAROLYN WEDIN SYLVANDER

"Making Love in the Midst of Mirrors":
Giovanni's Room *and* Another Country

While *Go Tell It on the Mountain* was a means by which Baldwin could deal with his own youth, religious background, and family relationships, particularly with his father, his next two novels, *Giovanni's Room*, 1957, and *Another Country*, 1962,[1] zero in more closely on another aspect of identity—sexuality. It might be even more accurate to say that, while *Go Tell It on the Mountain* uses religious experience as a prime metaphor for the search for identity, the next two novels use sexuality, particularly homosexuality, as the metaphor.

Giovanni's Room is the shorter, simpler, but somewhat more confusing and provisional of the two books. No Negro characters appear in *Giovanni's Room*. Settings are Paris and the south of France. Flashback is used here as it was in *Go Tell It on the Mountain*, but in a simplified way, with one character, David, a young white American, telling the entire story in first-person point of view.

The book is in two parts, with the first, shorter part, about 90 pages in the Dell paperback edition, made up of three chapters. The second part, 125 pages, consists of five chapters. The first part begins with David at the window of a "great house in the south of France" with night falling, looking at his increasingly distinct reflection in the glass. We learn immediately that he will be leaving for Paris the following morning, "the most terrible

---

From *James Baldwin*, pp. 45–66. © 1980 by Frederick Ungar Publishing Co., Inc.

morning of my life"; that his "girl," Hella, is on her way back to America; that Giovanni is "about to perish, sometime between this night and this morning, on the guillotine." From this portentous information, we move in the rest of Chapter 1 back with David to his early life up to his departure from America for France.

The events and personages of David's early life include most significantly a homosexual experience with a friend, Joe, an experience which David has since lied about, even to himself. "I repent now—for all the good it does— one particular lie among the many lies I've told, told, lived, and believed." In addition, his mother, dead when he was five,

> figured in my nightmares, blind with worms, her hair as dry as metal and brittle as a twig, straining to press me against her body, that body so putrescent, so sickening soft, that it opened, as a claw and cried, into a breach so enormous as to swallow me alive.

His father and Aunt Ellen fight and argue about the father's drunken affairs and David's own future, until he manages to escape from home in a job and in the Army. "I had decided to allow no room in the universe for something which shamed and frightened me. I succeeded very well—by not looking at the universe, by not looking at myself, by remaining, in effect, in constant motion."

Weary of alcohol, "meaningless friendships," "desperate women," and work, he leaves for France, to find himself. "If I had had any intimation that the self I was going to find would turn out to be only the same self from which I had spent so much time in flight," David now concludes, "I would have stayed home." And yet, inevitable for his identity, he knows, "at the very bottom of my heart," exactly what he is doing, as he sails off across the Atlantic.

Chapter 2 of *Giovanni's Room* gives a detailed description of David's meeting of Giovanni, a young Italian working in a Parisian bar frequented by gays. The setting and means of the meeting are important for contrast with the immediate, untainted, pure attraction and love Giovanni displays for David. David, out of money, is being fed by an American businessman, Jacques. Jacques and the Frenchman, Guillaume, who operates the bar, are repulsive, old homosexuals who spend their nights bribing and sampling the "knife-blade lean, tight-trousered boys" on the auction block. In contrast to the sordid buying and selling all around is Giovanni and his conversation with David, "so vivid, so winning, all of the light of that gloomy tunnel trapped around his head."

Chapter 3 of Part One takes us from the bar to a restaurant, for an early breakfast of oysters and wine, with, again, the purity of Giovanni's interest contrasted with the shopping around of Jacques and Guillaume. "And here my baby came indeed, through all that sunlight, his face flushed and his hair flying, his eyes, unbelievably, like morning stars." David and Giovanni end up in Giovanni's room—and "soon it was too late to do anything but moan" remembers David later. "He pulled me against him, putting himself into my arms as though he were giving me himself to carry, and slowly pulled me down with him to that bed. With everything in me screaming No! yet the sum of me sighed Yes."

Part One concludes back in the great house in the south of France, with unseasonal snow falling and with the landlady coming to inventory her property. David imagines her to be Giovanni's mother. "It is terrible how naked she makes me feel, like a half-grown boy, naked before his mother." After she leaves, David again remembers Giovanni, comparing his imminent death with their life together.

> I suppose they will come for him early in the morning, perhaps just before dawn, so that the last thing Giovanni will ever see will be that grey, lightless sky over Paris, beneath which we stumbled homeward together so many desperate and drunken mornings.

Part One of *Giovanni's Room* records David's growing acceptance of his sexuality, his acceptance of Giovanni's love. Part Two records his subsequent fall from acceptance, his denial of himself, his feeling, his possibility.

Much of the denial is expressed in terms of the growing repugnance David has for Giovanni's room, in which they now both live. "I remember that life in that room seemed to be occurring beneath the sea" begins Chapter 1 of Part Two. Soon negative imagery takes over in the descriptions of the room, just as springtime in their first coming together is overtaken by summer and then winter, as Giovanni kills Guillaume and hides, then is captured, tried, and executed. David fears the desire that Giovanni's love has awakened in him for other boys, and the images of Jacques's and Guillaume's perpetual and sordid seeking that the desire condemns him to.

> The beast which Giovanni had awakened in me would never go to sleep again; but one day I would not be with Giovanni any more. And would I then, like all the others, find myself turning and following all kinds of boys down God knows what dark avenues, into what dark places?

With this fearful intimation there opened in me a hatred for Giovanni which was as powerful as my love and which was nourished by the same roots.

Chapter 2 brings us back to David's growing feeling of entrapment in Giovanni's room. "It became, in a way, every room I had ever been in and every room I find myself in hereafter.... Life in that room seemed to be occurring underwater, as I say, and it is certain that I underwent a sea change there." The room is now closely described—its smallness, its curtainless and white-painted windows, its torn wallpaper on the floor together with dirty laundry, suitcases, tools, paint-brushes. It is not, as Giovanni calls it, the garbage heap of Paris but, as David now sees it, "Giovanni's regurgitated life." The room is tied with David's potential for saving Giovanni with his love: "I was to destroy this room and give Giovanni a new and better life. This life could only be my own, which in order to transform Giovanni's, must first become a part of Giovanni's room."

David's retreat from Giovanni and his room is aided by a letter from his girl, Hella, who had gone off to Spain to consider marriage to him. "I've decided to let two try it," she finally writes. "This business of loving me, I mean." To reassure himself that he is still capable of making love to a woman, he picks up and briefly uses a chubby American girl, Sue.

Chapter 3 narrates the best and worst of Giovanni's and David's life together. Giovanni loses his job because he will not submit to Guillaume's sex acts and despairingly clings to David. David feels "that Judas and the Savior had met in me." The intrusion of the present in his memory-flashback sees the hours of the night dwindle. "I know," says David, "that no matter what I do, anguish is about to overtake me in this house, as naked and silver as that great knife which Giovanni will be facing very soon." Giovanni's imprisonment in his body and in his prison cell are no different, it seems, than David's imprisonment in his body and his renounced responsibility. His reflections accuse him: "My executioners are here with me, walking up and down with me, washing things and packing and drinking from my bottle.... walls, windows, mirrors, water, the night outside—they are everywhere."

Chapters 4 and 5 tell the story of Hella's return to Paris, David's desertion of Giovanni, Giovanni's turning to Jacques and then other men for support, and his ultimate strangling of Guillaume in despair and rage after submitting to him in order to recover his barkeeping job. When David returns to Giovanni's room to pick up his things, we learn of Giovanni's past in the little Italian village, of the death of his young child, which caused him to leave. "And you will have no idea of the life there," he tells David, "dripping and bursting and beautiful and terrible, as you have no idea of my life now."

"You want to be clean," he accuses David. "You think you came here covered with soap and you think you will go out covered with soap—and you do not want to stink, not even for five minutes, in the meantime." David realizes that in "fleeing from his body, I confirmed and perpetuated his body's power over me."

Giovanni hides from the police for a week after the murder, but is ultimately found and in short order tried and convicted and sentenced. David tries fleeing with Hella to the south, where it should be, but isn't, warmer. He takes violent refuge in her body until it becomes "stale," "uninteresting," her presence "grating." Ultimately, Hella discovers him in a bar with a sailor and knows the truth of his relationship to Giovanni. She leaves for America.

Giovanni's Room concludes in the early morning in the "great house in the south of France," with David imagining Giovanni's advance to his execution as his own reflection in the large window panes becomes more and more faint. "I seem to be fading away before my eyes." He forces himself to look at his body in the mirror. "It is trapped in my mirror as it is trapped in time and it hurries toward revelation.... I long to crack that mirror and be free.... The key to my salvation, which cannot save my body, is hidden in my flesh."

David leaves the house, locks it, with the morning weighing "on my shoulders with the dreadful weight of hope." He tears up the blue envelope in which came the news of Giovanni's death sentence and throws the pieces into the wind. "Yet as I turn and begin walking toward the waiting people, the wind blows some of them back on me." So ends *Giovanni's Room*.

Some critics have described *Giovanni's Room* as a kind of first draft or trial run for *Another Country*, particularly in its use of sexuality, and especially male homosexuality, as a metaphor for the search for identity, for an understanding of life and responsibility to others within it, for the possibilities of rebirth.

The problem with *Giovanni's Room*, its provisional quality, lies in the personage of David. He cannot, and does not, as a character carry the weight of meaning Baldwin is apparently trying to place on his experience. Because he rejects the possibilities his relationship with Giovanni contains, he becomes a negative, and confusing, embodiment of homosexual experience, particularly for a reader already having negative images of that experience. The reader can't help but feel that David has perhaps made the right decision, even while he or she knows that, to Baldwin, the decision is cowardly.

Giovanni's statements to David about his wanting to get through life in soapy cleanliness, without "stink," and the selection of a white American for the main character of *Giovanni's Room* are of course related. Baldwin in his essays continually castigates the white American male for his refusal to admit or see or understand the "darker side" of life. And fear of "the terror within" has inevitably led to the easier and "safer" creating of external "evils"[2]—black men, homosexuals. Upright, defiantly heterosexual David, in his willful innocence of "the stink of life," is in explicit contrast with bisexual, southern European Giovanni and, in implied contrast, with the black American whose experiences early on force him into realistic confrontation of the "terror within."

The hope for David's rebirth into understanding is in Giovanni's room, womblike in its close, cluttered darkness, its watery imagery. But David, in this experience at least, refuses to be born the hard, messy way, so of course cannot be born at all. The slight suggestion of hope at the end of the novel, with the small bits of the blue envelope of the death sentence carried back onto David by the wind, means, perhaps, that he will have another chance to do what he has failed to do this time around—be reborn through terror and loss of innocence. He cannot love at all, the book tells us through Hella, until he undergoes that torturous rebirth. In a 1963 interview, Baldwin stated very clearly that because American men are afraid of homosexuality, "they don't know how to go to bed with women either." ("Disturber of the Peace," by E. Auchincloss and N. Lynch, *Mademoiselle*, May 1963, p. 206.)

The difficulty with *Giovanni's Room* is in its simplicity. The story of Giovanni is more melodramatic than realistic. It must be melodramatic, probably, to hold a reader's attention for the point of the book. The point of the book, too, while interesting, seems too simple. Even a reader cheerfully admitting the importance of sexuality in all forms is likely to find the weight of human identity carried by a homosexual affair not just simple, but simplistic.

Baldwin does not make the mistake of oversimplifying again. In *Another Country*, while the same meaning and potential are given to the homosexual experience, meaning and potential for identity do not lie only there, but in several ways of seeing the "darker side" of life—heterosexual experience, interracial experience, music and writing and death.

And the plot and characterizations of *Another Country* are nothing if not complex. The novel is divided into three books: "Easy Rider," "Any Day Now," and "Toward Bethlehem," with the third, the book of resolutions, much shorter than the other two. The characters and characters' relationships are carefully representative of black and white; male and female; married and unmarried; homosexual, bisexual, and heterosexual. Resolutions are also carefully spread between failure and death, love and happiness, and continuing struggle with no clear positive or negative outcome yet in sight.

The long first chapter of the first book belongs to a black jazz drummer, Rufus Scott. His story begins at Times Square, New York City, past midnight, in the late fall. He has been sitting in movies since 2:00; he has not eaten for days; he is broke. In characteristic Baldwin style, here in third-person point of view, we move back and forth in the chapter between this present tense—Rufus Scott at the end of his rope—and his mind's going back over the events of his life that have brought him there. His theme, the song line "You took the best, so why not take the rest?" occurs early, in connection with the "caterpillar fingers between his thighs" that he must fight off in the movie theater. He is "one of the fallen," under the "weight" of the "murderous" city, alone, "part of an unprecedented multitude."

Taking his memories not in the order in which they weave through his mind, but in chronological order, we find Rufus as an introduction to, a kind of negative touchstone for, the characters who make up the rest of the novel. Rufus grew up in Harlem, admired, talented, believed in, the idol of his younger sister, Ida, and hope of his parents. But the image in his memory is of a drowned boy being carried by his father from the garbage-filled Hudson River. And his memory of Army bootcamp in the South is "the shoe of a white officer against his mouth," which is on the ground, "against the red, dusty clay."

Back in New York, Rufus achieves some fame in hip circles as a drummer. He becomes friends with Vivaldo Moore, a struggling writer of Brooklyn Italian background; Cass and Richard Silenski, she an ex-New England debutante, he a Polish immigrant's son, English teacher, and writer; and Eric Jones, a red-headed actor from a well-to-do Alabama family. It is with Eric that Rufus's love–hate needs are acted out most violently and cruelly, in a triple reaction to Eric's whiteness, Southernness, and homosexuality. Later Rufus vents the same frustrated, tortured destructive drive on Leona, a poor Southern white woman who has been forced to leave her child behind in the South. Rufus's enactment of love and hate, tenderness and beatings, on the body of Leona leads eventually to her institutionalization and his degeneration to the state in which we find him at the opening of the novel. It is largely the hostile intrusion of "the big world" on Rufus that destroys his love relationships—"trouble with the landlord, with the neighbors, with all the adolescents in the Village," with his family, with the ever-menacing police. Rufus resents them all.

In total despair now—no job, money, home—Rufus finds the only friend he has left, Vivaldo, and eats and drinks with him, Cass, and Richard in a bar backroom. When Cass and Richard leave and Vivaldo is joined by an old girlfriend, Jane, Rufus wanders out to go to the bathroom, but instead heads uptown and eventually to the George Washington bridge. He jumps, as did Baldwin's young friend on whom Rufus Scott is based.

> He was black and the water was black....
>   The wind tore at him, at his head and shoulders, while something in him screamed, why? why? He thought of Eric.... *I*

can't make it this way. He thought of Ida. He whispered, I'm sorry, Leona, and then the wind took him, he felt himself going over, head down, the wind, the stars, the lights, the water, all rolled together, *all right.... All right, you motherfucking Godalmighty bastard. I'm coming to you.*

Chapter 2 brings us closer to understanding the world and the characters of Cass and Richard and Vivaldo. The chapter opens the following Sunday morning, amid Sunday papers and coffee cups in the Silenskis' living room in a Puerto Rican neighborhood in West Side Manhattan. Ida Scott calls and comes over, worried about her brother, and Vivaldo comes to read the novel Richard has just sold. The Silenskis' marriage looks idyllic—two sons, Richard on the verge of success and fame. Vivaldo is interested, from a distance, in Ida.

By Wednesday, the day before Thanksgiving, Rufus's body has been found. In Richard's and Cass's reactions to the suicide, we begin to see a crack, an uncertainty in the idyllic marriage, a menace to safety. At Rufus's funeral, Vivaldo and Cass are the only whites, and again, for Cass, there is a suggestion of danger, of depth, of worlds she is not familiar with or comfortable with. Simultaneously, she recognizes in Richard's book the extent of his talent and courage—"It had been written because he was afraid, afraid of things dark, strange, dangerous, difficult, and deep."

Rufus's funeral takes Vivaldo back to his own origins. "'You had to be a man where I come from, and you had to prove it, prove it all the time.... Well, my Dad's still there, sort of helping to keep the liquor industry going. Most of the kids I knew are dead or in jail or on junk.'" One of his boyhood proofs of manhood was beating up a "queer" from Greenwich Village. "'There were seven of us, and we made him go down on all of us and we beat the piss out of him and took all his money and took his clothes and left him lying on the cement floor, and, you know, it was winter.'"

Cass realizes that "Vivaldo's recollections in no sense freed him from the things he recalled." She mentally articulates a key to Rufus's failure and the struggles of the other characters:

Perhaps such secrets, the secrets of everyone, were only expressed when the person laboriously dragged them into the light of the world, imposed them on the world, and made them a part of the world's experience. Without this effort, the secret place was merely a dungeon in which the person perished; without this effort, indeed, the entire world would be an uninhabitable darkness.

Chapter 3 of "Easy Rider" opens several months later, in March of the following year. Vivaldo is struggling with characters of his novel who will not "surrender up to him their privacy"; "they were waiting for him to find the key, press the nerve, tell the truth." He realizes their similarity to himself and wonders "whether or not he had ever, really, been present at his life" or whether he, like others, had passed his life "in a kind of limbo of denied and unexamined pain." He reviews his relationship to women, to men, to blacks, and recalls his first meeting of Ida and his only meeting of Ida's and Rufus's mother.

Ida, whom Vivaldo is taking to lunch and a literary party at the Silenskis', reviews a different kind of life. "She was always waiting for the veiled insult or the lewd suggestion. And she had good reason for it, she was not being fantastical or perverse. It was the way the world treated girls with bad reputations and every colored girl had been born with one."

The Silenskis are "climbing that well-known ladder," with increasing unhappiness. They have moved to a "gray, anonymous building" with "functionless pillars" and "an immense plain of imitation marble and leather." "'He's not even famous *yet*,'" says Cass, "'and, already I can't stand it. Somehow, it just seems to reduce itself to having drinks and dinners with lots of people you certainly wouldn't be talking to if they weren't ... in the profession.'" Cass points out to Vivaldo and Ida that their acting friend, Eric Jones, is coming back from France to star in a Broadway production.

All goes well with Ida and Vivaldo this day. Their enjoyment of each other is broken only, and briefly, by Vivaldo's jealousy of Ida's attention to a TV producer, Mr. Ellis. They leave the Silenskis' party, however, go to Vivaldo's apartment, and make love for the first time. This chapter and Book One end appropriately on a Spring afternoon, with Ida making coffee and singing: "If you can't give me a dollar, / Give me a lousy dime— / Just want to feed / This hungry man of mine."

Book Two, "Any Day Now," opens in a kind of Eden, not in New York City. "Eric sat naked in his rented garden. Flies buzzed and boomed in the brilliant heat, and a yellow bee circled his head.... Yves' tiny black-and-white kitten stalked the garden as though it were Africa.... The house and garden overlooked the sea." Down below, in the Mediterranean, Eric's lover, Yves, is swimming. It is the day before their leaving this house to return to Paris, from whence Eric will go to New York, to be joined there later by Yves. The first chapter of this central book gives the reader a full history of Yves, of Eric's youth and early homosexual experiences in Alabama, and of their meeting and their growing love.

Significantly, Yves and Eric first become lovers after three months of seeing one another every day, in the town of Chartres, under the shadow of the great cathedral towers. Eric during these months "purified, as well as he could, his house, and opened his doors; established a precarious order in the heart of chaos," removing that "army of lonely men who had used him ... [as] the receptacle of an anguish which he could scarcely believe was in the world." He has thereby won Yves's trust, for Yves has also been used.

In a room above a stream, their first moment physically together "obliterated, cast into the sea of forgetfulness, all the sordid beds and squalid grappling which had led [them] here." "Eric felt beneath his fingers Yves's slowly stirring, stiffening sex. This sex dominated the long landscape of his life as the cathedral towers dominated the plains."

The key to Eric's importance in the novel lies in his exclusion from the standards of the world and the subsequent need for him to develop his own code of honor.

> He knew that he had no honor which the world could recognize. His life, passions, trials, loves, were, at worst, filth, and, at best, disease in the eyes of the world, and crimes in the eyes of his countrymen.... There were no standards for him because he could not accept the definitions, the hideously mechanical jargon of the age. There was no one around him worth his envy, he did not believe in the vast, gray sleep which was called security, did not believe in the cures, panaceas, and slogans which afflicted the world he knew; and this meant that he had to create his standards and make up his definitions as he went along.

Yves and Eric make love the last night above the sea—Yves "called Eric's name as no one had ever called this name before. Eric, Eric. Eric. The sound of his breath filled Eric, heavier than the far-off pounding of the sea." Chapter 1 of this second and central book of the novel ends in the peaceful, sunny morning with the two about "to make tracks."

The second chapter of the book sees Eric in New York eight days later. "Why am I going home? he asked himself. But he knew why. It was time. In order not to lose all that he had gained, he had to move forward and risk it all." The menace of New York is intensified for Eric after his French experience—its "note of ... buried despair," its "blighted" boys, its raging "plague," its people "at home with, accustomed to, brutality and indifference, and ... terrified of human affection."

Shortly, he sees the menace in the lives of his friends. He visits Cass and Richard. Their sons are beaten up in Central Park by black kids and the Silenskis fight in front of Eric. Richard releases his long resentment of Cass's reaction to his "success," and exhibits castration fear.

"You're just like all the other American cunts. You want a guy you can feel sorry for, you love him as long as he's helpless. Then you can *pitch in* .... you can be his *helper. Helper!* ... Then, one fine day, the guy feels chilly between his legs and feels around for his cock and balls and finds she's helped herself to them and locked them in the linen closet."

Eric goes to the bar where Ida has her singing debut. She is a success. "'My God,'" mutters Vivaldo, "'she's been working,'" implying "that he had not been, and held an unconscious resentment." As Ellis appears, there is, Eric senses, "something very ugly in the air." Ida has been in contact with Ellis without Vivaldo's knowledge. As the four walk to another bar for a drink and a "business deal" between Ida and Ellis, Eric is menaced also by the policemen encountered, by the gay men they meet, by everything, in the New York surroundings.

The following chapter, Chapter 3, develops these suggested complications further. Cass talks to Vivaldo about her marriage, goes off to sit in a movie alone, and then calls Eric and goes to his apartment. To Vivaldo's offer of company, she replies "'No, Vivaldo, thank you. I don't want to be protected any more.'" As she and Eric venture into an affair with no future, Eric says "'Something is happening between us which I don't really understand, but I'm willing to trust it. I have the feeling, somehow, that I must trust it!'" Eric introduces Cass to an unsafe, treacherous, but real "vision of the world" through his past experiences.

Meanwhile, Vivaldo is struggling with his doubts about, his battles with, Ida. The trust he feels compelled to have is based, however, not on admission of what he knows, but on blindness to it. She is not home; she is not at work; she is undoubtedly with Ellis. Vivaldo wanders through bars and ends up, eventually, at an all-night pot party, which seems to serve little function in the novel except to give Baldwin a chance to describe it before it becomes an American commonplace.

Vivaldo's soul-searching contains echoes of Gabriel's Bible passage in *Go Tell It on the Mountain* and of Eric's three-month preparation for Yves's love. "What order could prevail against so grim a privacy? And yet without order, of what value was the mystery? Order. Order. *Set thine house in order.*" He recognizes where he must go, in order to "break through" with Ida, with suggestions of Eric's and Yves's experience and of the surrender that David in *Giovanni's Room* refuses to make. "And something in him was breaking; he was, briefly and horribly, in a region where there were no definitions of any kind neither of color, nor of male and female. There was only the leap and the rending and the terror and the surrender." He confronts the chainlinks between sex and sin and color jangling through *Go Tell It on the Mountain*.

> How did he take her, what did he bring to her? ... If he despised his flesh, then he must despise hers—and *did* he despise his flesh? And if she despised her flesh, then she must despise him.... What were all those fucking confessions about? *I have sinned in thought and deed.*

Chapter 4 of "Any Day Now" takes the complications to climax. Ida's and Vivaldo's conflicts are exaggerated by the New York summer heat "there was [sic] speedily accumulating ... great areas of the unspoken, vast minefields which neither dared to cross." "'How can you love somebody you don't know anything about? You don't know where I've been. You don't know what life is like for me.... Nobody's willing to pay their dues,'" Ida accuses.

Cass's and Eric's affair continues, and Eric's theatrical success mounts— a movie role, a screen test for the lead in Dostoyevski's *The Possessed*. Eric's acting power is tied to his, by this time, clearly androgynous sexuality—"There was great force in [his] face, and great gentleness. But, as most women are not gentle, nor most men strong, it was a face which suggested, resonantly, in the depths, the truth about our natures."

On the climactic night, Vivaldo and Eric go off to Eric's apartment for searching conversation, and Ida and Cass, supposedly going home, are taken by Ida instead to Harlem to meet Ellis. Ida's most negative view of events is voiced in her warning to Cass.

> "What you people don't know ... is that life is a *bitch*, baby. It's the biggest hype going. You don't have any experience in paying your dues and it's going to be rough on you, baby, when the deal goes down. There's lots of back dues to be collected, and I know damn well you haven't got a penny saved."

And, indeed, Cass's promissory notes start coming in that night, as she comes home to face Richard's accusations and beating.

> When she had been safe and respectable, so had the world been safe and respectable; now the entire world was bitter with deceit and danger and loss; and which was the greater illusion? ... Richard had been her protection, not only against the evil in the world, but also against the wilderness of herself. And now she would never be protected again. She tried to feel jubilant

about this. But she did not feel jubilant. She felt frightened and bewildered.

The final book of the novel is called "Toward Bethlehem" and has a Shakespearean epigraph from Sonnet LXV: "How with this rage shall beauty hold a plea, / Whose action is no stronger than a flower?" The beauty of the first chapter of the final book is placed in a total physical and spiritual love experience between Eric and Vivaldo. "It was [Vivaldo's] first sexual encounter with a male in many years, and his very first sexual encounter with a friend." He is involved in a "blacker and more pure" mystery than ever before.

> He held Eric very tightly and covered Eric's body with his own, as though he were shielding him from the falling heavens. But it was also as though he were, at the same instant, being shielded—by Eric's love. It was strangely and insistently double-edged, it was like making love in the midst of mirrors, or it was like death by drowning.... Vivaldo seemed to have fallen through a great hole in time, back to his innocence; he felt clear, washed, and empty, waiting to be filled.

This beauty, surrender, and acceptance enable Vivaldo to go back to Ida, to listen to her confession, know her, trust her in a new way. Vivaldo is also now able to write, and Ida is relieved of her entirely isolated, negative view of the world—someone has heard.

Cass is left in the midst of struggle, with no clear outcome. She meets Eric, explains Richard's anger, wonders what she will do, fears losing her children. "'You did something very valuable for me, Eric,'" she tells him. "'You've been my love and now you're my friend.... That was you—you gave me for a little while. It was really you.'"

The ultimate beauty is reserved for the final three-page chapter of *Another Country*. Yves flies in to New York from Paris. Eric is there to meet him: "all [Yves's] fear left him, he was certain, now, that everything would be all right.... Then even his luggage belonged to him again, and he strode through the barriers, more high-hearted than he had ever been as a child, into that city which the people from heaven had made their home." So ends *Another Country*.

Since the central characters in *Another Country* are clearly Rufus Scott and Eric Jones, it is useful to explore their similarities and differences as Baldwin depicts them. Rufus dominates the first part of the book as Eric dominates the last part, with Rufus's memories introducing us to Eric and Eric's memories enabling us to understand more of Rufus. Rufus is black,

Northern, urban. Eric is white, Southern, small town. Rufus is a talented, personable musician; Eric is an actor. Rufus's life ends in suicide; Eric's is headed for love and success. Knowing these superficial facts, one might assume Rufus's failure to be a function of his race, Eric's success a function of his. Not so, or not entirely so.

Baldwin seems to suggest with these two characters that while pain and suffering are inevitable, acceptance of pain, necessary for being a fully aware, alive human, is not. And love, translated into *hearing* another person's pain, while necessary for accepting that pain, is hard to come by. The world gets in the way a lot. United States racism gets in the way a lot. New York streets, New York policemen get in the way a lot.

The key difference between Rufus's failure and Eric's success seems to lie in that otherworldly, other-country experience that Eric achieves only by leaving the United States and living in France. Yves is free of the racial and sexual hang-ups peculiar to American men. The love experience with Yves, blessed as it is by purification and cathedral-shadowing, enables Eric to come back to New York and bring with him some of that androgynous love that he gives Cass and Vivaldo. He must be out of the country, it seems, to formulate that code of honor of his own.

Eric's suffering because of his homosexuality is made excruciatingly clear in *Another Country*. But the shame and misery and fear he undergoes are his means to heroism because he does come out on the other side. His flesh is redeemed. He is heard and seen as his acting is empowered by his suffering. Rufus, on the other hand, suffers shame and fear and misery and is not heard, is not understood. His drumming art is in a code more difficult to translate than is Eric's. And Rufus's New York audience is less free or less willing to make the translation. Vivaldo makes the translation, through Ida, only after Rufus's death. Cass comes close to making it the night of Rufus's suicide. Ida does not need to translate, for Ida uses the same musical code. But Ida is not there during Rufus's last month. Richard's character is confirmed as weak and inadmirable by his willingness to condemn Rufus for his treatment of Leona. Richard is farthest from understanding.

Eric does understand, when he learns while abroad what has become of Rufus. Fittingly, it is the suffering that Rufus has put Eric through that is part of what enables Eric to bring blessing to Vivaldo and through Vivaldo to Ida. On the evening of their conversation and love, Vivaldo asks Eric about his relationship to Rufus, comparing it to his and Ida's. "'She never lets me forget I'm white, she never lets me forget she's colored. And I don't care, I don't care—did Rufus do that to you? Did he try to make you pay?'" "'Ah,'" Eric replies. "'He didn't *try*. I paid.... But I'm not sad about it any more. If it hadn't been for Rufus, I would never have had to go away, I would never have been able to deal with Yves.'"

It is also in Eric's and Vivaldo's post-lovemaking conversation that what could be called "the moral of the story" is articulated. "'I think that you can begin to *become* admirable if, when you're hurt, you don't try to pay back.... Perhaps if you can accept the pain that almost kills you, you can use it, you can become better,'" says Vivaldo. Eric agrees and adds, "'Otherwise, you just get stopped with whatever it was that ruined you and you make it happen over and over again and your life has—ceased, really—because you can't move or change or love any more.'"

The point, the moral, the lesson is not so new; but Baldwin's way of conveying it in *Another Country* has some positive and unique qualities. Making sex and racial conflict both explicit and significant; using the New York setting so thoroughly and skillfully; making music such an integral part of character and thought; using language with honesty and power—these are some of the ways Baldwin gives the novel and the moral his distinctive fictional stamp.

Honesty in language may bother some readers. But the bluntness of the language is part of Baldwin's message about facing up to reality. At one point in *Giovanni's Room*, David bemoans to Giovanni the fact that "'people have very dirty words for—for this situation.'" Giovanni replies in words we can take as Baldwin's explanation for his using language as he does: "'If dirty words frighten you, ... I really do not know how you have managed to live so long. People are full of dirty words. The only time they do not use them, most people I mean, is when they are describing something dirty.'"

If the ending of *Another Country* is a bit dangling and unconvincing, the attempts to convey "normal" American life a bit bland, the overall structure not realizably organic, and the sentiment of the sex scenes sometimes exaggerated, it is nevertheless a highly readable and memorable book. And the positive point it makes about love and hope, given the torturous means of attaining them, is positive indeed.

NOTES

1. James Baldwin, *Giovanni's Room* (New York: Dell, 1956), and *Another Country* (New York: Dell, 1960). All references to these novels will be to these editions.

2. See, for example, James Baldwin and Richard Avedon, *Nothing Personal* (New York: Atheneum, 1964). See also Chapter Two.

TRUDIER HARRIS

The Exorcising Medium:
Another Country

Guilt and suffering are paramount in *Another Country* (1962), where Baldwin again treats the relationship between a black woman and a white man. Less directly tied to the church, but still no less harsh in evaluating herself, Ida Scott is a paradox of stricture and freedom. She is unmarried and living away from home, so there is no relative or other authoritarian figure looking over her shoulder to keep her on the straight and narrow path. She can therefore act, and, minus the unrelenting conscience of a mother or an aunt, she can act more freely than an Elizabeth or a Florence can. At one of the final important scenes in the novel, however, we discover that she has been almost as strict in judging her own actions as a Sister McCandless would have been. Like Ruth Bowman in "Come Out the Wilderness," Ida may be out of the church, but she is not completely shed of the conscience that a church upbringing has bequeathed to her.

Baldwin has set up the novel in such a way that we can measure Ida's guilt only in direct proportion to the guilt she forces others around her to feel. Upon the death of her brother, Rufus, she moves into the circle of whites who have been closest to him and tries to make them assume responsibility for his suicide. She accomplishes her goal almost too well, for she suffers in direct proportion to her ability to inflict suffering upon them. She is guilty, her actions unconsciously show, of the same things of which she accuses Rufus'

From *Black Women in the Fiction of James Baldwin*, pp. 96–127. © 1985 by Trudier Harris.

friends—having failed to see that Rufus was suffering, or if she saw, having failed to do something about it. Her assertions in the novel are often contrary to this evaluation, but her actions suggest otherwise. Since a major premise of the novel is the need to experience other people's suffering in order to know one's own, and since Ida works so hard to make other people suffer, their suffering becomes a measure of her own. She has no narrative voice assigned to her in the story; therefore, the white characters and the narrative voices following them become mirror images for the pain and guilt she feels for having literally failed to be her brother's keeper. Indeed, her nearly fanatical perpetuation of Rufus' memory hints at the incestuous connection between brother and sister that Baldwin will develop symbolically in *If Beale Street Could Talk* and explicitly in *Just Above My Head*. Rufus' and Ida's case provides the psychological antecedent for what becomes a major theme in Baldwin's later fiction.

Ida's notion that she should have felt responsibility for Rufus has grown in part from the church-centered family of which her mother is head. Both she and Rufus have grown up in the church and both can attribute the earliest expressions of their musical talents to opportunities provided for them by that church environment. For Ida, therefore, there is the double guilt associated with the fact that she has moved from sacred to secular expressions of her talent and, within that secular environment, she has failed to be honest in her singing; she has used her body to try to further her career as a singer. There is a more pervasive guilt, therefore, in having failed her mother and her brother by turning from their good little sister and daughter to "the biggest whore around." All of the places where Ida finds herself as an adult are a contrast to the safety of the church in which she found herself as a child and as a teenager.

Ida becomes the burden bearer for Baldwin's major theme in the novel, a function that allows her character to develop—within severely compressed space—but that also places her at the center of Baldwin's overall purpose for the novel. That purpose can be capsulized in a comment about one of the other characters in the novel. Vivaldo, Ida's white lover, roams the streets one night wondering where she is and rehearsing the excuses she will present to him when she does arrive. He is distraught, unable to face Ida with his fears about their rapidly deteriorating relationship and equally unable to understand Ida's vengeful approach to their affair. Baldwin says of Vivaldo at this point: "Love was a country he knew nothing about."[1] That sentence serves as a metaphor not only for what happens to Vivaldo and Ida, but for all of the sexual love relationships in the novel. In a world where numerous copulations and infidelities occur,[2] and in which people are forever trying to commune with their bodies but are limited by them, Baldwin suggests that each individual is more than an island: he or she is a country apart from everyone else around him or her. This is true in love, and it is especially true when one experiences suffering and pain.

Baldwin's metaphor suggests that human beings are isolated from each other by sex, race, culture, and nationality as well as by some existential loneliness of the human spirit. For any human being to reach out to another, therefore, great effort is necessary. The effort intensifies in direct proportion to the level of involvement. Little is needed for impersonal cocktail party conversation; more is needed for casual sexual involvement, the passing fulfillment of physical need; but the greatest effort must be exerted between people who would truly love, care for, and commit themselves to each other. When Rufus (black) meets Leona (white) at a jazz set, for example, he is smugly confident that she is attracted to him. When she accompanies him to the party afterward and he sees her as a possible sexual outlet, she becomes slightly more individualized for him, and he must concentrate on his "line" to the extent necessary to seduce her. After the seduction and beginning with the growth of the affair, Rufus is forced to see Leona as a person, not merely as an outlet. To love her would be to exert the greatest effort possible toward going into her country and in turn allowing her into his. Race and culture make such openness impossible for Rufus. Instead of opening up and sharing with Leona, he becomes closed to such an extent that he drives her insane and destroys himself.[3] The negative example with Rufus and Leona will be replayed with Ida and Vivaldo as we watch to see if Ida will be more giving and forgiving than her brother.

To Baldwin, love relationships mean responsibility and, more important, exposing one's self: vulnerability. At the heart of vulnerability is a trust that the loved one will understand whatever is revealed to him or her and will not use that knowledge as a weapon. The lover, in turn, has the responsibility to keep the weapon of his or her knowledge sheathed. These are lessons that Ida and Vivaldo must learn. Because human beings instinctively seek their own survival and usually prefer pleasure to responsibility, the distance from one country to another is often too great a leap for them to undertake. Thus, they use each other as receptacles of their passion, or to advance careers, or to play the roles of wives and husbands—for marriage does not dissolve the distance between the countries.

This basic tendency in human beings to protect themselves from each other is complicated by several things, but especially by race. Though Baldwin's novel treats the distance between white males and white females, between Americans and Frenchmen, and between heterosexuals and homosexuals, the greatest distance he explores is that between blacks and whites. That engulfing distance informs Rufus' suicide a few pages into the novel and his sister Ida's vengeful reaction to the whites she accuses of having passively watched her brother die. Rufus kills himself because of his physical, moral, and mental degeneration, because he watches himself become an animal in his relationship with Leona. Except for a few scenes with Leona, his racial dilemma is full blown at the novel's opening rather than dramatized in it, but we quickly realize that the differences between blacks and whites form the basis of his problem. He has already "received the blow from which he never would recover" (p. 14), and his memory of racial incidents clearly shows that his depression is beyond alleviation. Has Ida received the same blow?

Ida enters the novel after Rufus' death to accuse Vivaldo, Cass, and Richard, Rufus' long-standing friends, of having failed to understand him well enough to save him. It is because he was black that he died, Ida maintains, and they, downtown in his presence, could not see about Rufus what she, uptown in Harlem, had no problem in seeing. They were too concerned about themselves (Vivaldo and Richard are writers and Cass is Richard's wife) to make that trip into Rufus' troubled country. Although they shared a bohemian or near bohemian life-style with Rufus, they never really made the effort to understand him. Later, Eric, a former lover of Rufus who was in Paris at the time of the suicide, will also be drawn into the circle of implied guilt.

For all its actions, the novel is really more of a treatise on the ideas of isolation, communication, and understanding that the actions are designed to dramatize. Ida, as black woman in a bohemian, sometimes middle-class, white world, becomes one of the focuses of the distance human beings must cross to know each other truly and thoroughly. Few critics have considered Ida worthy of extensive commentary *in her own right*; they usually comment on her only passingly in relation to other characters' development and fulfillment. George Kent, though, considers her one of "the more adequately developed characters" in *Another Country*—along with Rufus and Eric—but his short article does not allow for extensive commentary. Colin MacInnes maintains that Rufus and Ida "redeem the book," and Fred L. Standley asserts that "the narrative strand of Vivaldo and Ida is central to the novel's movement; it is, after all, the presence of these two characters which runs through all three sections."[4] Ida certainly has individuality in the novel, but she serves too as a way for the white characters, especially Vivaldo and Cass, to learn more about themselves and more about Ida and Rufus, and thereby about blacks in general.

Ida comes into the novel with a purpose, then; she wants vengeance for Rufus' death. She wants to induce guilt in the whites at the same time she wants to use them, especially Ellis, a white television producer, to further her career as an aspiring singer. She makes constant references to the need for whites to pay dues, but the nature of the dues paying is more often surmised than articulated. Certainly she wants Vivaldo to feel guilt, to experience mental suffering, but she has little idea of the ultimate purpose of her vengeance. Is guilt enough, or is the guilt designed to alter consciousness? Does she simply want to make Vivaldo uncomfortable by wielding sexual and racial power over him, or does she really want to effect some essential change in him? And she does not appear to have thought out where the relationship with Ellis will take her if and after she becomes a singer.

Ida grows into personhood as the novel progresses; she is, Eckman maintains, "the figure with whom Baldwin was most concerned."[5] Initially, she is Rufus' little sister who sets out to taunt, and if possible punish, those she considers responsible for his death. She becomes, as Stanley Macebuh concludes, "the personification of Baldwin's rage."[6] Therefore, though she has a recognizable presence, she is more a medium, a vehicle for the memory of Rufus and the medium through which the whites can exorcise their guilt for having somehow failed Rufus. Her relationship to Rufus points back to the earlier Baldwin fiction and forward to the later fiction; it resembles the brother/sister relationship Baldwin implied would be ideal in *Go Tell It on the Mountain*—if Florence would submit to expectations—and that he develops as such in *If Beale Street Could Talk* and *Just Above My Head*. To Ida, Rufus is the most important male image in her life; in fact, it could safely be advanced that Ida, unlike Florence, worships her brother. To Ida, Rufus is the quintessential big brother. The fact that Rufus is older and the assumed protector, unlike Gabriel, may be relevant. Rufus becomes a godlike figure to Ida personally and symbolically in that he dies in order that she may live, grow, and blossom into her full potential. Rufus as brother takes on dimensions of the Polyneices role; like Antigone, Ida ensures a peaceful death for her brother by forcing those who have had most intimate contact with him to remember him well even if they have not buried him properly. As a sacrificed Christ figure, Rufus is a constant reminder of the need to live fully, but to keep one's life in order for that final reckoning. Rufus is central; Ida is an extension of that centrality after his early disappearance from the novel: thus, a major problem from the beginning is how much of Ida is Ida and how much of Ida is Rufus. She becomes a priestess keeping vigil at the altar of her brother, a servant to his memory. Of secondary importance in comparison to Rufus, she is nonetheless the major focus for the themes of guilt and redemption that are worked out in the novel.

The earliest scene we have to support the notion that Rufus is more legend than flesh and blood to Ida occurred when she was still a teenager in pigtails. This scene is apparently one of many in which Ida cherished the occasions on which her big brother appeared from his romantic life downtown to rescue her from her parents' apartment. On those outings, she was a princess and Rufus the wand carrier who made her wishes come true.

The scene under consideration occurred the one time Vivaldo accompanied Rufus to visit his parents and Ida, and her glorification of Rufus is apparent. She is delighted to see her brother and gives Vivaldo the aura of a "glamorous stranger" (p. 120) because he is in Rufus' presence. Mrs. Scott explains that when Ida and Rufus were younger, "Rufus just couldn't do no wrong, far as Ida was concerned" (p. 121), that Ida had crawled into bed with him on nights when she felt afraid because "she just felt *safe* with him." To the young Ida, Rufus was her ticket away from the physical ugliness of her neighborhood as well as from the many traps it held for young people, away from "cans, bottles, papers, filth" (p. 118), away from the likes of Willie Mae, a former girlfriend of Rufus, who has had "some cat turn ... her on, and then he split" (p. 122). Ida clearly disapproves of Willie Mae, but who can say that the fourteen-year-old girl will not be a Willie Mae in two or three years? Those are the kinds of things from which, perhaps unconsciously, she expected Rufus to remove her. She says later: "I'd counted on Rufus to get me out of there—I knew he'd do anything in the world for me, just like I would for him. It hadn't occurred to me that it wouldn't happen. I *knew* it would happen' (p. 349). And when Rufus killed himself, that expectation was shattered. "I felt that I'd been robbed," Ida says, "and I *had* been robbed—of the only hope I had" (p. 350).

Presented as one of Vivaldo's reminiscences after Rufus' death, the scene of the visit to the Scott home serves not only to establish Ida's relationship to Rufus; it also serves to establish the guilt that Vivaldo will increasingly feel for having failed Rufus, especially after having been granted such an intimate look into Rufus' private world. The fact that Vivaldo is encouraged to recall the scene after his renewed acquaintance with Ida, and following Rufus' funeral, underscores her value as tangible penance. Vivaldo's guilt for having failed Rufus is compounded by the fact that he has helped not only to remove Rufus from his own life, but that he has also caused him to be removed from Ida, for whom he occupied such a special space.

To Ida, Rufus had represented Dream with a capital D, and his death meant a reality she was not ready to face. Near the end of the novel, when Cass asks what one should replace dreams with, Ida says with reality. Throughout most of her sordid adventures, however, she is unable to follow her own advice. She consciously sets out to pay those who were around Rufus back for what she thinks they have done to him. Her commitment to Rufus is shown in two emblems that she uses to remember him; both serve as talisman by which the priestess of the altar keeps the candles lit for the god she worships. If she serves him faithfully enough, perhaps she will exorcise her own guilt for the moments when she has briefly allowed the flame to die. The two emblems are metaphors for vengeance and both suggest the extent to which Ida has little life of her own. Her major objective is to live for Rufus.

The more prominent of the two emblems is a ruby-eyed snake ring Rufus brought to Ida when he returned from the navy. The most tangible sign of her desire for vengeance, it is simultaneously the symbol of her own imprisonment. As long as she wears the ring, there can be no Ida; there can only be Rufus' little sister who will not allow herself to grow into a person or a woman. The ring is first mentioned when Rufus is wandering around on the night he commits suicide. He thinks of the good times as opposed to his current circumstances, of the gifts he has brought to Ida, of the startling discovery that she is growing into a beautiful woman. He thinks of watching her twist "the ruby-eyed snake ring" (p. 12) on her long little finger as she thanked him for a shawl he had brought her, and he is glad she cannot see him now, for he is acutely aware of how his family, like John Grimes's mother Elizabeth, had been "counting" on him.

Encircling Ida's finger, the ring extends its imprisoning power to her mind and body as she uses both to make Vivaldo and others pay their dues for taking Rufus away from her. She says she has been robbed; through the memory of the ring, she expects to have her coffers replenished. The ring is a prominent adornment, a tangible memory in most of Ida's dealings with whites, and it becomes the identifying characteristic by which she is remembered. When she calls Cass asking for information about Rufus because the family has been out of touch with him for so long, it is Ida's ring that Cass recalls most vividly: "She remembered a very young, striking, dark girl who wore a ruby-eyed snake ring" (p. 79). Combining both higher and baser qualities in its precious stone and the venomous snake image, the ring will increasingly become a symbol of Ida's tortured relationship with whites, of the mixture of goodness she attaches to her brother and the destruction she attaches to whites. But even as she herself is in many ways a precious rarity, she allows the memory of her brother to poison all of her relationships. Only when she is able to separate her life from her brother's, her desire for vengeance from her need for love, is she able to take off the ring.

Meanwhile, it binds her to Rufus, and it keeps her voluntarily isolated within her own country. Her arrival at Cass and Richard Silenski's house on the afternoon following Rufus' suicide (but before his death has been discovered) shows her clinging to the ring because she cannot cling to her absent brother. Since Cass, Richard, and Vivaldo, who is also present, have seen Rufus last, Ida comes seeking more information about him. Her concern about where he is and how he looked is tied to the ring. "He's the only big brother I got," she explains, after she has spent some time haunting the streets trying to find Rufus. "She sipped her drink, then put it on the floor beside her chair. She played with the ruby-eyed snake ring on' her long little finger" (p. 88). Rufus is always present, sometimes subconsciously, in Ida's memory. Even at the gayest of times, or so it would seem to others, Ida twists, plays with, or strokes the ring on her finger.

Cass remembered it immediately, and it is what Vivaldo sees most vividly after he first makes love to Ida. Ida sleeps restlessly and stirs, "as though she had been frightened. The scarlet eye on her little finger flashed" (p. 148). Even in giving her body to Vivaldo, she does not give of herself; she shuts him farther away from her even at those moments she is presumably most private with him. The essential gulf she sees between them, what will continue to make them two countries instead of one, is that she is black and he is white.

The ring is no less striking when Eric meets Ida for the first time. His attention goes from the ring to features in Ida that remind him painfully of his affair with Rufus. "On the little finger of one hand, she wore a ruby-eyed snake ring.... She was far more beautiful than Rufus and, except for a beautifully sorrowful, quicksilver tension around the mouth, she might not have reminded him of Rufus. But this detail, which he knew so well, caught him at once" (p. 211). Eric can see Ida's resemblance to Rufus, but she is also a walking monument to his memory. She is wearing the shawl he has given her, and the ring; both point to her desire for vengeance.

In difficult moments, when she is unsure or when she is in the process of making a decision, Ida uses the ring as a touchstone to reinforce her determination. On the night that she and Vivaldo watch a movie with Cass and Eric, who has a bit part in it, Ida is anxious to get rid of the men so she can go to Harlem to meet Ellis. She persuades Cass to go with her: "I wish you'd come up and have one drink with me up there," she says to Cass, and "she kept twisting the ring on her little finger" (p. 291). Because Cass is having an affair with Eric and Ida knows it, Cass feels Ida uses that knowledge to force an outing that might otherwise have been considered casual. Ida may twist her ring, as if undecided, but she is resolved to use Cass to cover her own assignation. As they talk in the cab on the way to Harlem, Ida emphasizes to Cass the distance between herself and Vivaldo: "'I'll never marry Vivaldo, and'—she tapped her ring again—'it's hard to see what's coming, up the road. But I don't seem to see a bridegroom'" (p. 292). She will continue to shut herself out in part because she does not believe either Vivaldo or Cass is capable of understanding her and in part because there is something in her that does not desire exposure even if she were capable of opening up to someone; her fondling of the ring heightens her separateness.

Twin symbol of vengeance and isolation, the ring can only lose its significance when Ida ventures into someone else's country and allows that someone to enter hers. That someone is Vivaldo. Only when Ida stops punishing Vivaldo and allows him to become spiritually intimate with her can she take off the ring. That growth and progression occurs near the end of the novel. In a scene with Vivaldo in which she decides to tell all, Ida slowly begins to distance herself from the destructive side of Rufus' memory. She reveals her affair with Ellis, explains what Rufus has meant to her, and analyzes why she has been driven to hurt Vivaldo. She must reexamine her actions because, unexpectedly, she has fallen in love with Vivaldo. She makes that announcement, then sits "perfectly still, looking down, the fingers of one hand drumming on the table. Then she clasped her hands, the fingers of one hand playing with the ruby-eyed snake ring, slipping it half-off, slipping it on" (p. 345). Her gesture indicates the last step she must make to be truly one with Vivaldo. She recognizes her love for him, but she still clings to Rufus. Her confession of love leads to other confessions and explanations and finally to cleansing tears. Not yet able to part with the ring, Ida tells Vivaldo of still other affairs with white men, releasing heart-wrenching tears. "She covered her mouth, her tears spilled down over her hand, over the red ring" (p. 355), which is the last reference to the ring. It is still a strong enough reference to indicate future direction—that Ida will soon take it off. At least the snake-eyed reference is diminished here and, more important, Ida's tears are washing over the ring, which may suggest that the cleansing of her soul will extend to the associations she connects with the ring. Nothing has touched it before; by allowing the tears to taint it, so to speak, she simultaneously allows them to cleanse it of unpleasant connotations. Her resolve, after all, is to stay with Vivaldo and try to make their relationship work.

The second emblem that ties Ida to Rufus and that receives more than passing reference is a pair of earrings she wears. They are cufflinks made into earrings and, though Ida does not know it, were originally a gift of love from Eric to Rufus. In a way, therefore, while Ida claims to have known empirically and intuitively much more about Rufus than his friends did, there are still some things she does not know. The cufflinks are also mentioned on the night when Rufus wandered the streets before his suicide. Being picked up and fed by a homosexual on the prowl forced Rufus to remember the cruelty with which he had made Eric pay for loving him and the special things that Eric had done for him. Eric, rich white boy from Alabama who discovered it was his fate to love men, had given up the last vestige of heterosexuality for Rufus. Eric

> had had a pair of cufflinks made for Rufus, for Rufus's birthday, with the money which was to have bought his wedding rings: and this gift, this confession, delivered him into Rufus's hands. Rufus had despised

him because he came from Alabama; perhaps he had allowed Eric
to make love to him in order to despise him more completely. Eric
had finally understood this, and had fled from Rufus, all the way to
Paris. But his stormy blue eyes, his bright red hair, his halting drawl,
all returned very painfully to Rufus now. (p. 43)

His guilt forces Rufus to give the cufflinks to Ida, and he thinks that they are
"now in Harlem, in Ida's bureau drawer" (p. 44). Ida wears them proudly, thus
exhibiting another tie to Rufus' past and stifling her future.

Eric notices the earrings on the night he stands at the bar waiting for
Vivaldo and Ida. Ida throws back her head laughing at something one of the
musicians has said and

her heavy silver earrings caught the light. Eric felt a pounding
in his chest and between his shoulder-blades, as he stared at the
gleaming metal and the laughing girl. He felt, suddenly, trapped
in a dream from which he could not awaken. The earrings were
heavy and archaic, suggesting the shape of a feathered arrow:
Rufus never really liked them. In that time, eons ago, when they
had been cufflinks, given him by Eric as a confession of his love,
Rufus had hardly ever worn them. But he had kept them. And
here they were, transformed, on the body of his sister. (p. 211)

It is a painful memory for Eric and, unknowingly, Ida succeeds in making
at least one of Rufus' friends remember him intensely. Later, Eric finds the
courage to mention the earrings: "They're very beautiful ... your earrings."
"Do you like them?" she asks. "My brother had them made for me—just before
he died" (p. 218). And she uses the occasion to perpetuate her legendary view
of Rufus and her own philosophy developed as a result of what has happened
to Rufus. She says to Eric:

"He was a very beautiful man, a very great artist. But he made"—
she regarded him with a curious, cool insolence—"some very bad
connections. He was the kind who believed what people said. If
you told Rufus you loved him, well, he believed you and he'd stick
with you till death. I used to try to tell him the world wasn't like
that." She smiled. "He was much nicer than I am. It doesn't pay
to be too nice in this world." (p. 218)

Included in that "cool insolence" is a hint that Eric, since he has confessed
to knowing Rufus, may also be guilty of having abused him in some way.

Ironically, it is Eric who could testify to Rufus' abuses, because Rufus hated himself and the world too much ever to allow anyone to get close to him.

Ida's shortsightedness about Rufus' true personality and his past life shows again that she does not know him as well as she professes, for she has seen him only in the family context in Harlem, when he was decidedly on his best behavior. She never learns, for example, that it was just as important for Rufus to keep the romance going with her as it was for her to believe in that romance, even if it meant he had to borrow money from Vivaldo to play the big man with his younger sister. Too busy blaming the whites in the novel for having seen only a portion of Rufus' personality, Ida fails to see that she herself is guilty of the same failing. Rufus' trips to Harlem have probably been infrequent, even more so in the last couple of years of his life, so there are many gaps, from the earlier period as well as from the latter one, when Ida really did not know her brother's true status and frame of mind. Her need to implicate others forestalls her confrontation with her own guilt, and she gets away with so much precisely because she is black. The whites are uncomfortable with her and don't really know what to do with her anger; their own guilt, compounded by Ida's accusations and insinuations, enables Ida to get away with a lot that she might not otherwise. It is partly a breakdown of Baldwin's thesis about guilty, blind, insensitive whites and innocent, knowledgeable, suffering blacks in that Ida is one of the blacks who is not so very innocent or knowledgeable about some things (though the corollary to this would suggest that her whoring activities are in part due to the system perpetuated by whites).

In many ways a personification of Rufus' anger and in other ways a distortion of what he actually was, Ida serves to tweak everybody's conscience or at least to dredge up their unpleasant memories. The function Ida serves coincides with the way in which her character is revealed in the novel. The story is Ida's story only in as much as she comes into contact with Cass, Vivaldo, and Eric, for point of view is theirs, not hers. We must learn of her affair with Ellis through others; we do not follow her to those meetings. What we learn of her early in the novel is reflected in Vivaldo's memory of his visit to Rufus' home and in the gathering at Cass's when Ida comes seeking information about Rufus. The only time Ida is revealed to us directly is when she speaks; otherwise, she is seen through someone else's vision and in someone else's space. This technique of presenting Ida ties her to Rufus as well. She, like Rufus, is outside the circle of whites who know them both, yet she touches all of them. To know themselves, they have to learn more of Ida, and she does not make it easy for them. She is just as elusive narrationally as she is personally to the white protagonists in the novel.

To give Ida a point of view would be comparable to giving Caddy a section of *The Sound and the Fury*. Though we learn much about Caddy through Benjy, Quentin, Jason, and Dilsey, she is still as far from us at times as the myth of the South that she is drawn to represent. We see her actions, we know what she looks like and what she wears, but we do not really *know* her; the outside, the form of her existence and of her being, will forever shield the essence of her personality from us. So too with Ida. We know how she looks, what kind of effect she has upon people and how they respond to her. Until the very last scenes of the novel, however, we are left to speculate upon her motives, upon what truly drives her to be what she is. The whites must work to get to know her, just as the reader must, for Baldwin lays most of the responsibility for the ugliness surrounding the racial situation in America upon whites. To give Ida a point of view would reduce blackness to a commonplace level where it could be easily dismissed. Instead, the whites, especially Vivaldo, must reach out to that other country and understand Ida and encourage her to forgive and understand them; that is the only path that will allow them to understand and save themselves.

For Vivaldo and Cass, Ida becomes a touchstone for racial understanding, and for Vivaldo she becomes the black woman through whom he learns more about himself. His sexual experiences before his liaison with Ida consisted primarily of clandestine visits to Harlem to deposit his white seed in black whores. Most black women have been whores to him, and he has not thought about the political, racial, or moral implications of his actions. In order to save his relationship with Ida, he must grow at the same time he must encourage her to grow. For Eric and Richard, Ida reveals to them the pitfalls that lie in wait for all human beings. Her affair with Ellis mirrors Cass's affair with Eric and perhaps forces Richard to see connections between his wife and a black woman that he would not otherwise have seen.

What we see of Ida, then, comes through her relationships with these four white characters. How the discussion of her character must be approached reflects again the kind of role black women usually play in Baldwin's fiction. They are subordinate to other characters, sacrificing for them, or like Ida, "sandwiched" in between them. Ida is therefore a thoroughly dependent character in terms of critical evaluation of the novel; she is always to be treated in someone else's orbit, not necessarily other people in her own. Her life choices are made in reaction to others, how she lives is dictated by others, and ultimately her pain and suffering are as much external as they are internal. Primarily reactive, the little portion of Ida's personality that is not can almost be overlooked.

From her entry into the novel, Ida reacts to the whites and makes them react to her. She may force them to see herself (and Rufus retrospectively) in a different light, but she almost loses her soul in the process. She represses her emotion to control others, then finds herself trapped by an equally powerful emotion, that of love. The fine line she has walked between love and hate is represented on one level by men and women and on a more important level by blacks and whites. In order for love and understanding to triumph, each character, and Ida most of all, must be baptized in suffering. Since they could not or would not witness Rufus' suffering, they must witness their own, and some of them must witness Ida's. Those who survive and grow do so because they pay the dues of cathartic identification with other suffering human beings. By immersing themselves in those other countries of suffering, they accept the vulnerability and the responsibility inherent in unselfish love.

To Cass, Ida is initially a beautiful black girl concerned about her brother, and, to us, Cass is initially the mothering center of the certified middle-class white American family. Both impressions change. When Ida arrives at Cass's door, Cass sees her as a beautiful young woman whose eyes remind her of Rufus (different characters will recognize different features of Rufus in Ida). She comments on Ida's beauty and "realized, for the first time, that a Negro girl could blush" (p. 86). That single, revisionist approach to Ida is only the first of many things Cass will discover about her and, through her, about herself. During the conversation about Rufus' whereabouts, Cass realizes "that something in Ida was enjoying this—the attention, the power she held for this moment. This made Cass angry, but then she thought: Good. It means that whatever's coming, she'll be able to get through it" (p. 90). The manipulative hardness Cass sees in Ida will take her not only through Rufus' suicide and funeral, but through the affair with Ellis and her bid to be a singer. Ida is a mixture of the kitten and the tigress; just as she combined a solemn occasion with a sense of detachment, a sense of enjoyment, she will also waver between destroying Vivaldo and loving him. She works as hard to induce guilt in him as she works to manipulate Ellis, through the pleasure of her body, to further her singing career.

Cass is willing to admit Ida into her circle of companions as a friendly gesture. She sees no harm in being generous to Rufus' little sister because Ida has no real meaning for her, except perhaps that Vivaldo is interested in Ida and that fact briefly raises the question about how Cass feels about interracial affairs. But Cass goes on with her neat little life, and the parties and gatherings with Ida and Vivaldo, until she discovers one day that Richard has compromised his writing talent and published a second-rate novel, and that she no longer believes in his ability or respects what he has accomplished. She finds herself safe, secure, the mother of two growing boys, and terribly unfulfilled and unhappy. In an effort to salvage something of her self, she engages in an affair with Eric, often using Vivaldo and Ida as the smokescreen to get away from Richard. Her stepping out of safety enables her to see Ida's situation more clearly, just as Tod Clifton's stepping out of a kind of security enables him to see in *Invisible Man*. Because Cass has risked her reputation, her children, and her husband, she begins to see a bit of the predicament in which most black women find themselves quite frequently.

These revelations come to Cass on the night that she and Eric go to the movie with Vivaldo and Ida. The men and women separate afterwards, Cass agreeing to go to Harlem for one drink with Ida, then home to Richard:

> As she said this, both she and Ida laughed. It was almost the first time they had ever laughed together; and this laughter revealed to Cass that Ida's attitude toward her had been modified by Ida's knowledge of her adultery. Perhaps Ida felt that Cass was more to be trusted and more of a woman, now that her virtue, and her safety, were gone. And there was also, in that sudden and spontaneous laughter, the very faintest hint of blackmail. Ida could be freer with Cass now, since the world's judgment, should it ever be necessary to face it, would condemn Cass yet more cruelly than Ida. For Ida was not white, not married, nor a mother. The world assumed Ida's sins to be natural, whereas those of Cass were perverse. (p. 291)

A closed chapter of female history is now opening up to Cass as she is forced to see a black woman in a specific, more than superficial way. Her descent from her middle-class pedestal opens her eyes to what women experience who have never had the pedestal available to them. As the moment of enlightenment continues, Ida and Cass respond to each other more as women, not as females connected through their men, and Cass begins to see into another country.

Through this conversation, which takes place in the cab on the way to Harlem, Baldwin explores what Jacqueline Orsagh calls "the polarity of whore and virgin" with Ida and Cass. This part of Orsagh's discussion is revealing, but it is still somewhat limited by her extremes of interpretation. Neither Ida nor Cass is ultimately as destructive to her man as Orsagh suggests, and Ida's negative side does not need to be exaggerated to the extent Orsagh does for her point about whores and virgins to be made. It is striking to observe, too, that Orsagh sees black women in Baldwin's fiction only as they are relevant to her comments on the white females. Thus, only Ida receives any special treatment—because of her relationship to Cass.[7]

The polarity in the two women develops in the way they see themselves and the world. Ida, at twenty-two, finds it "hard to imagine" that Cass, at thirty-four, has "dealt with—two men" in her "whole life" (p. 291). Cass readily admits that she has been sheltered, while we will later learn from Ida that she has slept with many men, several of them white. Cass thinks Ida can marry Vivaldo just because she loves him, but Ida recognizes that love can be "a goddamn pain in the ass" (p. 292). The romantic vision of shelter gives way to the reality of life. To Cass's comment that Ida does not know what it is like to have a baby, Ida responds that such knowledge is easily available to her, but babies are not her "kick." What Cass sees as a part of her shelter, Ida sees in a different light:

> "You don't know, and there's no way in the world for you to find out, what it's like to be a black girl in this world, and the way white men, and black men, too, baby, treat you. You've never decided that the whole world was just one big whorehouse and so the only way for you to make it was to decide to be the biggest, coolest, hardest whore around, and make the world pay you back that way.... I bet you think we're in a goddamn park. You don't know were in one of the world's great jungles. You don't know that behind all them damn dainty trees and shit, people are screwing and sucking and fixing and dying." (p. 293)

Cass, aware of her perceptual and visual limitations, "looked out at the park, trying to see what Ida saw; but, of course, she saw only the trees and the lights and the grass and the twisting road and the shape of the buildings beyond the park" (p. 293).

The safety not available to Ida and that Cass has put in jeopardy forces them to continue their discussion—not in anger, but in a kind of revelation that would be impossible under other circumstances. Ida bluntly tells Cass she will not marry Eric because she is not "that crazy" (p. 294), and Cass is forced to admit that the best she can hope for in five years is that she and Eric will be friends. As it turns out, she tells Richard about the affair later that night, and the connection with Eric dissolves very shortly. Perhaps it has been in part as a result of the conversation with Ida that Cass decides to tell the truth to Richard. She willingly submits to the suffering Ida has predicted for her. When they were getting out of the taxi, Cass had insisted on paying the driver; "'Let me.... It's just about the only thing that a poor white woman can still do.' Ida looked at her, and smiled. 'Now, don't you be like that,' she said, 'because you can suffer, and you've got some suffering to do, believe me'" (p. 296). Even though Cass has shared a spiritual intimacy with Ida, she still relies on her economic advantage, which has been presented as the way of escaping some of the poverty and ugliness Ida has been talking about.

From love and life, however, there is no shelter, no safety. Eventually, the soul must be bared to the loved one, as Cass does with Richard, and that vulnerable baring can only bring suffering.

Yet their conversation has drawn them close enough for Cass to defend Ida against insinuations by a member of Ellis' party. When the woman wonders "if his wife knows where he is" as Ida and Ellis are dancing, Cass retorts: "Mrs. Ellis and Miss Scott have known each other for quite a longtime, long before Mrs. Ellis's marriage" (p. 302), and when the woman continues by observing "how strange that is," Cass responds with "Not at all ... they both worked in the same factory." Cass is being deliberately reckless, but she understands enough by this point to be daring in Ida's defense. What Cass does may be admirable, but her one trip down from the pedestal has not enabled her to see all that goes on in Ida's world. She fails to see that Ellis and Ida are having an affair. That knowledge is revealed to her later that evening by Richard, when he tells her to quit using Ida and Vivaldo as excuses for her absences because he knows Ida has been meeting Ellis. Though Cass senses, at one point in the conversation in the Harlem barroom when Ida and Ellis are present, "the knowledge that black people had of white people" (p. 301), her perception does not apply uniformly to all areas of life. As Ida has said of Vivaldo earlier, in connection with Rufus, there are some things one does not want to know about a friend. Cass does not see Ida's affair with Ellis because she does not want to see it. Knowledge would bring conscience, which in turn would demand action; she would have to think of her friend Vivaldo and whether or not he should be told. So she prefers to think that Ida has met Ellis only for business purposes; she is genuinely surprised when Richard tells her the truth.

Although she does not know of the affair, she does understand that, as she had used Ida and Vivaldo as "smoke screens to cover her affair with Eric," Ida has used her to cover her meeting with Ellis:

> Why should not Ida use *her*, then, to cover from Vivaldo her assignation with Ellis? She had silenced *them*, in relation to Richard—now she was silenced, in relation to Vivaldo. She smiled, but the smoke she inhaled was bitter. When she had been safe and respectable, so had the world been safe and respectable; now the entire world was bitter with deceit and danger and loss; and which was the greater illusion? (p. 304)

Reflecting as she is riding home in a taxi with a young driver to whom she is very much attracted, she is forced again to realize the exposure stepping off her pedestal has brought to her: "Richard had been her protection, not only against the evil in the world, but also against the wilderness of herself. And now she would never be protected again" (p. 305). It was necessary to step off the pedestal, however, in order to grow, to learn more about herself, about Ida, and about others.

The measure of her growth is her confrontation with Richard about her affair with Eric. She begins to see some of the absence of safety that has been Ida's lot every day of her life. She willingly submits, from her point of view, to the ultimate potential destruction, which would be complete loss of the pedestal and everything that goes along with it. But she makes that journey and survives. She and Richard are not completely reconciled by the end of the novel, but indications are that they will be, and they will both be stronger. Just as Cass tells Richard the truth, and causes him to suffer, she must also face an additional truth of her own: that she is partly responsible for Richard's failures because she has encouraged him to attempt things he was incapable of accomplishing.

Perhaps it is too late for Richard to change the kind of work he does, but it is not too late for reconciliation. Cass's final words to Eric that it's "too late now" (p. 341) for Richard's and her marriage are really less fatalistic than they seem, for although she denies hope in one breath, in the next she talks of weathering things out with Richard. The safety of the pedestal has been shattered, but the reality with which it has been replaced is not ultimately destructive, and that reality has been shaped in part by Cass's contact with Ida.

To Richard, Ida is also Rufus' little sister, someone who must be accepted because of circumstances. Since Richard's point of view, like Ida's, is submerged to those of Cass, Vivaldo, and Eric, he provides little more knowledge about her other than being on the scene at many of the gatherings Ida attends. His attitude toward blacks, and therefore perhaps toward Ida, is revealed in two incidents related in the novel—Rufus' treatment of Leona and the beating up of Richard's sons by a group of black boys; the baser side of black people has been revealed to him, so he does not find it at all surprising that Ida engages in the affair with Ellis.

During the scene in which Richard announces Rufus' death to Cass and in the conversation following it, he says:

> "I don t love Rufus, not the way you did, the way all of you did. I couldn't help feeling, anyway, that one of the reasons all of you made such a kind of—*fuss*—over him was partly just because he was colored. Which is a hell of a reason to love anybody. I just had to look on him as another guy. And I couldn't forgive him for what he did to Leona. You once said you couldn't, either." (p. 93)

On the one hand, his honesty about not loving Rufus is commendable, but on the other hand, he is lying when he says he does not associate the lack of love or the violence with Rufus' color. Consider his reaction when his two sons come in from a fight. He pretends to be calm and explains, when one of his sons asks if the fight has occurred because "they're colored and we're white," that "the world is full of all kinds of people, and sometimes they do terrible things to each other, but—that's not why" (p. 206), yet when his sons are settled and he returns to the living room with Eric, he mutters: "Little black bastards ... they could have killed the kid. Why the hell can't they take it out on each other, for Christ's sake!" (p. 207). Parental anger is certainly justified in the situation, but Richard's anger focuses on violence done by blacks, not simply on violence. His comment about the boys taking it out on someone reveals, too, his subconscious admission that there is something amiss in race relations that blacks *should* take out on someone.

Richard's revelation of Ida's affair with Ellis is more functional than perceptive. It shows how far Cass has been away from people with whom she has spent a great deal of time. Ida, Richard tells Cass after the excursion to Harlem, has been with Ellis the many nights Cass has maintained she was with Vivaldo and Ida. "And it's been going on a long time," Richard concludes. When Cass asks how he knows, his question is penetrating: "How do *you*—*not* know it?" (p. 311), and adds that Cass and Vivaldo are "the only two in town" who do not know about the affair. What Cass and Vivaldo have failed to see with Ida and Ellis is another incident comparable to what all of his friends have failed to see with Rufus, or what they have refused to see. Vivaldo deliberately blinds himself to Ida's affair with Ellis, and Cass has similarly blinded herself subconsciously. She has not been suspicious the many times Ellis has been out without his wife and apparently enjoying the company of Ida. And she has not been suspicious earlier that evening in Harlem, even when the woman in the group made such unpleasant insinuations. Cass's desire to defend Ida has been admirable, but it has also been flawed by the fact that Cass is so willfully blind and selectively supportive. Richard can see the truth, and Ellis has confirmed it, because he has no personal, human interest in Ida that would conclude that her actions should be otherwise. For him, even though she is Rufus' little sister, and perhaps because of that fact, Ida is still a member of the nameless black mob capable of any violence or any whorish manipulation.

Eric, too, is forced to see Ida initially as Rufus' younger sister. Through her, he is forced to realize that the suffering he has gone to Paris to escape is only a minuscule portion of the pain of life, from which there is no escape. Initially, the cufflinks/earrings evoke painful memories for him of his affair with Rufus. Later, also through Ida, he is forced to come into contact with other blacks, and he is forced to witness the painful triangular development of the relationship between Ida, Vivaldo, and Ellis. His reaction to the other blacks perhaps illustrates what has happened to his relationship with Rufus. Rufus certainly made Eric suffer, but instead of understanding the agonies in Rufus that caused him to inflict suffering, Eric ran away from his pain as well as from that of Rufus. On the night he meets Ida and Vivaldo at a bar to hear Ida sing, he must sit and listen to the blues that have personified Rufus' suffering; it is something he cannot do, so he "did not really listen to the music, he could not; it remained entirely outside him, like some minor agitation of the air" (p. 214). The musicians can be ignored because they are not the best, but Ida's stronger rendition of a bluesy song "made Eric look up" (p. 215). Eric has literally gone to another country in order to escape the painful suffering Ida sings about, and to which he must now listen and witness, thus emphasizing again the lack of protection for anyone who would truly love another.

Eric at least knows the potential for suffering, even if he has tried to escape it, and he sees that potential in Ida's treatment of Vivaldo and in Vivaldo's reaction to how other men respond to Ida. Eric sees that Ida's smiles at Vivaldo hold "some hint of the vindictive" and her lips curl sardonically at the same time he sees "how desperately one could love" Ida, "how desperately Vivaldo was in love with her" (p. 215). That desperation causes a jealousy in Vivaldo in the way Eric observes him stormily looking at a young man who watches Ida being lifted onto the stand with the musicians. Eric sees, too, that Ida clings to Vivaldo, but "there was something in it which was meant for Ellis. And Vivaldo seemed to feel this, too. He moved slightly away from Ida and picked up her handbag from the table—to give his hands something to do?" (p. 219). Eric can feel in Ida's careless maneuvers some of what Rufus has done to him, and he can see in Vivaldo's helplessness one similar to his own. That tension Eric has noticed curling around Ida's lips when he first met her personifies the tension that existed in his relationship to Rufus.

The memory of that tension continues as they walk from one bar to another. Eric is further forced to see the ugliness in the relationship between Ida and Vivaldo as they, walking ahead, engage in a conversation which drifts backward to Eric.

> He heard Ida. "—sweetie, don't *be* like that."
> "Will you stop calling me *sweetie*? That's what you call every miserable cock sucker who comes sniffing around your ass."
> "*Must* you talk that way?"
> "Look, don't you pull any of that *lady* bullshit on me."

"—you talk. I'll never understand white people, never, never, never! How *can* you talk that way? How can you expect anyone else to respect you if you don't respect yourselves?"

"*Oh*. Why the fuck did I ever get tied up with a *house* nigger? And I am not *white people!*"

"—I warn you, I warn you!"

"—*you're* the one who starts it! You *always* start it!"

"—I knew you would be *jealous. That's* why!"

"You picked a fine way to keep me from being—jealous, baby."

"Can't we talk about it *later?* Why do you always have to spoil everything?"

"Oh, sure, sure, I'm the one who spoils everything, all right!" (p. 222)

In a determined effort to blot out what he would rather not hear, Eric turns to talk with Ellis, whom he has earlier maintained that "he had no desire to talk to" (p. 221). His conscious mind may not yet have registered it, but, through Ida, he is constantly made to confront the unpleasantnesses of life. Of course, we can say that Eric's determination not to hear the conversation is a matter of politeness, of not wanting to intrude upon someone else's privacy. But it is also a function of his approach to life; he prefers the peaceful, the idyllic, to disturbances, even minor ones. Earlier, he has been pictured in an Edenic setting in his farmhouse in the South of France with Yves, his lover. Basking, swimming, drinking, and loving were the order of the day, and that is the kind of life Eric has come to appreciate following his affair with Rufus. Now he is forced to see another black person suffer and induce suffering, a black person who is tied to Rufus not only racially, but biologically.

Ever-vengeful Ida also questions Eric's relationship with Rufus, thus forcing him further back into the past he does not want to remember. At a table in another bar, Ida asks Eric if he had found it hard to be Rufus' friend, and his response in the negative causes "sweat in his armpits, on his forehead, between his legs." Intuitively sensing something more, Ida will not let the matter rest:

"You may have wanted more from him than he could give. Many people did, men *and* women." She allowed this to hang between them for an instant. Then, "He was terribly attractive, wasn't he? I always think that that was the reason he died, that he was too attractive and didn't know how—how to keep people away." She sipped her drink. "People don't have any mercy. They tear you limb from limb, in the name of love. Then, when you're dead, when they've killed you by what they made you go through, they say you didn't have any character. They weep big, bitter tears—not for you. For themselves, because they've lost their toy." (pp. 224–25)

Her racial politics are harshly uncompromising, and they apply to all aspects of life. She has said earlier, of the attack upon Cass's and Richard's children: "I imagine ... that it was in some kind of retaliation for something some other boys had done to them" (p. 221), and Eric, for the sake of peace, had agreed. With Ida's "grim" view of love, though, he is forced to disagree by maintaining that he loved Rufus, that they "really were very good friends," and that it was an "awful shock" (p. 225) to him in Paris when he heard of Rufus' death. Subconsciously, Eric uses the physical distance he had hoped would diminish his own pain as the excuse for not knowing Rufus was suffering. Eric's defense comes, too, because Ida's view of Leona, Rufus' known lover, is so dismal. To Ida, Leona is "a terrible little whore of a nymphomaniac, from Georgia" and a "filthy white slut" (p. 225), images from which the sensitive Eric, who is from Alabama, would like to dissociate himself. Eric may be, as Donald Gibson suggests, "the most understanding, best adjusted character" in the novel, but Ida is still able to make him feel uncomfortable.[8]

Eric's ability to suppress things also comes out when he gets confirmation of Ida's affair with Ellis. Eric and Vivaldo become lovers on the same night Cass and Ida go to Harlem. Cass goes home, confronts Richard about her affair, learns of Ida's, then calls Eric the next morning with both pieces of news. The beautiful sexual experience Vivaldo and Eric have just shared, in which Eric discovered the surprising depth of feeling he has for Vivaldo, will not allow him to hurt Vivaldo further by telling him of Ida's long-standing infidelity, for Vivaldo has spent a great part of the evening discussing the punishing things Ida has done to him. So Eric ignores what Cass tells him about Ida and Ellis; only after Ida tells Vivaldo of her affair does Eric admit to Vivaldo that he has been told about it. At least concern for Vivaldo would make Eric's silence altruistic. Otherwise, he might seem more callous than he is, since he is more passive than active, more acted upon than doing, more the pleasure seeker than the willing sufferer. Even when things are presented from his point of view, he serves more as a medium, a reflector; he is not very reflective. What he learns from Ida's conversations can be surmised more than concluded definitively, and what he says serves as a measure of the reflection that must be going on in his mind.

To Vivaldo, the character most touched by her, Ida is the black woman with whom he falls in love and to whom he submits to be punished for the guilt he feels about all of his previous interracial relationships and for his negligence of Rufus. Before he becomes involved with Ida, his primary sexual preference had been for black whores in Harlem. To go to Harlem is to "screw" without commitment, to possess a body without being the least bit touched in return. It is the ultimate in islandized isolation that Ida's presence will destroy, and his guilt about the lack of commitment to the bodies he uses is what makes him defenseless against her. "In Harlem," Baldwin writes, Vivaldo "had merely dropped his load and marked the spot with silver" (p. 115). The pleasure soon backfires, however, and he begins to encounter girls he wishes he had met elsewhere, or he despises the ones he meets. Ambivalence Vivaldo feels toward the girls and toward his desire and need for them is intensified because he is Rufus' friend and must see, from Rufus' point of view, the day-to-day oppression of blacks. It is when he goes to rescue Leona from a beating by Rufus that he remembers being conned in Harlem, and it is when he is trying to come to grips with the sexual habits of his neighbors that he thinks of other whores; their plight in turn directs his thoughts toward Rufus. The whores and Rufus are one in that they have both been screwed by the world at large.

Such connections, however, do not go far in informing Vivaldo's reaction to Ida. He is very much attracted to her, and says he loves her, but he has difficulty separating her from other whores he has known. His own insecurity causes him to believe almost anything of Ida, primarily because whoring black women are what he has been most exposed to. At a party at Cass's, Vivaldo insinuates that Ida is willing to use Ellis to further her singing career. She tearfully responds that he thinks she is "nothing but a whore" (p. 145). Maybe Ida has not yet considered using her body to get what she wants from Ellis, but Vivaldo's insinuation that she is capable of such an action is perhaps more devastating, in the freshness of their romance, than anything else could possibly be. Vivaldo still has in the back of his mind the mental trash that suggests that black women are unconsciously free with their bodies.

After Ida has told Vivaldo of her affair with Ellis, he reacts in a familiar way: to him, Ida is the ultimate whore who has conned him not only out of his money, but out of his affection. While he is trying to absorb all Ida tells him about Ellis, he "looked over at her, and a wilderness of anger, pity, love, and contempt and lust all raged together in him. She, too, was a whore; how bitterly he had been betrayed!" (p. 361). Sadly, Ida has not betrayed Vivaldo; he has betrayed himself. He has done so by refusing to face up to problems he and Ida have had, by choosing to believe the lies he knows she has told him about her absences, and by refusing to suffer openly what he has painfully suffered in private.

Vivaldo's guilt about having failed Rufus and about having used black women allows him to give Ida an unbridled license to cause him pain. His guilt is apparent as he and Cass are on their way to Rufus' funeral. He had earlier gone to Rufus' house, and he describes to Cass how he wanted to take Ida into his arms and kiss the accusatory look off her face; he wanted her and her family to know that, though they are black and he is white, "the same things have happened, really the *same* things" (p. 99). Cass correctly points out that the same things have not happened to Vivaldo *because* he is white. That is the essential difference between him and Rufus. So Vivaldo sits crying, feeling inadequate, wanting to protect and soothe Ida. Shortly after the service, he comments to Cass that he would like to "prove" to Ida one day "that the world's not as black as she thinks it is," and Cass adds, "or as white" (p. 108). Color consciousness, therefore, informs Vivaldo's sense of guilt. He will present himself to Ida as a fledgling Christ from whom she can exact the blood of dues paying she believes that white people owe to blacks.

When Vivaldo goes into the relationship with Ida, therefore, she easily takes advantage of his compromised position. Her vengeance is easily effected. Vivaldo understands what she is doing to him, but he lacks the power or the will to stop her. At one point, he asks Ida: "You're never going to forgive me, are you? for your brother's death" (p. 273), and her answer is silence. He says to Eric on the night they spend together: "She never lets me forget I'm white, she never lets me forget she's colored. And I don't care, I don't care—did Rufus do that to you? Did he try to make you pay?" (p. 287). He says to Ida during their final, revealing conversation: "What I've never understood ... is that you always accuse me of making a thing about your color, of penalizing you. But you do the same thing. You always make me feel white. Don't you think that hurts me? You lock me out. And all I want is for you to be a part of me, for me to be a part of you. I wouldn't give a damn if you were striped like a zebra" (p. 348). And when he finally knows she is going to open herself up to him, he admits he is afraid, but asks her to tell him all because, he says, "I can't take any more of your revenge" (p. 351). The body he has presented to be crucified has suffered beyond death; his only hope of restoration is to bring it back to the realm of the living.

Vivaldo's submission to silent suffering has been infinitely more destructive to his psyche than anything he could have suffered openly. He has paralyzed himself with thoughts of Ida alone with Ellis and has flagellated himself with the excuses Ida could make to him for her absences. All of her imagined excuses are an insult to his intelligence; still, he prefers those to facing the truth of Ida's affair with Ellis. He imagines her not going home from work because she has gone to see her family or is otherwise engaged in innocent activity, and "even though he knew that she was using him against himself, hope rose up hard in him, his throat became tight with pain, he willed away all his doubts" (p. 250). He torments himself, wandering the streets one night waiting for Ida to come home, only to discover when she does that "he lacked the courage to mention the name of Steve Ellis" (p. 270).

Vivaldo is unable to effect the protection he sought for Ida or that he desperately needs for himself, As Ida has accused him of doing earlier with his response to Rufus, Vivaldo has blocked out information he does not wish to know, but those things, "like demons in the dark," "reveal themselves" when least expected (p. 331). Those demons rise to chase Vivaldo into that other country he has been trying so desperately to avoid. As Ida tells her story, he can no longer escape commitment and responsibility; nor is he invulnerable to the final, crashing pain Ida heaps upon him.

Two incidents are relevant to the baring of herself Ida undergoes before Vivaldo and the reaction he has to it. First of all, Vivaldo has made love with Eric. He has been attracted to men before and sensed on one occasion that Rufus needed him to make love to him, or at least to hold him,[9] yet it is only when he tells Eric of the pain Ida has caused him is he able to love Eric. Pain, suffering, and removal of safety, Baldwin suggests, enable one to begin the opening-up process. By immersing oneself in "sins" uglier than those one is already guilty of, a certain kind of enlightenment emerges. As he embraces Eric, Vivaldo becomes "involved in another mystery, at once blacker and more pure" (p. 324). The choice of color imagery would be unfortunate but for its relevance to the blacks and whites in the novel. Vivaldo, who has been so pedestalized in his manliness and heterosexuality, is initiated into understanding Ida's sexual promiscuity by engaging in his own "perversion." Homosexuality can be considered, more degenerate, "blacker" to some, and it is by going into this unknown territory that Vivaldo is better prepared to understand where Ida has been as a black person also maligned and outside the mainstream of acceptability. By being unfaithful to Ida with Eric, Vivaldo can also no longer stand in a position of absolute morality and judge her. His action with Eric is therefore purer because it is an act of love, free of using and taking, free of domination and exploitation.[10] Because he and Eric trust each other enough to be open and honest, there can be no negative evaluation attached to what they do, at least not by themselves. Vivaldo's anger with Ida is understandable, but we are presented with it against the backdrop of Vivaldo's and Eric's liaison, and that mitigates his anger and his judgment.[11]

The other incident relevant to Ida's and Vivaldo's final conversation is the discovery of Eric's and Cass's affair. Cass calls to tell Eric of her discussion with Richard just as he and Vivaldo finish making love, and the two men discuss Richard's position in the mess that Cass and Eric have created. Eric emphasizes that Richard has been wounded and that no one has to be admirable to feel pain, and Vivaldo responds with a comment that is relevant to his own situation with Ida: "But I think that perhaps you can begin to *become* admirable if, when you're hurt, you don't try to pay back.... Do you know what I mean? Perhaps if you can accept the pain that almost kills you, you can use it, you can become better" (p. 329). Armed with these two signs of wisdom and growth, Vivaldo goes home and walks into the pain that Ida uses to almost kill him. He stays with her, as Richard stays with Cass, but his trial by cross is acutely exacting.

Ida's growth in the novel is important, but it continues to be subordinated to what happens to the white characters. The final confession she makes to Vivaldo is still put in his territory, in the context of how he will respond to her. It is important that she understand what she has done and what it has cost her, but Baldwin sets up the scene so that Ida's revelation of her suffering is still done in mirror image. We measure how much she has suffered on the basis of Vivaldo's response to her suffering. Her subordination is revealed in her posture and in the fact that she begs for forgiveness; Vivaldo is not similarly driven to do so. In this connection, Donald Gibson raises some provocative questions about the racial logic of the novel, especially in its requirement that Ida, black, confess her infidelity to Vivaldo, white, but does not compel Vivaldo to confess similarly.[12] Such a turn of events emphatically places the burden of guilt upon the woman, and Ida, continuing in the tradition in which she has been conceived, finally finds herself weeping at the altar in a scene comparable to that in which Florence Grimes was involved. Unlike Florence, though, Ida does not have to wait for her lord to forgive her, for she is physically in his presence.

Vivaldo's assumption of that godlike role ties into Baldwin's theme on the need to identify with someone else's suffering. The beginning of Ida's exposure of her "sins" makes Vivaldo feel that "she was not locking him out now ... he was being locked in" (p. 349). The process has started; he is on his way to that other country. His pain is an echo of her suffering as she explains how she hated him for allowing the affair with Ellis to continue because he was afraid of the consequences if he tried to stop it; she hates him for "pretending" to believe her because he did not want to know what was happening to her. She tells him of sleeping with white men before she left Harlem, of scorning their puniness and their sexual deviancies. Finally, she tells him of the last encounter with Ellis when she realized she could no longer endure the power he had over her. She falls to the floor in spasms of weeping as Vivaldo stands in a moment of revulsion: "He was afraid to go near her, he was afraid to touch her, it was almost as though she had told him that she had been infected with the plague" (p. 358).

Where he has been and what he has done recently force his moment of indecision resolutely into the other country.

> And yet, at the same time, as he stood helpless and stupid in the kitchen which had abruptly become immortal, or which, in any case, would surely live as long as he lived, and follow him everywhere, his heart began to beat with a newer, stonier anguish, which destroyed the distance called pity and placed him, *very nearly, in her body*, beside the table, on the dirty floor. (p. 358—my emphasis)

To feel, vicariously, cathartically, the ultimate suffering of another human being, to put oneself in that person's place, is the final stage toward closing the gap between those isolated countries. Vivaldo makes that leap; he still has a few unpleasantnesses to digest, but he at least makes that important leap. It is a sign that things will be all right when a detail Vivaldo has been seeking for his novel "fell, neatly and vividly, like the tumblers of a lock, into place in his mind" (p. 359).

With Ida and Vivaldo, as with Richard and Cass, there is still a question about what one does *after* arriving in the other country. Certainly commitment and responsibility are there, but for Ida and Vivaldo, so is reality. They are still a black woman and a white man living together in a semiartist community way ahead of permissible mores of the society. Their triumph does not end in sounding brass, but in work for Vivaldo and sleep for Ida. Their ending is much like that of the Younger family in *A Raisin in the Sun*: there are no conclusions; there is only commitment to new levels of personal and public struggle.

Ida, this mixture of love, hate, and vengeance who has been revealed to us through many characters as well as through her own presence, is not so unlike other black women in Baldwin's fiction as her spitfire personality would suggest. We have seen defiance brought low in the person of Florence, and no less is Ida's fiery spirit dampened. She had set out to hate everyone and to punish everyone, only to find herself helplessly in love with Vivaldo, or so she maintains; how she can reconcile her hatred with her professed love is questionable. She had also set out to use Ellis, only to discover, in an ironic reversal, that she, like all of Baldwin's black heroines, is really at the mercy of the men in her life, from Vivaldo to Ellis. She deluded herself into thinking that she, at twenty-two, could manipulate a veteran of sexual politics like Steve Ellis. He has been in the television and producing business long enough to have seen many little Idas who thought their talent commanded attention. And perhaps he has helped them, but he has assuredly used them as well.

Ellis' power over Ida may be in terms of prestige and influence, but it manifests itself at a sexual level. Ida tries to use the weapon of her sex against Ellis, as Rufus has earlier used his against Leona (p. 24), only to discover that Ellis manipulates and controls her more thoroughly than she ever imagined controlling him. The climactic revelation comes on the night Cass accompanies her to Harlem. Ellis wants Ida to sing with the group, but the musicians do not; they reject her because they see her as Ellis' whore, a good sister turned bad who has spoiled her brother's memory. Ellis has the power to command acquiescence from both parties, but the musicians punish Ida by not backing her up properly. It is their distaste, Ellis' ruthless power, and her realization that she has indeed defiled Rufus' memory that drive her to the decision to break with him and to share her secrets with Vivaldo.

The role she plays in relation to Ellis and to Vivaldo has its seeds in the esteem in which Ida has held Rufus. He was big brother who could rescue, and she was little sister who needed rescuing. That presupposed a kind of passivity on her part, or at least a recognition that she could not save herself without someone's aid, and that someone, Rufus, was identified with romance and power; he has the power to remove her from the pitfalls that she may encounter in Harlem. By attributing such power to him, Ida places him in the mythic role of Big Brother that Baldwin explores at length in *Just Above My Head*.

With this basic attitude toward Rufus' power, it is easy for Ida to transfer such beliefs to Ellis, who has the economic counterparts attached to Rufus' romantic power. It is understandable that she sees herself, sometimes unconsciously, as a servant before the male lords and masters in her life and that she, like Ruth, punishes herself through involvement with them. She humorously refers to Vivaldo on one occasion as "the lord and master" (p. 226), but her humor backfires when it turns out that he is indeed her lord and master. Even the reference serves to echo the plight of the women in *Go Tell It on the Mountain*. And Vivaldo is no less aware of the mastering image that has both religious and sexual connotations. He thinks of his making love to Ida: "When he entered that marvelous wound in her, *rending and tearing! rending and tearing!* was she surrendering, in joy, to the Bridegroom, Lord, and Savior? or was he entering a fallen and humiliated city, entering an ambush, watched from secret places by hostile eyes?" (p. 260). The lower case in Ida's comment gives way to the upper case in Vivaldo's, for finally Ida does submit to be soothed, cleansed, renewed, and saved through the sharing encounter with Vivaldo. She becomes completely powerless before him, and it is he who must decide to be generous, grant forgiveness, and reincorporate her into the union she has violated.[13]

For all her resolve, Ida is as much victim as she is victimizing. Stanley Macebuh shares the evaluation of the peculiar position into which Ida is placed in the novel:

> Ironically, one is confronted with a curious situation in which Ida's and Rufus' anger directly elicits the regeneration of the other characters in the novel while at the same time leading to their own demoralisation. Rufus commits suicide apparently because he is consumed by fury and self-pity, and Ida herself degenerates towards the end of the novel into a whining, self-conscious adolescent unduly intent on explaining away the moral compromises she is compelled to make in order to survive.[14]

I would add as a further commentary that Ida's need for confession ties her to the Florences and Elizabeths of Baldwin's fictive world. She has certainly progressed beyond them in her ability to act, but she is no less exacting in her measure of her own guilt, no less willing to indict herself for clearly tangible sins than are these earlier women for indicting themselves for imaginary sins. They have the same basis of creation, and they ultimately fall into the same pattern of passing judgment upon themselves, though their notions of the measurement of their punishment may differ slightly.

Just as Elizabeth and Florence have been subordinate to other characters, so has Ida. Baldwin allows his characters to find parts of themselves by coming into contact with Ida, and she serves well in developing his thesis about isolation of blacks and whites. In fact, she serves almost too well, because the flesh-and-blood Ida must be deciphered through so many mediums. She is Black Woman at the same time that she is more individualized than that burden. She inflicts pain, but she is ultimately more suffering than avenging. As a representative of the blacks Baldwin believes his whites should understand in order to live with themselves and with blacks, Ida gets saddled with too much responsibility. As an individual black woman, it is precisely that responsibility that keeps us from seeing Ida, except through several cloudy lenses.[15]

By focusing his thesis on Ida, Baldwin can deal with her less as *a* black woman than as *the* black woman that exists in Cass's mind, or Eric's, or Vivaldo's, or the reader's. Ida grows, certainly, and we learn more about her, but she is still an elusive entity. At times she is a mysterious, larger-than-life personage, much like Nella Larsen's Helga Crane in *Quicksand*; she becomes a peacock paraded before the white characters' notions of black womanhood. Once she leaves Harlem, she is cut adrift from the black community except in brief excursions to the bars in which she sings. Her family becomes irrelevant; even the memory of Rufus becomes diffused and loses force without Ida growing in direct proportion to that loss. Though Ida sings the blues, and even lives them, she is still not wholly at home in that tradition. Like Ruth Bowman in "Come Out the Wilderness," she has no black friends, and the only time she attends church as an adult is for Rufus' funeral. Ida's character is developed solely in the small white community in which she assumes a part. Though their influence may still be felt, her ties to the black community and to her own familial heritage are short-circuited.[16] And Baldwin never really explains how a black woman from those beginnings could so thoroughly sever connections with all the bases of support contained there. Certainly Ida's desire to better her condition is understandable, but not *everything* in her past was so ugly as to be rejected completely, and she fast discovers that economic and spiritual poverty, ugliness, violence, and abuse are not limited to Harlem. Ida becomes, then, a black woman who exists, to a large extent, in a cultural vacuum, who is misguided by the economic glitter of the American Dream, but who is sensitized, nonetheless, through her integrationist contact with other suffering human beings.

We leave Ida in a peaceful sleep at the end of the novel. She has been cleansed through tears, which evokes comparison to baptism, but the question can be asked, Baptism to what? Her severed connections to the black community do not suggest that she will return there. Her baptism suggests that she has been permanently incorporated into the problematic relationship with Vivaldo. We are left wondering if Ida has really been cleansed of her tendency to guilt and to involving herself in situations for which she will feel guilty. We are left at the pinnacle of her resolution, before it has been tested by the fire of everyday existence. We may feel good about the change, but we cannot judge its depth beyond the moment. Therefore, Ida becomes a transitional figure in terms of the development of the progression away from the church. She is out physically, but questions still arise about her mental resolution in terms of ridding herself of the vestiges of the church-based ties that lead her to confession and remorse about her actions. Her ambivalent state provides a natural transition to the women in *If Beale Street Could Talk*, several of whom are not only out of the church, but who have no church-based consciences.

NOTES

1. James Baldwin, *Another Country* (Dial Press, 1962; rpt. New York: Dell, 1963), p. 250. Further references to this source will be parenthesized in the text.

2. Many critics have commented upon or directly complained about such occurrences in the novel. "As for sexual episodes," writes Colin MacInnes, "although there are glorious

moments ... the effect is frequently turgid and high-flown: the worst passages being almost like inflated parodies of the best"; see "Dark Angel: The Writings of James Baldwin" in Donald B. Gibson, *Five Black Writers* (New York: New York Univ. Press, 1970), p. 135. In *The Furious Passage of James Baldwin*, Fern Marja Eckman comments: "Undeniably there are powerful and beautiful passages in *Another Country*. Just as undeniably, the less standard varieties of sex are consistently sugared over and sentimentalized, with many—but not all—of the couplings between homosexual and heterosexual, Negro and white, in most of their possible equations, glorified as the apotheosis of love" (New York: Evans, 1966, p. 165). Eugenia Collier maintains that *Another Country* has "something offensive for everyone," including "the sordidly graphic descriptions of sex"; see "The Phrase Unbearably Repeated" in Therman B. O'Daniel, ed., *James Baldwin: A Critical Evaluation* (Washington, D.C.: Howard Univ. Press, 1977), p. 38.

3. Eckman (p. 113) mentions the suicide of Baldwin's friend, Eugene Worth, who, like Rufus, jumped off the George Washington Bridge. See also p. 162.

4. See George Kent, "Baldwin and the Problem of Being," in Gibson, *Five Black Writers*, p. 156; MacInnes, p. 136; and Fred L. Standley, "*Another Country*, Another Time," *Studies in the Novel* 4 (Fall 1972): 506.

5. Eckman, p. 159.

6. See Stanley Macebuh, *James Baldwin: A Critical Study* (New York: Joseph Okpaku Publishing, 1973), p. 87.

7. See Jacqueline E. Orsagh, "Baldwin's Female Characters: A Step Forward" in O'Daniel, pp. 62–65.

8. Donald B. Gibson, "James Baldwin: The Political Anatomy of Space," in O'Daniel, p. 12.

9. John S. Lash maintains that Rufus "has on occasion sought refuge from the whiplashes of the Negro life in New York in sexual indulgences with Vivaldo Moore, his best friend," but there is no explicit evidence in the novel to validate that statement; see "Baldwin Beside Himself: A Study in Modern Phallicism," in O'Daniel, p. 53.

10. Lash suggests that Eric is "the phallicist to whom men—and one woman—turn in their hours of bafflement and exaltation, the ministering angel, as it were, of the phallic god residual in the flesh of every man" (ibid., p. 50). He also maintains that "phallic confrontation" between men in Baldwin's works is "a normal or supernormal behavior pattern" and that Baldwin distinguishes between "phallic confrontation and overt effeminacy." Gibson also discusses the sometimes negative attitude Baldwin has toward homosexuality. Of *Giovanni's Room*, he asserts: "The novel makes clear the author's disgust with fairies, with males who assume feminine guise of dress or manner, and with males who are not at least bisexual" (ibid., p. 9). In *Another Country*, all of the prominent male characters who engage in homosexual acts—Rufus, Vivaldo, Eric—are bisexual. The ultimate fulfillment of sexual contact is between Eric and Yves, whose name, as Lash points out, is significantly pronounced "Eve," reinforcing the sometimes paradisal contact between males and males.

11. The level of communion between Eric and Vivaldo anticipates the religion of love through sex that Fonny and Tish will create in *If Beale Street Could Talk*.

12. See Gibson, "James Baldwin: The Political Anatomy of Space" in O'Daniel, p. 13.

13. Macebuh calls Vivaldo's role "priestlike" in the face of Ida's confession (p. 95).

14. Macebuh, p. 88.

15. Eckman comments on the alternative ending Baldwin had planned for the novel and for Ida: "And Ida herself, the figure with whom Baldwin was most concerned, simmering with his own rage, swathed in his own bafflement, was to have wound up as a

patient in a psychotic ward, a fate reserved in the published version for a white girl" (p. 159).

16. Addison Gayle maintains that the assimilationist approach to the novel demands that blacks give up their blackness. "Strip away the more sensational features of *Another Country*," he writes, "and the integrationist ethic is revealed; to be elevated to human kind, Blacks must be made one with the society, must desert the legacy of the cultural past." Gayle, *The Way of the New World* (Garden City, N.Y.: Doubleday, 1976), p. 267.

IRVING HOWE

A Protest of His Own

Twelve years ago a young Negro writer named James Baldwin printed an impassioned essay. "Everybody's Protest Novel," in which he attacked the kind of fiction from "Uncle Tom's Cabin" to "Native Son," that had been written in America about the sufferings of Negroes. The "protest novel," said Baldwin, began with sympathy for the Negro but soon had a way of enclosing him in the tones of hatred and violence he had experienced all his life; and so choked up was it with indignation, it failed to treat the Negro as a particular human being. "The failure of the protest novel * * * lies in its insistence that it is [man's] categorization alone which is real and which cannot be transcended."

To transcend the sterile categories of "Negro-ness," whether those enforced by the white world or those erected defensively by Negroes, became Baldwin's central concern as a writer. He wanted, as he says in "Nobody Knows My Name," his brilliant new collection of essays, "to prevent myself from becoming *merely* a Negro; or, even merely a Negro writer." He knew how "the world tends to trap and immobilize you in the role you play," and he knew also that for the Negro writer, if he is to be a writer at all, it hardly matters whether this trap is compounded of hatred or uneasy kindness.

From *The New York Times*, July 2, 1961. © 1961 by The New York Times Co.

Avoiding the psychic imprisonment of a fixed role, however, is more easily said than done. It was one thing for Baldwin to rebel against the social rebelliousness of Richard Wright, the older Negro novelist, who had served him as a literary hero, and quite another to establish his personal identity when there was no escaping that darkness of skin which in our society forms a brand of humiliation. Freedom cannot always be willed into existence; and that is why, as Baldwin went on to write two accomplished novels and a book of still more accomplished essays, he was forced to improvise a protest of his own: nonpolitical in character, spoken more in the voice of anguish than revolt, and concerned less with the melodrama of discrimination than the moral consequences of living under an irremovable stigma.

This highly personal protest Baldwin has released through a masterly use of the informal essay. Writing with both strength and delicacy, he has made the essay into a form that brings together vivid reporting, personal recollection and speculative thought. One of his best pieces, for example, begins as an account of his return to the streets of Harlem where he was raised; moves toward a description of why Negroes living in housing projects resent the liberal authoritarianism with which these are often managed; rushes to some sharp observations about the residents of Harlem who "know they are living there because white people do not think they are good enough to live anywhere else"; and comes to a reflective climax with an outburst of eloquent speech: *"Negroes want to be treated like men * * *. People who have mastered Kant, Hegel, Shakespeare, Marx, Freud, and the Bible find this statement utterly impenetrable * * *. A kind of panic paralyzes their features, as though they found themselves on the edge of a steep place."*

There are other essays in "Nobody Knows My Name" composed with equal skill: a saddening account of Baldwin's first visit South, a report on an international conference of Negro intellectuals debating whether they share a common culture, a chilling polemic against William Faulkner's views on segregation. And especially noteworthy are three essays on Richard Wright, which range in tone from disturbed affection to disturbing malice and reflect Baldwin's struggle to achieve some personal equilibrium as writer and Negro by discovering his true feelings toward the older man.

That Baldwin has reached such an equilibrium it would be foolish to suppose, and he himself would surely be the first to deny it. One great merit of his essays is their honesty in reflecting his own doubts and aggressions, and in recording his torturous efforts to find some peace in the relations between James Baldwin the lonely writer and James Baldwin the man who suffers as a Negro. This honesty, I would suggest, has driven him to abandon some of the more sanguine assumptions of "Everybody's Protest Novel"—it is, alas, not so simple to shed the categories imposed by society—and to come closer to Richard Wright's anger than he might care to admit. For if he began by attacking Wright for writing as a Negro rather than an individual artist, the pressures of experience have forced Baldwin to do his best work as an individual artist precisely when writing as a Negro.

I have only one complaint to register against "Nobody Knows My Name." Partly because his work relies so heavily on a continuous scrutiny of his own responses, Baldwin succumbs at times to what Thorstein Veblen might have called the pose of conspicuous sincerity. In the essays on Wright, and especially in a piece on Norman Mailer, the effort to expose the whole of his feelings slips occasionally into a mere attitude, and the confessional stance reveals some vanities of its own.

These are small blemishes on a splendid book. James Baldwin is a skillful writer, a man of fine intelligence and a true companion in the desire to make life human. To take a cue from his title, we had better learn his name.

JULIUS LESTER

Some Tickets Are Better:
The Mixed Achievement of James Baldwin

With the publication of *The Price of the Ticket*, James Baldwin presents the work on which he wants to be judged and by which he would like to be remembered. The volume contains fifty-one essays, twenty-five of them previously uncollected. The remaining twenty-six represent the entire contents of five previously published books: *The Devil Finds Work*, *No Name in the Street*, *Notes of a Native Son*, *Nobody Knows My Name*, and *The Fire Next Time*.

Arranged chronologically from February 1948 to January 1985, the essays are overpowering in their intensity and brilliance. Particularly in the essays from 1948 to *The Fire Next Time* (1963), Baldwin reveals himself to be a tremendously eloquent humanist.

His is not a romantic humanism, however, but a hard-edged, uninviting, and terrifying one. "But our humanity is our burden, our life; we need not battle for it; we need only to do what is infinitely more difficult—that is, accept it. The failure of the protest novel lies in its rejection of life, the human being, the denial of his beauty, dread, power, in its insistence that it is his categorization alone which is real and which cannot be transcended" ("Everybody's Protest Novel").

In the essays of the first fifteen years Baldwin writes not only as a black writer pleading the cause of blacks, but as a black pleading the cause

From *Critical Essays on James Baldwin*, Fred L. Standley and Nancy V. Burt, ed., pp. 244–250. Originally published in *Dissent* 33 (1986):189–192. © 1986 Julius Lester.

of humanity. Baldwin startles one by his use of "we," because sometimes he speaks not as a black but as an American. "Our dehumanization of the Negro then is indivisible from our dehumanization of ourselves: the loss of our own identity is the price we pay for our annulment of his" ("Many Thousands Gone").

Baldwin's power as a writer lies in his ability to weave the deeply autobiographical with the political and social. There is no separation between Jimmy Baldwin, black child of Harlem, and James Baldwin, American. For him, the personal is never just personal, and the political never just political. Because he perceives himself not only as the individual James Baldwin but also as the black Everyman, his writing has a moral authority that would be dismissed as arrogant if so many had not affirmed what he wrote.

To call Baldwin a black writer, then, is not only to relegate him to a literary ghetto, it is to dismiss his testimony. In these early essays no writer is more American than this tiny black man who first saw light in Harlem in 1924. Despite all he has seen, despite all that has been done to him, his response is not a literature delineating the emptiness and alienation in which so many Americans live. His response is not a literature of smug ridicule or clever satire. He responds with that most intangible, bothersome and intrusive of emotions—love. And the object of his love is not only blacks; its object is the republic itself. If words alone could redeem, Baldwin's would have placed us all in that "shining city on a hill" to which the current occupant of the White House deludes himself into thinking his presidency shows the way.

From 1948 to 1963 Baldwin's message was more spiritual than political, more psychological than ideological, and it had two central elements: (1) The necessity for blacks to free themselves from white imposed definitions; and (2) The necessity for whites to free themselves from their own definitions. As long as this mutual interdependence is unrecognized, blacks and whites will be unable to be human to themselves. And if one cannot be human to oneself, it is impossible to be human to another.

By 1960 Baldwin had honed this theme into one well-crafted sentence: "It is a terrible, and inexorable, law that one cannot deny the humanity of another without diminishing one's own: in the face of one's victim, one sees oneself" ("Fifth Avenue Uptown").

Witness. That is how James Baldwin describes himself. Not many writers would be comfortable with that self-definition, or understand it, even. Elie Wiesel is the only one who comes to mind, and perhaps that is not coincidence. Both have dedicated—or is it sacrificed?—themselves to the sacred act of giving testimony to what they have seen. Yet, they write, not as prosecutors of those who inflicted the horrors, but as prophets praying to God to be merciful, a God neither is sure is really there, and if He is, whether He is listening or really cares. But they pray, nonetheless, for humanity to transform itself before God metes out His terrible justice.

Once when I pressed Baldwin to define witness, he said:

> I am a witness to whence I came, where I am, witness to what I've seen and the possibilities that I think I see. I began using the word when I began to be called a spokesman. I'm certainly not a spokesman and the only word I could find is that I'm trying to be a witness. A spokesman assumes that he is speaking for others. I never assumed that I could. What I tried to do, or to interpret and make clear was that what the republic was doing to black people it was doing to itself. No society can smash the social contract and be exempt from the consequences and the consequences are chaos for everybody in the society. In the church in which I was raised you were supposed to bear witness to the truth. Now, of course, later on you wonder what in the world the truth is, but you do know what a lie is.

It is this need to "bear witness" that gives Baldwin's writing its urgency and passion, its rhetoric the all-encompassing generalization and the long and, sometimes, too-complex sentences. Baldwin's prophetic voice is a melding of those of the preacher he once was and of the King James version of the Old Testament. The reader is left wondering if he or she is in the presence of a person putting words to paper, or of a force unleashed by history that howls outside our windows.

The publication of *The Fire Next Time* in 1963 was an important event in the history of the civil rights movement and of America. It was the year when Bull Connor unleashed police dogs and fire hoses on blacks demonstrating in Birmingham, Alabama: images that were seen on the nightly news and horrified the nation. *The Fire Next Time* was Baldwin's warning of the black violence that would inevitably come if white America did not confront its racism.

The book became a best-seller and made Baldwin a celebrity, because he was able to combine anger and humanism in such a way that whites could receive the anger, not as an unqualified condemnation of themselves, but as angry tears of righteousness for us all..... if the word integration means anything, this is what it means: that we, with love, shall force our brothers to see themselves as they are, to cease fleeing from reality and begin to change it.... We cannot be free until they are free."

Yet, in *The Fire Next Time* there is a small, but perceptible shift in Baldwin's humanism that becomes more pronounced and obvious in many of the essays after 1963. "I could not share the white man's vision of himself for the very good reason that white men in America do not behave toward black men the way they behave toward each other" (*The Fire Next Time*).

But is that really true? "One cannot deny the humanity of another without diminishing one's own," Baldwin had written a few years earlier. If that is so (and I believe that it is), then white men in America do "behave toward each other" in the same way they behave toward blacks, but perhaps the ways are not so evident. Baldwin does not make the effort to get at what is not apparent.

The sweeping generalization has always been a hallmark of Baldwin's essays. He never questions or doubts that what he is witness to represents more than subjective experience. While this is the source of his power in *The Fire Next Time*, it is also the source of a weakness that will become more evident, a weakness wherein Baldwin will see, more and more, only what he wishes to see, and less and less make the effort to see what is.

In *The Fire Next Time* the humanistic Baldwin wrote of his concern for the "dignity" of blacks and for the "health" of their souls, and declared that he "must oppose any attempt that Negroes may make to do to others what has been done to them.... It is so simple a fact and one that is so hard, apparently, to grasp: *Whoever debases others is debasing himself.* This is not a mystical statement but a realistic one, which is proved by the eyes of any Alabama sheriff and I would not like to see Negroes ever arrive at so wretched a condition." Many of the later essays of *The Price of the Ticket* are evidence that Baldwin has not been a voice of opposition—at least not publicly—when blacks have sought to do to others what has been done to them.

He did not oppose publicly the rhetorical excesses of the Black Power movement in the late 1960s. Nor has he sought to examine the meaning of Louis Farrakhan, the glint of whose eyes bears no small resemblance to those "of any Alabama sheriff."

Baldwin is more than eloquent when articulating that the sole salvation for whites is to take responsibility for the evil they have wrought: "It has always been much easier (because it has always seemed much safer) to give a name to the evil without than to locate the terror within. And yet, the terror within is far truer and far more powerful than any of our labels: the labels change, the terror is constant" ("Nothing Personal"). Yet, he does not take the next step and say that blacks, too, must take responsibility, not only for the evil they have wrought, but even for the evil they have endured.

What has happened to James Baldwin since *The Fire Next Time* is that a black vision of the world has slowly gained precedence over his humanistic one. The roots of this lie, perhaps, in Baldwin's definition of himself as a witness and the responsibilities of a witness. In a taped conversation I had with him a year and a half ago, I asked if Richard Wright had had a responsibility to him and did he have a responsibility to younger black writers.

> I never felt that Richard had a responsibility for me, and if he had, he'd discharged it. What I was thinking about, though, was the early fifties when the world was breaking up, when the world of white supremacy was breaking up. I'm talking about the revolutions all over the world, specifically since we were in Paris—Tunisia, Algeria, the ferment in Senegal, the French loss of their Indo-Chinese empire. A whole lot of people—darker people for the most part—came from all kinds of places to Richard's door as they do now to my door. And in that sense he had a responsibility which he didn't know—well, who can blame him? A boy from Ethiopia, a boy from Senegal—they all claimed him. They had the right to claim him like they have the right to claim me.

What is that right? I asked. Why did they have a right to claim him? Why do they have the right to claim you?

> Well, right or not, there he was to be claimed. He was the most articulate black witness of his moment.... Richard was known in Paris and they had a right to claim him, much more right than those who did claim him—Sartre, de Beauvoir, etcetera.... I was in a very funny position. The people who knocked on his door ended up sleeping on my floor. I knew something about it which Richard didn't know ... someone who is not white and has managed to survive somehow and attempts to be in some way responsible—of course you're going to be claimed by multitudes of black kids. There's no way around it.

But can one be claimed without eventually being enslaved? It would be presumptuous of me to maintain that this is what has happened to Baldwin. Yet, reading *No Name in the Street* (1972) one is stunned by his lack of insight into the dangers represented by the Black Panther party as well as his sycophantic attitude toward Huey Newton and Eldridge Cleaver. In many of the essays of the 1970s and 1980s, it is not only what Baldwin says that is distressing, but, equally, that he fails to demand that blacks risk the terror and burden of being human as he demands it of whites.

His review of Alex Haley's *Roots* could have been written by any black writer beating the drum of blackness. It is not James Baldwin in fearful pursuit of truth but Baldwin imitating himself poorly. At the end of the review one sees the philosophical consequences of allowing one's self to be claimed: "It [*Roots*] suggests, with great power, how each of us, however unconsciously, can't but be the vehicle of the history which has produced us." This kind of historical determinism is damaging, because it denies human responsibility, not for history itself but for what we do with history.

The most disturbing of the later essays is "An Open Letter to the Born Again." Published in the *Nation* (September 29, 1979), it was written in the bitter aftermath of Andrew Young's resignation as U.N. ambassador, when black leaders excoriated Jews for their perceived role in that resignation. Throughout his career Baldwin has written thoughtfully and insightfully about black–Jewish relations. While he has sometimes come close to what some consider anti-Semitic statements, one always gave him the benefit of the doubt because he was James Baldwin. With "An Open Letter to the Born Again" one can do so no longer. "But the State of Israel was not created for the salvation of the Jews; it was created for the salvation of the Western interest. This is what is becoming clear (I must say that it was always clear to me). The Palestinians have been paying for the British colonial policy of "divide and rule" and for Europe's guilty Christian conscience for more than thirty years." Regardless of one's views on Israel, Baldwin's assertions have the uninformed certainty of barbershop opinion. His propensity for cosmic generalizations leads him to conclude that: "The Jew, in America, is a white man. He has to be, since I am a black man, and, as he supposes, his only protection against the fate which drove him to America. But he is still doing the Christian's dirty work, and black men know it."

Yet, in Baldwin's earlier essays there are noble statements which argue against defining others solely on the basis of one's own experience, which challenge us to live on the razor's edge of risk and vulnerability.

As one follows the journey of James Baldwin over the past thirty-seven years, one must wonder if the terror within has worn him down, if he no longer has the strength to throw himself into the abyss to find the tiny nuggets of truth which only he was able to find.

Or, is it that, having permitted himself to be claimed by black people, he has abdicated the lonely responsibility of the artist and intellectual to be claimed by nothing but that futile and beautiful quest for Truth?

It was Baldwin himself who wrote in 1962 that "... the truth, in spite of appearances and all our hopes, is that everything is always changing and the measure of our maturity as nations and as men is how well prepared we are to meet these changes and, further, to use them for our health" ("The Creative Process").

It is not easy to be so critical of Baldwin. That his writings have made a significant difference in the way many of us, black and white, view ourselves and each other is indisputable. Read as a body, the essays of James Baldwin are a sustaining act of love and faith of which America has not been worthy.

Perhaps it is too much to ask that any one writer sustain love and faith throughout a life of terror. Perhaps it is too much to ask him to return again and again to the abyss. The price of such excursions is high and one pays in one's soul and body. Perhaps, then, no one asks another to do more than he or she can, and instead lovingly laments the absence of the growth that we would want for that person—and ourselves.

In the last essay of *The Price of the Ticket* there are these words: "The object of one's hatred is never, alas, conveniently outside but is seated in one's lap, stirring in one's bowels—and dictating the beat of one's heart. And if one does not know this, one risks becoming an imitation—and, therefore, a continuation—of principles one imagines oneself to despise."

If *The Price of the Ticket* is to be the summation of Baldwin's career, then we must be grateful for the wisdom contained in its early essays and take as a warning the latter ones which are, all too often, "an imitation" and "a continuation of principles" Baldwin taught us to despise.

DAVID LEEMING

Africa and The Fire Next Time

I will make my words in thy mouth fire.
    —Jeremiah 5:14

On July 7, 1962, Baldwin, accompanied by his sister Gloria, arrived in Africa. For some time he had felt he "should see Africa" but had resisted the trip because of a persistent feeling, expressed, for example, in the "Princes and Powers" essay, that he had infinitely more in common with his compatriots, even his white compatriots, than he did with Africans. He was frankly skeptical of the interest among American blacks at the time in their African "homeland." He had, for instance, been almost scornful of Richard Wright's movement in that direction. An important part of Baldwin's message to this point, as indicated in speeches like "In Search of a Majority," was based on the idea of unbreakable, if painful, "blood ties" between white and black Americans and the notion that the unique American experience, for all its problems, was the best hope for the future. To "return" to African roots was to return to a distant past and to a relationship that was based on shared color rather than on shared experience. He had written to a friend from Israel that he knew instinctively what he might experience in Africa, that this frightened him, and that this was why he had put off the trip for so long. To Fern Eckman he confessed that he was "afraid" of being looked

From *James Baldwin: A Biography*, pp. 207–215. © 1994 by David Leeming.

down upon as an American and afraid that something American in him might look down on Africans.

At first it seemed as though such fears might be justified. In the usual confusion surrounding his travels, Baldwin had forgotten about visas. Arriving at the airport passport control in Dakar, he was confronted for the first time by official bureaucracy wearing a black mask. In front of him in line was a white European being dealt with somewhat harshly, and this "rattled" him. When his turn came he could not understand the official and attempted to explain who he was by showing him a picture of himself in a magazine. The official told him he would have to buy a ticket for some other destination before he could be issued a temporary transit visa. Where did he want to go? Baldwin suggested Brazzaville, having no plans beyond Dakar. The policeman laughed and suggested Conakry. Eventually, with the help of a taxi driver, he and Gloria were able to negotiate the visa problem, and soon they found themselves in downtown Dakar.

One pleasant surprise was their being mistaken at first for Africans. A small child had left her mother's side and presented herself to Gloria to be lifted up. Gloria complied and the mother watched with evident pleasure and pride. When the father came over to Baldwin and asked if they were from Dahomey, he suddenly had a sense that he belonged in the scene, that he had roots here and need no longer be "afraid." The style of the people on the streets even reminded him of Harlem. The robes, the colors, the turbans, the colorful caps, the women wrapped in cloths of bright prints, their babies tied to their backs, were at once wildly exotic and oddly familiar. Dakar was strange, a European city surrounded by a culture it had worked so hard to undermine. The people he saw seemed at once at home and out of place; he began to identify with them and perhaps to wish he were somehow more like them in appearance. He found that his external "white consciousness," his sense of the appropriate instilled in him by a long history as a minority race, was challenged by a physical representation of a way of perceiving that had its source in prehistoric times, before humans began to think about who or what they were. The visitor from America longed for the easy unself-conscious self-assurance he thought he saw in the streets of Dakar.

Baldwin was experiencing his version of *The Heart of Darkness* and he found in it—its exoticism, its marketplace scents and sounds, its beggars, its lame, its colors, its emotional expressiveness—something of the depth, the ability to touch, the willingness to accept the "stink of love" that he had chastised his nation for suppressing. Africa in all of its turmoil, in all of its pain, was teeming with the essence of what it was on the most basic level to be human, and Africa was, above all, black.

During the time in Africa he made a point of talking to whites—especially white Americans—in the diplomatic and information services as well as to Africans. He had dinner with the American ambassador to Senegal, went to the beach with other white diplomats, and got to know United States Information Service officials. When one USIS man suggested to Baldwin that Africans had all of the Western vices but none of the Western virtues, he listened, but he wondered whether the USIS's ideas of the nature of vice and virtue would be his.

A few days after his arrival in Dakar, Baldwin was asked to speak at the U.S. cultural center. He talked on a favorite theme—the goal of "liberation" for whites as well as blacks in the American civil rights struggle. When a white USIS officer asked whether whites or blacks in America would be liberated first, a young Senegalese answered for Baldwin in a manner that coincided completely with his point of view. The fact that a white American could ask a black American such a question was itself an answer to the question.

After a seminar on Senghor and *Négritude* on another day, Baldwin was taken out for dinner by a prestigious, wealthy, and rather intoxicated African man through whom he was exposed to an aspect of Africa that somewhat undermined the appealing qualities he had noted in the public marketplace and among students at the cultural center. The man talked of nothing but money, the quality of various scotch whiskeys, and the laziness of his "help." The rich African was a horrifying parody of "white consciousness" and a living representation of those black slave-trading middlemen who were so much a part of his history.

The Baldwins were met in Conakry, where they went next, by the head of USIS, and they were introduced to President Sekou Touré, who seemed to Baldwin to be proud, impressive, but unsympathetic. The atmosphere in Guinea was markedly different from that of Senegal and contributed to his negative attitude towards its president. Escaping from his hosts, Baldwin wandered the streets and was struck by their relative barrenness and by the attitude of wariness that prevailed in the city. He sensed he was being watched. Later, back among the American officials, he heard stories of the influence of the Russians and Chinese. One USIS man told of the mysterious arrest of his houseboy. The American center had been closed, and there were very few books to be found in Guinea. Christianity and capitalism were not the only white ideologies to have left their painful marks on Africa.

It was with some relief that Baldwin and Gloria arrived late in July in Freetown, Sierra Leone. This was to be the most important stop on the African tour, primarily because of an introduction to Frank Karefa-Smart, a USIS employee who became, in effect, their guide and host. Frank was the younger brother of Dr. Joseph Karefa-Smart, a leading politician and the head of one of the most influential families in Sierra Leone. Baldwin took an instant liking to both Karefa-Smarts, especially to Frank, in whom he saw the kind of complexity to which he was invariably attracted in another human being—sensitivity and intelligence combined with a certain sadness and skepticism, an essential "privacy." He could not have known then that in a few years Gloria would marry Frank Karefa-Smart.

Through their new friends the Baldwins learned a great deal about the Sierra Leonean version of the peculiar legacy of colonialism. The Karefa-Smarts were English-speaking people of the old British protectorate, while the majority of Freetown's citizens were Creole descendants of the original settlers of the Freetown colony. The gap between the colony and the protectorate was evident in all areas of life in Sierra Leone, not least in the parliament itself, a session of which Baldwin attended with Frank Karefa-Smart, where the protectorate-based Speaker wore a British judicial wig, carried a mace, and exhibited pure arrogance in relation to the much less sophisticated parliamentarians from the colony. Baldwin was finding that "discovering" Africa would mean sifting through not only the ancient tribal differences but the modern ones artificially created by the white oppressor. Color could not in itself make a "nation."

The rest of the African trip included stops in Monrovia, Abidjan, and Accra. But everything after Freetown was anticlimactic, and Baldwin realized he did not want to write the article on Africa commissioned by *The New Yorker*. As was the case with his trips to the South, he was uncomfortable in the role of reporter. The pages of notes on the diamond trade in Sierra Leone left him cold, and an agricultural station outside of Monrovia had something of the same effect. His interest was always in the inner workings of people, and he was finding himself more and more the captive of American officials whose company he enjoyed well enough but who could provide him only with a predictable outlook on Africa. Throughout the notes he kept on Africa there are indications of the things that really attracted him but which he was unable to pursue in any depth. He comments frequently on the sheer beauty of the landscape, the farms, the people—"especially the children, the openness and gentleness.... *The Children*."

Baldwin left Africa glad he had been there but with his eyes firmly focused on America. What he had seen—the political turmoil, the poverty, the pride, the physicality, the failure of the whites in Africa to understand—led him directly to the essay that he had left unfinished before the trip and which he knew now he must finish before he could do anything else. "Down at the Cross" would, he thought, be his consideration of Western culture from the perspective of the people oppressed by that culture. In it he would expose the real "moral history of the West." After Africa he was more convinced than ever that America's—and the West's—only hope of survival lay in a liberation from the hypocrisy that had made oppression and subjugation in the name of democracy and religion possible. It was time for a "redefinition" of our myths in the context of our deeds. Africa had cemented his belief that to be of African descent in the West was "to be the 'flesh'. of white people—endlessly mortified."

Baldwin had gone to Turkey to finish *Another Country*. Now, a little less than a year later, after picking up Lucien in Paris, he went back there to finish "Down at the Cross." Several years before, Bald win had promised an article on the Black Muslims to Norman Podhoretz at *Commentary*, at about the same time he had committed himself to writing the African piece for William Shawn at *The New Yorker*. As there was no African travel essay, he decided that *The New Yorker* should be offered "Down at the Cross," which, in any case, since it included a long segment on his early life in the church, had developed into something more than an essay on the Muslims. Podhoretz considered, with some reason, that he had been treated badly, but Baldwin also wanted a wider audience than *Commentary* would provide, and short of money, as always, he needed the higher fee that *The New Yorker* could pay.

The twenty-thousand-word essay, unlike anything *The New Yorker* had ever printed before, was published as "Letter from a Region in My Mind" and almost immediately became, literally, the "talk of the town," causing the magazine's sales to soar. *Time* magazine called it "compelling" and "bitterly eloquent." There were also detractors—and friends—who resented Baldwin's placing such a work in *The New Yorker* among the elitist ads for expensive cars and clothes. Many of the same people complained of his selling serious articles to *Playboy* and *Mademoiselle*. Baldwin's not altogether tongue-in-cheek reply was always that his audience were the "publicans and tax-collectors" as well as the righteous.

Meanwhile, in commemoration of the one hundredth anniversary of the Emancipation Proclamation, he wrote an open letter to his nephew James, his brother Wilmer's son. This was published in *Progressive* as "A Letter to My Nephew." Both pieces were received with enthusiasm. It was James Silberman at Dial who recognized the larger importance of the two articles and their essential connection. Against the advice of Shawn at *The New Yorker*, he suggested using the "Letter to My Nephew" as an introduction to the longer essay. *The Fire Next Time*, then, became a book which contained "My Dungeon Shook: Letter to My Nephew on the One Hundredth Anniversary of the Emancipation" and "Down at the Cross: Letter from a Region in My Mind."

The "Letter to My Nephew" is an impassioned cry to the African-American youth represented specifically by Baldwin's nephew and more generally by the young people challenging the old guard in the rights movement. It is a direct and clear articulation of the Baldwin philosophy, as much a manifesto as *Notes of a Native Son* had been in 1955, but a much angrier one.

The idea for the open letter had taken hold during a visit to an elementary school classroom in Dakar on the second day of Baldwin's recent trip. When he entered the room the children were reciting in unison from a history textbook. The words seemed to have little to do with the lives of those in the room, and upon reading the opening passage of the book (published and written in France)—"Our ancestors, who came from Gaul..."—he was enraged by the irony. These children were being denied their own heritage; the object was to turn them into absurd replicas of their colonizers. He thought of the analogous situation of millions of black children in American classrooms reading about "our ancestors," the Europeans, the pilgrims, the writers of the Constitution, and the pioneers. African-American children must not be "educated" into the myths of the oppressor; they must not be denied their own identity.

The greatest danger, Baldwin announces to his nephew, is "believing that you really are what the white world calls a *nigger*." As for the white oppressors, their greatest crime is their "innocence"; they "have destroyed and are destroying hundreds of thousands of lives and do not know it and do not want to know it." Ida had told Vivaldo in *Another Country* that he had no right not to "know." Baldwin reminds his nephew of the results of the failure to know, the results of this white innocence: "You were born where you were born and faced the future that you faced because you were black and *for no other reason*."

Then Baldwin turns to the question of the role of black people in reeducating whites. Integration does not mean that you have to become like white people, he tells, his nephew, or that they must accept you. The point is that "we, with love, shall force our brothers to see themselves as they are, to cease fleeing from reality and begin to change it.... We cannot be free until they are free."

In "Down at the Cross" Baldwin considers the question of the relationship between religion and the love he had spoken of in the letter to his nephew. He begins with a wonderfully vivid description of his own church experience, emphasizing that his desire to be saved as a teenager was in reality a desire to be saved from the call of the body and from the agony of racial oppression. He describes how he began, however, even in the church, to recognize the importance of *sensuality*: "To be sensual ... is to respect and rejoice in the force of life, of life itself, and to be *present* in all that one does, from the effort of loving to the breaking of bread." But finally there had been no choice but to leave the church. Christianity was more concerned with the soul than the body, "to which fact the flesh (and the corpses) of countless infidels bears witness."

In Africa he had found the same struggle between the sensual and the repressive that he had found in his own church. It was as evident in the African colors, sounds, and smells surrounded by the French and English buildings of Dakar and Freetown as it was in the saints in their Sunday best "down at the cross" of the white God. And once again he had come to an anti-Christian position. "Whoever wishes to become a truly moral human being," Baldwin writes,

> must first divorce himself from all the prohibitions, crimes, and hypocrisies of the Christian church. If the concept of God has any validity or any use, it can only be to make us larger, freer, and more loving. If God cannot do this, then it is time we got rid of him.

Having disposed for the moment of the old religion of the black diaspora, Baldwin turns his attention to the new religious hope of the black dispossessed, the religion of Elijah Muhammad. This was a religion that had in many ways succeeded where Christianity had failed. It had reached out to junkies, to drunkards, to prostitutes, to the poor, and had inspired pride, self-respect, and the possibility of material achievement. Yet, behind these achievements was a parody of a familiar point of view: "God is black. All black men belong to Islam; they have been chosen. And Islam shall rule the world. The dream, the sentiment is old; only the color is new."

During his visit to Elijah Muhammad, Baldwin had felt "I was back in my father's house," back in a set of puritanical taboos and totems that could not speak to the real nature of our problems as a nation, that, like all ideologically based forms, could only serve to imprison us further, to keep us from the "sensuality" which is an acceptance of life: "Perhaps the whole root of our trouble, the human trouble, is that we will sacrifice all the beauty of our lives, will imprison ourselves in totems, taboos, crosses, blood sacrifices, steeples, mosques, races, armies, flags, nations, in order to deny the fact of death, which is the only fact we have.... One ... ought to *earn* one's death by confronting with passion the conundrum of life." To accept death—and, therefore, life—in this way is to be free, but "freedom is hard to bear." The Nation of Islam's call for a separate nation is no less ironical or dangerous than the de facto establishment of exactly that by the white power structure in America.

At the end of his essay Baldwin points, as he had elsewhere, to the power of love as our only hope, love "not in the infantile American sense of being made happy but in the tough and universal sense of quest and daring and growth," the sense represented metaphorically in *Another Country*. The final words are a Jeremiah-like last-chance charge to a nation on the brink of disaster; they are James Baldwin's "I have a dream":

> If we—and now I mean the relatively conscious whites and the relatively conscious blacks, who must, like lovers, insist on, or create, the consciousness of the others—do not falter in our duty now, we may be able, handful that we are, to end the racial nightmare, and achieve our country, and change the history of the world. If we do not now dare everything, the fulfillment of that prophecy, re-created from the Bible in song by a slave, is upon us: *God gave Noah the rainbow sign, No more water, the fire next time!*

The reviews of *The Fire Next Time* were highly favorable and the book went to the top of the nonfiction best seller lists all over the country, and for the first time Baldwin became an internationally recognized writer. The reception in England was especially enthusiastic. In *The Guardian* Marcus Cunliffe wrote, "James Baldwin has become world-famous ... he speaks with an appalling authority, as one at the head of a multitude." Ved Mehta, writing in *The Observer*, said "*The Fire Next Time* is an extraordinary human document—a classic." Most important was a letter from Beauford Delaney, in which his old mentor summed up what Baldwin had hoped would be the reaction of black Americans: The work "reveals for all of us so much that we feel but cannot put into words." The prophet had been heard by the whole nation.

NOTES

207–11   Trip to Africa: DL conversations with JB and Gloria Karefa-Smart (1963–66); JB's notes on trip.
207JB on being American in Africa: Eckman, 166–67; JB notes.
207–8JB affected by trip: Eckman, 167.
208–9Africa and color: Eckman, 167.
209USIS incident: JB notes.
210JB on Frank Karefa-Smart: JB notes.
JB in Sierra Leone parliament: JB notes.
JB on "the children": JB notes.
211JB on writing "Down at the Cross": JB letter to Mary Painter, Dec. 1961.
JB on being of African descent in this world: JB letter to "Dan," Dec. 1961.
"Letter from a Region ...": *New Yorker*, 17 Nov. 1962, 59–144 (*Fire*).
211–13   "Letter to My Nephew ...": *Progressive*, Dec. 1962, 19–20 (*Fire*).
The publication of *Fire*: *Dial*, 1963; DL interview with James Silberman.
214–15   Reviews of *Fire*; *Guardian*, 17 July 1963; *Observer*, 14 July 1963.

JOHN M. REILLY

"Sonny's Blues":
James Baldwin's Image of Black Community

A critical commonplace holds that James Baldwin writes better essays than he does fiction or drama; nevertheless, his leading theme—the discovery of identity—is nowhere presented more successfully than in the short story "Sonny's Blues." Originally published in *Partisan Review* in 1957 and reprinted in the collection of stories *Going to Meet the Man* in 1965, "Sonny's Blues" not only states dramatically the motive for Baldwin's famous polemics in the cause of Black freedom, but it also provides an esthetic linking his work, in all literary genres, with the cultures of the Black ghetto.[1]

The fundamental movement of "Sonny's Blues" represents the slow accommodation of a first-person narrator's consciousness to the meaning of his younger brother's way of life. The process leads Baldwin's readers to a sympathetic engagement with the young man by providing a knowledge of the human motives of the youths whose lives normally are reported to others only by their inclusion in statistics of school dropout rates, drug usage, and unemployment.

The basis of the story, however, and its relationship to the purpose of Baldwin's writing generally, lies in his use of the Blues as a key metaphor. The unique quality of the Blues is its combination of personal and social significance in a lyric encounter with history. "The Blues-singer describes first-person experiences, but only such as are typical of the community and

From *James Baldwin: A Critical Evaluation*, Therman O'Daniel, ed., pp. 163–169. © 1977 by Howard University Press.

such as each individual in the community might have. The singer never sets himself against the community or raises himself above it."[2] Thus, in the story of Sonny and his brother an intuition of the meaning of the Blues repairs the relationship between the two men who have chosen different ways to cope with the menacing ghetto environment, and their reconciliation through the medium of this Afro-American musical form extends the meaning of the individual's Blues until it becomes a metaphor of Black community.

Sonny's life explodes into his older brother's awareness when the story of his arrest for peddling and using heroin is reported in the newspaper. Significantly the mass medium of the newspaper with the impersonal story in it of a police bust is the only way the brothers have of communicating at the opening of the story. While the narrator says that because of the newspaper report Sonny "became real to me again," their relationship is only vestigially personal, for he "couldn't find any room" for the news "anywhere inside ..." (P. 103)

While he had had his suspicions about how Sonny was spending his life, the narrator had put them aside with rationalizations about how Sonny was, after all, a good kid. Nothing to worry about. In short, the storyteller reveals that along with his respectable job as an algebra teacher he had assumed a conventional way of thinking as a defense against recognizing that his own brother ran the risk of "coming to nothing." Provoked by the facts of Sonny's arrest to observe his students, since they are the same age as Sonny must have been when he first had heroin, he notices for the first time that their laughter is disenchanted rather than good-humored. In it he hears his brother, and perhaps himself. At this point in the story his opinion is evidently that Sonny and many of the young students are beaten and he, fortunately, is not.

The conventionality of the narrator's attitude becomes clearer when he encounters a nameless friend of Sonny's, a boy from the block who fears he may have touted Sonny onto heroin by telling him, truthfully, how great it made him feel to be high. This man who "still spent hours on the street corner ... high and raggy" explains what will happen to Sonny because of his arrest. After they send him someplace and try to cure him, they'll let Sonny loose, that's all. Trying to grasp the implication the narrator asks: "You mean he'll never kick the habit. Is that what you mean?" He feels there should be some kind of renewal, some hope. A man should be able to bring himself up by his will, convention says. Convention also says that behavior like Sonny's is deliberately self-destructive. "Tell me," he asks the friend, "why does he want to die?" Wrong again. "Don't nobody want to die," says the friend, "ever." (P. 108)

Agitated though he is about Sonny's fate the narrator doesn't want to feel himself involved. His own position on the middle-class ladder of success is not secure, and the supporting patterns of thought in his mind are actually rather weak. Listening to the nameless friend explain about Sonny while they stand together in front of a bar blasting "black and bouncy" music from its door, he senses something that frightens him. "All this was carrying me some place I didn't want to go. I certainly didn't want to know how it felt. It filled everything, the people, the houses, the music, the dark, quicksilver barmaid, with menace; and this menace was their reality." (P. 107)

Eventually a great personal pain—the loss of a young daughter—breaks through the narrator's defenses and makes him seek out his brother, more for his own comfort than for Sonny's. "My trouble made his real," he says. In that remark is a prefiguring of the meaning the Blues will develop.

It is only a prefiguring, however, for the time Sonny is released from the state institution where he had been confined, the narrator's immediate need for comfort has passed. When he meets Sonny he is in control of himself, but very shortly he is flooded with complex feelings that make him feel again the menace of the 110th Street bar where he had stood with Sonny's friend. There is no escaping a feeling of icy dread, so he must try to understand.

As the narrator casts his mind back over his and Sonny's past, he gradually identifies sources of his feelings. First he recalls their parents, especially concentrating on an image of his family on a typical Sunday. The scene is one of security amidst portentousness. The adults sit without talking, "but every face looks darkening, like the sky outside." The children sit about, maybe one half asleep and another being stroked on the head by an adult. The darkness frightens a child and he hopes "that the hand which strokes his forehead will never stop." The child knows, however, that it will end, and now grown-up he recalls one of the meanings of the darkness is in the story his mother told him of the death of his uncle, run over on a dark country road by a car full of drunken white men. Never had his companion, the boy's father, "seen anything as dark as that road after the lights of the car had gone away." The narrator's mother had attempted to apply her tale of his father's grief at the death of his own brother to the needs of their sons. They can't protect each other, she knows, "but," she says to the narrator about Sonny, "you got to let him know you's *there*." (P. 119)

Thus, guilt for not fulfilling their mother's request and a sense of shared loneliness partially explain the older brother's feeling toward Sonny. Once again, however, Baldwin stresses the place of the conventional set of the narrator's mind in the complex of feelings as he has him recall scenes from the time when Sonny had started to become a jazz musician. The possibility of Sonny's being a jazz rather than a classical musician had "seemed—beneath him, somehow." Trying to understand the ambition, the narrator had asked if Sonny meant to play like Louis Armstrong, only to be told that Charlie

Parker was the model. Hard as it is to believe, he had never heard of Bird until Sonny mentioned him. This ignorance reveals more than a gap between fraternal generations. It represents a cultural chasm. The narrator's inability to understand Sonny's choice of a musical leader shows his alienation from the mood of the post-war bebop subculture. In its hip style of dress, its repudiation of middle-brow norms, and its celebration of esoteric manner the bebop subculture made overtly evident its underlying significance as an assertion of Black identity. Building upon a restatement of Afro-American music, bebop became an expression of a new self-awareness in the ghettos by a strategy of elaborate nonconformity. In committing himself to the bebop subculture Sonny attempted to make a virtue of the necessity of the isolation imposed upon him by his color. In contrast, the narrator's failure to understand what Sonny was doing indicates that his response to the conditions imposed upon him by racial status was to try to assimilate himself as well as he could into the mainstream American culture. For the one, heroin addiction sealed his membership in the exclusive group; for the other, adoption of individualistic attitudes marked his allegiance to the historically familiar ideal of transcending caste distinctions by entering into the middle class.

Following his way, Sonny became wrapped in the vision that rose from his piano, stopped attending school, and hung around with a group of musicians in Greenwich Village. His musical friends became Sonny's family, replacing the brother who had felt that Sonny's choice of his style of life was the same thing as dying, and for all practical purposes the brothers were dead to each other in the extended separation before Sonny's arrest on narcotics charges.

The thoughts revealing the brothers' family history and locating the sources of the narrator's complex feelings about Sonny all occur in the period after Sonny is released from the state institution. Though he has ceased to evade thoughts of their relationship, as he had done in the years when they were separated and had partially continued to do after Sonny's arrest, the narrator has a way to go before he can become reconciled to Sonny. His recollections of the past only provide his consciousness with raw feeling.

The next development—perception—begins with a scene of a revival meeting conducted on the sidewalk of Seventh Avenue, beneath the narrator's window. Everyone on the street has been watching such meetings all his life, but the narrator from his window, passersby on the street, and Sonny from the edge of the crowd all watch again. It isn't because they expect something different this time. Rather it is a familiar moment of communion for them. In basic humanity one of the sanctified sisters resembles the down-and-outer watching her, "a cigarette between her heavy, chapped lips, her hair a cuckoo's nest, her face scarred and swollen from many beatings.... Perhaps," the narrator thinks, "they both knew this, which was why, when, as rarely, they addressed each other, they addressed each other as Sister." (P. 129) The point impresses both the narrator and Sonny, men who should call one another "Brother," for the music of the revivalists seems to "soothe a poison" out of them.

The perception of this moment extends nearly to conception in the conversation between the narrator and Sonny that follows it. It isn't a comfortable discussion. The narrator still is inclined to voice moral judgments of the experiences and people Sonny tries to talk about, but he is making an honest effort to relate to his brother now and reminds himself to be quiet and listen. What he hears is that Sonny equates the feeling of hearing the revivalist sister sing with the sensation of heroin in the veins. "It makes you feel—in control. Sometimes you got to have that feeling." (P. 131) It isn't primarily drugs that Sonny is talking about, though, and when the narrator curbs his tongue to let him go on, Sonny explains the real subject of his thoughts.

Again, the facts of Sonny's experience contradict the opinion of "respectable" people. He did not use drugs to escape from suffering, he says. He knows as well as anyone that there's no way to avoid suffering, but what you can do is "try all kinds of ways to keep from drowning in it, to keep on top of it, and to make it seem ... like *you*." That is, Sonny explains, you can earn your suffering, make it seem "like you did something ... and now you're suffering for it." (P. 132)

The idea of meriting your suffering is a staggering one. In the face of it the narrator's inclination to talk about "will power and how life could be—well, beautiful," is blunted, because he senses that by directly confronting degradation Sonny has asserted what degree of will was possible to him, and perhaps that kept him alive.

At this point in the story it is clear that there are two themes emerging. The first is the theme of the individualistic narrator's gradual discovery of the significance of his brother's life. This theme moves to a climax in the final scene of the story when Sonny's music impresses the narrator with a sense of the profound feeling it contains. From the perspective of that final scene, however, the significance of the Blues itself becomes a powerful theme.

The insight into suffering that Sonny displays establishes his priority in knowledge. Thus, he reverses the original relationship between the brothers, assumes the role of the elder, and proceeds to lead his brother, by means of the Blues, to a discovery of self in community.

As the brothers enter the jazz club where Sonny is to play, he becomes special. Everyone has been waiting for him, and each greets him familiarly. Equally special is the setting—dark except for a spotlight which the musicians approach as if it were a circle of flame. This is a sanctified spot where Sonny is to testify to the power of souls to commune in the Blues.

Baldwin explicates the formula of the Blues by tracing the narrator's thoughts while Sonny plays. Many people, he thinks, don't really hear music being played except so far as they invest it with "personal, private, vanishing evocations." He might be thinking of himself, referring to his having come to think of Sonny through the suffering of his own personal loss. The man who makes the music engages in a spiritual creation, and when he succeeds, the creation belongs to all present, "his triumph, when he triumphs, is ours." (P. 137)

In the first set Sonny doesn't triumph, but in the second, appropriately begun by "Am I Blue," he takes the lead and begins to form a musical creation. He becomes, in the narrator's words, "part of the family again." (P. 139) What family? First of all that of his fellow musicians. Then, of course, the narrator means to say that their fraternal relationship is at last fulfilled as their mother hoped it to be. But there is yet a broader meaning too. Like the sisters at the Seventh Avenue revival meeting Sonny and the band are not saying anything new. Still they are keeping the Blues alive by expanding it beyond the personal lyric into a statement of the glorious capacity of human beings to take the worst and give it a form of their own choosing.

At this point the narrator synthesizes feelings and perception into a conception of the Blues. He realizes Sonny's Blues can help everyone who listens be free, in his own case free of the conventions that had alienated him from Sonny and that dimension of Black culture represented in Sonny's style of living. Yet at the same time he knows the world outside of the Blues moment remains hostile.

The implicit statement of the esthetics of the Blues in this story throws light upon much of Baldwin's writing. The first proposition of the esthetics that we can infer from "Sonny's Blues" is that suffering is the prior necessity. Integrity of expression comes from "paying your dues." This is a point Baldwin previously made in *Giovanni's Room* (1956) and which he elaborated in the novel *Another Country* (1962).

The second implicit proposition of the Blues esthetics is that while the form is what it's all about, the form is transitory. The Blues is an art in process and in that respect alien from any conception of fixed and ideal forms. This will not justify weaknesses in an artist's work, but insofar as Baldwin identifies his writing with the art of the singers of Blues it suggests why he is devoted to representation, in whatever genre, of successive moments of expressive feeling and comparatively less concerned with achieving a consistent overall structure.

The final proposition of the esthetics in the story "Sonny's Blues" is that the Blues functions as an art of communion. It is popular rather than elite, worldly rather than otherwise. The Blues is expression in which one uses the skill he has achieved by practice and experience in order to reach toward others. It is this proposition that gives the Blues its metaphoric significance. The fraternal reconciliation brought about through Sonny's music is emblematic of a group's coming together, because the narrator learns to love his brother freely while he discovers the value of a characteristically Afro-American assertion of life-force. Taking Sonny on his own terms he must also abandon the ways of thought identified with middle-class position which historically has signified for Black people the adoption of "white" ways.

An outstanding quality of the Black literary tradition in America is its attention to the interdependence of personal and social experience. Obviously necessity has fostered this virtue. Black authors cannot luxuriate in the assumption that there is such a thing as a purely private life. James Baldwin significantly adds to this aspect of the tradition in "Sonny's Blues" by showing that artful expression of personal yet typical experience is one way to freedom.

NOTES

1. James Baldwin, "Sonny's Blues," *Partisan Review* 24 (Summer, 1957): 327–58. And in *Going to Meet the Man* (New York: Dial Press, 1965), pp. 103–41. Citations in the text are from the latter publication of the story.

2. Janheinz Jahn, *Neo-African Literature: A History of Black Writing*, trans. Oliver Coburn and Ursula Lehrburger (New York: Grove Press, 1968), p. 166

RICHARD N. ALBERT

The Jazz-Blues Motif in
James Baldwin's "Sonny's Blues"

James Baldwin's "Sonny's Blues," a popular selection among editors of
anthologies used in introductory college literature courses, is one of his most
enduring stories because it is less polemical than many of his later efforts and
because it offers several common literary themes: individualism, alienation,
and "Am I my brother's keeper?" The story has also generated some
perceptive critical views, some of which emphasize Baldwin's metaphorical
use of the blues. However, none of the criticism bothers to look more closely
at the significance of the jazz and blues images and allusions in relation to the
commonly-agreed-upon basic themes of individualism and alienation.

A closer examination of Baldwin's use of jazz and blues forms and of
Louis Armstrong, Charlie Parker, the character Creole, and the song, "Am
I Blue?" reveals some solid support for the basic themes, as well as some
possible important thematic and structural flaws that might cause some
readers to question whether Baldwin really understood the nature of the
jazz/blues motif that he used. On the other hand, he may have intentionally
injected "contraries" that imply an interpretation which emphasizes a coming
together in harmony of *all* people—not just Sonny's brother and his people
and culture.

The blues, both as a state of being and as music, are basic to the structure
of the story. In *Stomping the Blues* (1976) Albert Murray says, "The blues as

From *College Literature* Vol. XI, No. 2 (1984), pp. 178–185. © 1984 by West Chester
University.

such are synonymous with low spirits," and both the narrator and his brother Sonny have had their share. The narrator's major source of discontent has been his selfish desire to assimilate and lead a "respectable," safe life as a high-school algebra teacher. When he learns of Sonny's troubles with drugs and the law, he feels threatened. Sonny, on the other hand, has a stormy relationship with his father. He is unhappy in Harlem and hates school. He becomes alienated from his brother because of his jazz-oriented life style and his continued attraction to Greenwich Village. Finally, Sonny's using and selling heroin leads to a jail sentence.

The blues as music, as opposed to "the blues as such," take into account both form and content. In this story, content (message) is all important. As music, the blues are considered by many blacks to be a reflection of and a release from the suffering they endured through and since the days of slavery. In *The Jazz Book* (1975) Joachim Berendt says, "Everything of importance in the life of the blues singer is contained in these [blues] lyrics: Love and racial discrimination; prison and the law; floods and railroad trains and the fortune told by the gypsy; the evening sun and the hospital ... Life itself flows into the lyrics of the blues...." When Sonny plays the blues at the end of the story, it is the black heritage reflected in the blues that impresses itself upon Sonny's brother and brings him back into the community of his black brothers and sisters.

Beyond this basic use of the blues motif as background for the unhappiness of the narrator and Sonny and their resultant alienation from one another, Baldwin uses the jazz motif to emphasize the theme of individualism. Sonny is clearly Thoreau's "different drummer." He is a piano player who plays jazz, a kind of music noted for individuality because it depends on each musician's ability to improvise his or her own ideas while keeping in harmony with the progression of chords of some tune (often well-known). It has often been described as being able to take one's instrument, maintain an awareness of one's fellow players in the group, and in this context spontaneously "compose a new tune" with perhaps only a hint of the original remaining, except at the beginning and end of the number. In his *Shadow and Act* (1964) Ralph Ellison refers to this as the jazz musician's "achieving that subtle identification between his instrument and his deepest drives which will allow him to express his own unique ideas and his own unique voice. He must achieve, in short, his self-determined identity."

One of the greatest jazz improvisers of all time was Charlie Parker, Baldwin's choice as the jazz musician that Sonny idolizes. No better choice could have been made. Parker was one of a group of young musicians in the late 1940s and early 1950s who played what was called bebop, or bop. They developed new and difficult forms—faster tempos, altered chords, and harmonies that involved greater ranges of notes which were frequently played at blistering speeds. Parker was more inventive and proficient than any of the others. His records are widely collected today, especially by young, aspiring jazz musicians, and he remains an inspiration to many. An individualist beyond compare not only in his music, but also in his life style, he died in 1955 at the age of 34, the victim of overindulgence in drink, drugs, and sex.

That Sonny should have Parker, whose well-known nickname was "Bird," as an idol is important. Parker flew freely and soared to the heights in all aspects of his life. He was one of a kind and he became a legend ("Bird Lives" is a popular slogan in jazz circles even today). Sonny's life begins to parallel Parker's early. In *The Jazz Book*, Joachim Berendt says of Parker: "He lived a dreary, joyless life and became acquainted with narcotics almost simultaneously with music. It is believed that Parker had become a victim of 'the habit' by the time he was 15." So also, it seems, had Sonny. A further reference to Parker is made when the narrator thinks of Sonny when he hears a group of boys outside his classroom window: "One boy was whistling a tune, at once very complicated and very simple, it seemed to be pouring out of him as though he were a bird, and it sounded very cool and moving through all that harsh, bright air, only just holding its own through all those other sounds." The key words in this passage are "complicated," "bird," and "holding its own through all those other sounds," all of which evoke the image of Bird Parker blowing his cool and complicated improvisations over the accompaniment of the other members of a jazz combo.

When Sonny tells his brother that he is interested in playing *jazz*, the essential difference of the two brothers becomes evident. Sonny expresses his admiration for Charlie Parker, whom the older brother had never heard of. For the narrator, jazz means Louis Armstrong. Armstrong certainly was a highly-regarded, popular jazz musician—probably the best known in the world, having become known as Ambassador Satch because of his frequent trips abroad—but among bop musicians he represented the older, more traditional form of jazz.

Baldwin's equating Sonny with Parker and his brother with Armstrong is important because it emphasizes the difference between the two brothers with reference to both individualism and knowing oneself. Sonny refers to Armstrong as "old-time" and "down home." There is a strong Uncle Tom implication in this and it is true that Armstrong was viewed this way by many of the young black musicians in the 1940s and 1950s. Had Armstrong become "the white man's nigger"? Had Sonny's brother? Probably so. He had tried, as best he could, to reject his black self through becoming a respectable math teacher and dissociating himself from black culture as much as possible. He was careful not to do those things that he felt whites expected blacks to do. Baldwin understood this attitude, acknowledging that only when he went to Europe could he feel comfortable listening to Bessie Smith, the well-known black blues singer of the 1920s and early 1930s. However, in fairness to Sonny's brother, it must be noted that after World War II bop musicians and their music were the subject of considerable controversy. In their *Jazz: A History of the New York Scene* (1962) Samuel Charters and Leonard Kunstadt observe: "The pathetic attempts of Moslem identification, the open hostility, the use of narcotics—everything was blamed on bop. It was the subject of vicious attacks in the press, the worst since the days of 'Unspeakable Jazz Must Go,' and the musicians were openly ridiculed." It is in this context that we must consider the narrator's concern about Sonny and the life style that he seems to be adopting.

Up to the final section of the story, Baldwin uses jazz references well, but then some surprising "contraries" begin to appear. As Sonny begins to play his blues in the last scene, he struggles with the music, which is indicative of how he struggles with his life: "He and the piano stammered, started one way, got scared, stopped; started another way, panicked, marked time, started again; then seemed to have found a direction, panicked again, got stuck." As Sonny flounders about, Baldwin brings into play two key references that lead and inspire Sonny to finally find himself through his music: The character of Creole and the playing of the song "Am I Blue?" Baldwin's use of these two elements is, to say the least, unusual.

The use of Creole as the leader of the group Sonny plays with in this last and all-important section of the story is paradoxical. Baldwin seems to be emphasizing Sonny's bringing his brother back to a realization of the importance of his roots as epitomized in Sonny's playing of the blues. Why did Baldwin choose a leader who is not strictly representative of the black heritage that can be traced back through the years of slavery to West Africa with its concomitant blues tradition that includes work songs, field hollers, and "African-influenced spirituals"? According to James Collier in *The Making of Jazz* (1979), Creoles were generally regarded as descendants of French and Spanish settlers in Louisiana. Over the years, many Creole men took as mistresses light-skinned girls and produced that class referred to as black Creoles, many of whom passed for white and set themselves above the Negroes. From the early 1800s they were generally well-educated and cultured, some even having gone to Europe to attend school. Music was also an important part of life among the Creoles. According to James Collier (and this is very important for the point I am making),

> ... The black Creole was what was called a "legitimate" musician. He could read music; he did not improvise; and he was familiar

with the standard repertory of arias, popular songs, and marches that would have been contained in any white musician's song bag. The point is important: The Creole musician was entirely European in tradition, generally scornful of the blacks from across the tracks who could not read music and who played those "low-down" blues. [*The Making of Jazz: A Comprehensive History*, 1979].

After the Civil War, the advent of Jim Crow laws deeply affected the status of black Creoles. In particular, the passage of Louisiana Legislative Code III was devastating in that it declared that any person "with any black ancestry, however remote, would be considered black." Many Creoles with musical training were hard hit and sought work as musicians. The competition with Negroes was keen and unpleasant, but eventually, Leroy Ostransky notes (in his *Jazz City: The Impact of Our Cities on the Development of Jazz*, 1978), both groups "discovered each other's strengths and the resulting synthesis helped bring about the first authentic jazz style, what came to be called the New Orleans style."

Though Creoles did contribute to the development of jazz as it is played in Baldwin's story, it must be remembered that the story seems to emphasize the importance of the strictly black experience and tradition, which for most people means the heritage that includes not only post-Emancipation Jim Crow laws, but also the indignities of slavery, the horrors of the middle-passage, and the cruelties of capture and separation from families in West Africa. The black Creoles were not distinctly a part of that culture.

The second confusing element in the last section of the story is Baldwin's use of the song "Am I Blue?" It is certainly not an example of the classic 12-bar, 3-lined blues form. However, it might be pointed out that in the context of this story it would not have to be, because Sonny is part of a jazz movement that is characterized by new ideas. Nevertheless, we must not forget the main thrust of the last scene: The narrator's rebirth and acceptance of *his* heritage. Certainly most musicologists would agree that blues music has a complexity that includes contributions from many sources, but the choice of song is questionable for other reasons.

It would have seemed appropriate for Baldwin to have chosen some song that had been done by one of his favorite blues singers, Bessie Smith. In *Nobody Knows My Name* he says: "It was Bessie Smith, through her tone and her cadence, who helped me dig back to the way I myself must have spoken when I was a pickaninny, and to remember the things I had heard and seen and felt. I had buried them very deep." In relation to the idea of the narrator's rebirth through his experience of hearing Sonny play the blues, choosing a song made famous by Bessie Smith would have been fitting and would have reflected Baldwin's personal experiences. But this is not the case.

Why did Baldwin choose "Am I Blue?" a song far-removed from the black experience? It was written in 1929 by composer Harry Akst and lyricist Grant Clarke, who were both white, as far as I can determine. Akst was born on New York's East Side, the son of a classical musician who played violin in various symphony orchestras and wished Harry to become a classical pianist. However, Harry became a composer of popular music and eventually worked with well-known show business personalities like Irving Berlin and Fred Astaire. One of his best-known songs is "Baby Face." Grant Clarke was born in Akron, Ohio, and worked as an actor before going to work for a music publisher. In 1912, his "Ragtime Cowboy Joe" became a hit.

Akst and Clarke wrote "Am I Blue?" specifically for Ethel Waters, an extremely popular black singer who had paid her dues and sung her share of the blues through the years, but who had by 1929 achieved fame on the stage and in films. The song was written for the film musical "On With the Show." Ethel Waters received a four-week guarantee in the making of the film at $1,250 per week. Bessie Smith never achieved a comparable fame among general audiences. Ethel Waters seems to have been more in a class with Louis Armstrong in terms of general entertainment value and popularity. The bop musician's point of view was antithetical to the Uncle Tom image they had of Armstrong. Ralph Ellison observes: "The thrust toward respectability exhibited by the Negro jazzmen of Parker's generation drew much of its immediate fire from their understandable rejection of the traditional entertainer's role—a heritage from the minstrel tradition— exemplified by such an outstanding creative musician as Louis Armstrong. Why would Baldwin choose a song made popular by Ethel Waters, rather than one by his favorite, Bessie Smith?

All of this is not to say that "Am I Blue?" is not in the blues tradition in terms of message. The lyric expresses the sadness of a lonely woman whose man has left her, not unusual content for all forms of blues songs through the years. But it is what Paul Oliver refers to, in *The Meaning of the Blues* (1963), as one of those "synthetic 'blue' compositions of the Broadway show and the commercial confections of 52nd Street that purport to be blues by the inclusion of the word in the titles." Therefore, in view of the song's origin, Baldwin's fondness for Bessie Smith, and the possible intent of Sonny's playing the blues to bring the narrator back to an acknowledgment and affirmation of his roots, the choice of this particular song seems inappropriate.

And yet Baldwin may have known what he was doing. Is it possible that in "Sonny's Blues" he is indicating that tradition is very important, but that change is also important (and probably inevitable) and that it builds on tradition, which is never fully erased but continues to be an integral part of the whole? Ellison is again relevant here: "Perhaps in the swift change of American society in which the meaning of one's origins are so quickly lost, one of the chief values of living with music lies in its power to give us an orientation in time. In doing so, it gives significance to all those indefinable aspects of experience which nevertheless help to make us what we are." Both Ellison and Baldwin seem to be saying that we are an amalgam of many ingredients that have become fused over the centuries. We cannot separate ourselves, *all* people, from one another. Having Sonny, inspired by Creole, playing "Am I Blue?" for what we must assume is a racially mixed audience in a Greenwich Village club gives credence to these ideas and helps to explain what might otherwise appear to be some inexplicable incongruities.

ARTHENIA BATES MILLICAN

Fire as the Symbol of a Leadening Existence in "Going to Meet the Man"

James Baldwin's collection of short stories, *Going to Meet the Man*, was published in 1965, a year after *Blues for Mister Charlie*, his first published play. The title story in the collection and the play sing the blues for "Mister Charlie," the white racist, who is intent on keeping the black man in his place—more specifically in the Southern region of the United States. Baldwin has drawn attacks on these works from several critics[1] who consider the "blues" effect "trivial" because he labors to bring new light to the same-old-story-worth-telling-once-more of whites against blacks. Furthermore, he has employed the everlasting, inescapable symbol as the locus for both works. In fact, Joseph Featherstone expresses the opinion that the whole "racial fuss" in *Blues for Mister Charlie* and "Going to Meet the Man" stems from the author's concern for the white man's inability to display his sexual virility at will.[2]

The chronology of works in an author's canon may have everything or nothing to do with the ordering of his perception. But to build a premise, we will assume that *Blues for Mister Charlie* was written a year before "Going to Meet the Man." That way we can assume that Baldwin portrayed a white racist in the play who is freed of his crime (murder) by the law. In the meantime he informs us that something happens to that man, the human being, who is freed by the law of the land. Escape from crime in this manner places the absolution from that crime on the back of the criminal. He will either

From *James Baldwin: A Critical Evaluation*, Therman O'Daniel, ed., pp. 170–180. © 1977 by Howard University Press.

repent in humility or remain adamant in the decision of the law and lose his humanity. We are left with the white racist, unshaken and unredeemed in *Blues for Mister Charlie*. If there is any vestige of justice in the South, which is based on Christian ethics or secular morals, Lyle Britten is lost. He is, like the protagonist in William Melvin Kelley's *Dem*, left smarting in a tub of hot water gazing at the ceiling—not the sky. Jesse, the lawman, is one step above them.

Perhaps no one who witnesses the spectacle of a man "in fire," "on fire," or "under fire" can resist voicing the simple query—"Why?" "Going to Meet the Man" gives the case history of Lyle Britten, in broader dimensions, to answer that query. Fire is used in "Going to Meet the Man" as a symbol of frustration, which Jesse, the protagonist, experiences as a boy of eight, as a young adult (no doubt in his twenties), and as a deputy sheriff forty-two years old. Through Jesse's reverie, we can rebuild the framework for his destruction, which, of course, exempts the decadence of the racist society that helped to form him. Baldwin does this by grafting upon Jesse's consciousness the necessity for him to keep the black man in *his* place.

Fire, in a literal and symbolic sense, is frequently used by Baldwin in his nonfiction as well as in his fiction. The ready example in nonfiction is *The Fire Next Time*, which emerges as a searing, torturous personal account of the writer as a youth growing up in Harlem. Besides, there is a candid, mind-jolting portrayal of what America has done to the black man. The ready example in fiction is *Go Tell It on the Mountain*, where the saints, one by one, give vent to the lightning power of the Holy Ghost that purifies the sinner's heart with tongs of fire. So often implications in Baldwin's works take us to the fire and brimstone of hell, to the overwhelming heat of passion and lust, to the well-fed bonfire set to scorch the black criminal hanging from a tree. Notwithstanding the power of Baldwin's literal engagement with fire, we want to touch upon realities that transcend the limitations of the obvious. By way of symbolism, Baldwin uses fire in "Going to Meet the Man" as a device to achieve coherence as he dissects the inner mind of Jesse, the deputy sheriff who must cope with black civil-rights demonstrators because he is the *law*.

The story begins and ends in Jesse's nuptial bed. The "nighttime reverie" is at first a recapitulation of his "brutal day" among the blacks who staged a demonstration while voter-registration took place at the county court house. What had annoyed him most of all was the singing—the continuous singing of the blacks, which pierced his consciousness so severely that he longed to escape from "the castle of his own skin." But he could not escape, though he had the desire to escape. The memories of the day opened a vista to past encounters—the not-so-distant past, and the distant past, where the white–black encounter began for him. The reverie, borne upon the device of a remembered song, has a "simple river-run structuring that is flawless," according to David Littlejohn.[3]

To measure the descent of Jesse, who is "nameless" though not fatherless, let us select two referents that will allow us to sense the leadening weight that attends him as he rises or grows from boyhood into manhood. If he moves in space, it is a "descent into the maelstrom"—Poe's phrase. The platform of white supremacy on which Jesse must stand is a maelstrom—simply defined as "a powerful, often violent whirlpool sucking in objects within a given radius." To reconstruct Dante's cosmography in order to establish a hierarchy of ethical, moral or religious (spiritual) values, let us consider the cone, the artist's rendering of the Inferno, as a plane representing the complex of heaven, purgatory and hell. The top, or the wider area, may represent heaven; the middle area, purgatory; the bottom area, hell. In the area of hell, at the lowest point, according to Dante, Satan is frozen in a pool of ice. The chill, Jesse's temporary impotence the night of the reverie, intimates that he is frozen in hell. If heaven symbolizes warmth, happiness, enlightenment, joy, or peace, hell symbolizes the absence of these "virtues." Therefore, the "river-run structure" of Jesse's reverie is flawless in the artistic sense; but what Baldwin depicts in terms of Jesse's sense, ultimately the human sense, is overwhelmingly flawed. Jesse has been under fire—frustrated because of his engagement with the white–black, love–hate thing all of his life. Becoming a deputy sheriff at the age of forty-two, Jesse makes his ascendant step to a rage–sorrow thing that renders him the semblance of a man. And that is what the blacks will confront when they step out to vie for liberty, equality, and fraternity.

Jesse's experience of a lynching at the age of eight comes from a father's will to train a white boy the way he should go so that in later times he will be anchored to the moorings of white superiority. The initiation rites left Jesse, the boy, with too much burdensome knowledge. The coalescence of the good and bad, pleasant and unpleasant—picnic and fire, love and hate—opposites forged into what might be called a single wedge of experience, makes way for a continuum of unresolved conflict in his mind.

The love–hate entanglement that rests upon Jesse's mind is set forth in "Going to Meet the Man" through Baldwin's depiction of outright occurrences under review in Jesse's reverie.

The first important incident in Jesse's life is the lynching of the black man in Harkness who "knocked down old Miss Standish." The excitement in the air, the preparation of food, and the care his mother took in "dressing up" gave Jesse (then an eight-year-old boy) the impression that they were going on a Fourth of July picnic. When he asked his father if they were going on a picnic, his father replied: "That's right, we're going on a picnic. You won't ever forget this picnic."[4] At the lynching, Jesse sat on his father's shoulder so that he could see the black man hanging above the bonfire. The boy saw a man "bigger than his father and black as an African jungle cat, and naked." (P. 246) The boy sensed the value of his chance to observe the "stylized" lynching by the look on his father's face. "His father's face was full of sweat, his eyes were peaceful. At that moment Jesse loved his father more than he had ever loved him. He felt that his father had carried through a mighty test, had revealed to him a great secret which would be the key to his life forever." (P. 248) Later, his father said that he anticipated a night of conjugal bliss after enjoying the lynching and the picnic. The strange kind of horrified fulfillment experienced by Jesse as a boy with his father's prompting may suggest that "there is in this barbaric anti-human rite a genuine primeval satisfaction."[5]

This idea of love in a general and specific way, in connection with the lynching, stands in contrast to the idea of hate in the same way. The idea of love, which enabled the boy to understand his place in the scheme of a Southern bureaucracy, balances with the idea of hate, which he must perpetuate to maintain his place in that bureaucracy. When Jesse was coming home from the lynching, he realized that he had not seen Otis, a black playmate his age, for three days. He asked his father about Otis, and his father said that Otis' people were afraid to let him out. When Jesse said: "Otis didn't do nothing," his father replied: "Otis *can't* do nothing, he's too little.... We just want to make sure Otis *don't* do nothing.... And you tell him what your Daddy said, you hear?" And the boy answered, "Yes sir." (P. 240) Thus, Jesse is commissioned as a guardian of the white Southerner's trust at the age of eight.

Behind the scene, a moment of personal involvement with the black criminal intensified Jesse's sense of guilt and fear as potently as his father's personal involvement excited sexual passion. During the gelding scene, the crowd screamed because of the horrifying excitement. The sound of the boy's voice is enveloped with that of the crowd, but he is screaming for a different reason. Baldwin writes: "The dying man looked straight into Jesse's eyes—it could not have been as long as a second, but it seemed longer than a year. Then Jesse screamed and the crowd screamed as the knife flashed, first up and then down." (P. 248) The thought of Otis made Jesse sick after the Harkness experience. The pattern was set for Jesse's frustration in the coalescence of the love and hate entanglement. He had loved Otis (the black race), yet he must now hate him in order to perpetuate the ideals of *his* race.

If we follow a chronological sequence, the second phase of Jesse's reverie takes us to the not-too-distant past, when he worked as collector for a mail-order house. His dealings with "nigger" mail-order customers mark the state in his life when he is all-knowing and debonair about race relations. His lessons on race, taught well during the period of orientation, present him now as an authority on the "niggers"; he is sure of their love (respect) for him, and he is sure that they deserve disrespect (hate) because they deliberately choose to be brutes. The issues are seemingly clear: white is white and black is black. Yet the love–hate entanglement persists.

On one hand Jesse saw his black customers as a group of people who enjoyed laughing and talking and playing music when they were not "pumping out kids every five minutes." Seemingly they did not have a care in the world as they stood in the door in the sunlight just looking foolish—seemingly not thinking of anything but getting back to what they were doing. They seemed to appreciate him, greeting him with "Yes suh, Mr. Jesse. I surely will, Mr. Jesse. Fine weather, Mr. Jesse. Why, I thank you, Mr. Jesse." (P. 231) He could easily demonstrate his role then as a Southern patriarch whom they loved. Jesse was sure of that "love." Baldwin writes:

> Hell, they all liked him, the kids used to smile when he came to the door. He gave them candy, sometimes, or chewing gum, and rubbed their rough bullet heads.... (P. 231)

And of course, his nights in Black Town with black paramours came with the territory.

But on the other hand, he hated "niggers." They were not progressive: "They had been living in a civilized country for years but their houses were dark, with oil cloth or cardboard in the windows, the smell was enough to snake you puke your guts out." (P. 231) He was, therefore, justified (according to his orientation) in demonstrating his authority as a preserver and destroyer of his mail-order customers.

The unexpected assault of a fatherless and nameless black boy on Jesse's whiteness is not only preemptive of the rise of the black man in the generic sense, but also of his rise as an individual who demands dignity for himself (the black male) and for his women as a whole and for each of them, also, as individuals. The scene is brief but important in that it serves as a throttle to reverse the pattern of the love–hate entanglement. The nameless boy says, I love myself but I hate you Mister Charlie. The black boy's love, though, bears a closer relationship to love in its truest sense. It springs from a sense of personal loyalty and devotion instilled in him by "Old Julia" which is of course, untutored. He is able to see through the shambles of Jesse's "love" for blacks and denounces it outright. He considers the white man's "love" as the *raison d'être* for black hate.

"Old Julia," one of Jesse's mail-order customers, was to him "a nice old woman." He had not seen her for years so he stopped to ask a boy, about ten years old, if she still lived in the house.

JESSE: Old Julia home? ...
BOY: Don't no Old Julia live here.
JESSE: This is her house. I know her. She's lived here for years.
BOY: ... You might know a Old Julia some place else white man. But don't nobody by that name live here ....
JESSE: Hey! Old Julia! ... She's gone out? ... Well.... tell her I passed by and I'll pass by next week .... You want some chewing gum?
BOY: I don't want nothing you got, white man. (PP. 234–35)

The recollection of his encounter with the boy brought to memory his first assessment of the boy's action—disgust over the antics of a crazy black kid. But then an unspoken vigil between the two of them brought a different impression. Jesse broke the silent combat—their eyeing each other—by calling out, "Hey Old Julia!" He realized that in that moment

... only silence answered him. The expression on the boy's face did not change. The sun beat down on them both, still and silent; he had the feeling that he had been caught up in a nightmare dreamed by a child.... It had that feeling—everything familiar, without undergoing any other change, had been subtly and hideously displaced: the tree, the sun, the patches of grass in the yard, the leaning porch and the weary porch steps and the card-board in the windows and the black hole of the door which looked like the entrance to a cave, and the eyes of the pickaninny, all, all, were charged with malevolence. *White Man.* (P. 234)

The young, debonair salesman was made aware of the presence of a "New Negro" who would foster the same old love–hate scheme (thus the "familiar feeling"), but the love (respect) formerly reserved for him (the white race) had suddenly turned to hate (disrespect).

The civil-rights demonstration led by blacks in Jesse's hometown was a typical phenomenon of the 1960s. Blacks who had been in the army knew the tactics of combat and employed them during the rebellion. The sentiment was that dynamite had fallen into the wrong hands, for the once peaceful town was rocked by explosions every night. The night of the reverie, Jesse heard cars as they hit the gravel road not far from his house going to the black college. He knew that the cars were coming from everywhere, bringing people out of the state who would face the lawmen at the court house the next morning.

Baldwin exercises care in portraying Jesse, the deputy sheriff of forty-two who is now a lawman, "the lyncher" in special uniform. Despite the sheriff's faults,

> he tried to be a good person and treat everybody right: it wasn't his fault if the niggers had taken it into their heads to fight against God and go against the rules laid down in the Bible for everyone to read! Any preacher would tell you that. He was only doing his duty: protecting white people from the niggers and the niggers from them selves. (PP. 235–36)

He had never thought of blacks in relation to God or heaven before the confrontation, but the singing blacks helped him to decide that "God was the same for everyone, he supposed, and heaven was where good people went—he supposed." (P. 235) The Jesse who is "the law" must do his duty as a lawman; however, he is no longer the debonair Jesse. He is a refined version of the deputy sheriff in Rulesville, Mississippi, who became "the law" after he had assisted his brother in the Emmett Till murder of 1955.

Jesse, the deputy sheriff, has the job of stopping the black singers. He decides that they can be stopped by manhandling the leader, who might silence his followers to avoid physical harm to himself. His guess is wrong. He puts the prod to the ringleader, who jerks and screams. Big Jim C., Jesse's superior, and his boys had already whipped him severely. Jesse bullies the leader, commanding: "You make them stop that singing ... you hear me? ... and you are going to stop coming down to the court house and disrupting traffic—and molesting the people and keeping us from our duties and keeping doctors from getting to sick white women and getting all them Northerners in this town to give our town a bad name—!" As he talked, "he kept prodding the boy..... The boy rolled around in his own dirt and water and blood and tried to scream again as the prod hit his testicles." (PP. 232–33) He stopped because he had not been ordered to kill the black ringleader.

No doubt the continuous singing of the blacks, the haunting melodies that had dominated his consciousness during the Harkness experience, caused him to rage in order to mitigate his guilt and self-denigration. Even though the leader was still, maybe dead, Jesse continued to rave: "You hear me? ... You had enough? ... You had enough? You going to make them stop that singing now?" (P. 233) The singing went on. Impulsively,

His foot leapt out, he had not known it was going to, and caught the boy flush on the jaw. *Jesus*, he thought, *this ain't no nigger, this is a goddamn bull.* (P. 233)

Jesse tried to recall something deep within his memory as the youth passed out. As soon as the leader gained consciousness he spoke to Jesse:

"My grandmother's name was Mrs. Julia Blossom. Mrs. Julia Blossom. You going to call our women by their right names yet.—And those kids ain't going to stop singing. We going to keep on singing until every one of you miserable white mothers go stark raving out of your minds." (P. 233)

The youth passed out again and Jesse remembered that he was the black boy who had insulted him years before. He "wanted to go over to him and pick him up and pistol whip him until the boy's head burst open like a melon. He began to tremble with what he believed was rage, sweat, both cold and hot, raced down his body...." (P. 235)

For all his brutality, Baldwin considers Jesse, the deputy sheriff, a rightful American product. He says in "Notes for Blues,"

.. we, the American people, have created him, he is our servant; it is we who put the cattle-prodder in his hands and we are responsible for the crimes that he commits.[6]

He expresses the belief, also, that

it is we who have locked him in the prison of his color.... It is we who have forbidden him, on pain of exclusion from the tribe, to accept his beginnings, when he and black people loved each other, and rejoice in them, and use them....[7]

Finally, he says,

It is we who have persuaded him that Negroes are worthless human beings, and that it is his sacred duty, as a white man, to protect the honor and purity of his tribe.[8]

If Baldwin can muster the strength to issue these views to account for the making of Lyle Britten, it is certain then that the depiction of Jesse is meant to be sympathetic. His lack of a surname indicates that he is a scapegoat for the white-racist ideal.

The "sorrows" attending Jesse's outrage seem plausible. No one seemed capable of finding the right method to cope with the effects of the black demonstration on the white populace. The men who were his models and had been friends to his father "had taught him what it meant to be a man. He looked to them for courage now." (P. 236) But the ease of former years had vanished. "They were soldiers fighting a war, but their relationship to each other was that of accomplices in a crime." (PP. 238–39) "Each man in the thrilling silence which sped outward from their exchanges, their laughter, and their anecdotes, seemed wrestling, in various degrees of darkness, with a secret which he could not articulate to himself, and which, however directly it related to the war, related yet more surely to his privacy and his past." (P. 238)

Jesse remembered the man in the fire, the boy on the swing, the boy in the cell and realized as he looked forward to another day that the singing of the blacks did not have the obscure comfort of former years. He knew that the young people had changed the words to the song. He knew now that "they hated him, and that this hatred was blacker than their hearts, blacker than their skins, redder than their blood, and harder, by far, than his club." (P. 238) He came to the conclusion that when the young blacks sang they were singing white folks into hell rather than blacks into heaven. Even when he had gained the obscure comfort from the songs from other years, the blacks had perhaps intended to consign him and other white men to hell.

"Going to Meet the Man" dramatizes Baldwin's idea about the confrontation of forces outside and within ourselves to initiate a first step in redeeming our humanity. One virtue of Jesse, the deputy, is that, through the reverie, he faces his experiences and expresses the desire to be born again to more pleasant experiences if not to the reality of universal brotherhood. A somewhat lengthy statement from Baldwin's recent work, *No Name in the Street*, states the value of confrontation:

> The black and white confrontation, whether it be hostile, as in the cities and the labor unions, or with the intention of forming a common front and creating the foundations of a new society, as with the students and the radicals, is obviously crucial, containing the shape of the American future and the only potential of a truly valid American identity. No one knows precisely how identities are forged, but it is safe to say that identities are not invented: an identity would seem to be arrived at by the way in which the

person faces and uses his experience. It is a long drawn-out and somewhat bewildering and awkward process.[9]

Blacks, according to Baldwin's idea in *The Fire Next Time*, feel that if outright confrontation with whites fails to assure their rise to power, "at least they are well placed to precipitate chaos and to ring down the curtain on the American dream."[10]

For Jesse, chances seem slim for forging a new viable personality from his own experiences. He decides to use his experiences with black paramours to incite his wife to the abandonment that she might use with a black lover. His desire to be born again is suggested by his desire to drown his disturbing memories in the sensuality that he attributes to lovemaking with blacks. The very suggestion of his ordering his wife to imagine that he is a black lover to insure conjugal bliss from the virginal font, the source of Southern purity, substantiates Baldwin's claim that whites are victims of an uncertainty that leads them to distrust their own reactions. He writes:

> It is this individual uncertainty on the part of white American men and women, this inability to renew themselves at the fountain of their own lives, that makes the discussion, let alone the elucidation, of any conundrum—that is, any reality—so supremely difficult. The person who distrusts himself has no touchstone for reality—for the touchstone can be only oneself.[11]

Thus, the white man is himself in need of new standards to release him from the confusion that bars him from fruitful communion with the depth of his own being.[12]

The final comment on Jesse's desire to "die" in order to become once more a refreshed, if not a renewed, being, is based on his misreading of "sensuality" as a white interpreter of the black experience. Baldwin says that "ironic tenacity" in blacks is, to whites, synonymous with sensuality. "White Americans do not understand the depths out of which such an ironic tenacity comes, but they suspect that the force is sensual, and they are terrified of sensuality and do not any longer understand it. The word 'sensual' is not intended to bring to mind quivering dusky maidens or priapic black studs."[13] In its truest manifestations, "to be sensual," says Baldwin, "is to respect and rejoice in the force of life, of life itself, and to be *present* in all that one does, from the effort of loving to the breaking of bread."[14]

Fire is the symbol of the frustrations in the life of Jesse the boy, the young salesman, and the deputy. His frustrations have prevented him from priming the depths of his own personality because he must do what his forefathers ordained for him. Even though he desires to be freed from the unpleasant experiences caused by the white–black conflict in his native Southern town, he is unable to escape the burden of his heritage. His situation is almost hopeless. According to Baldwin, "the crimes we have committed are so great and so unspeakable that the acceptance of this knowledge would lead literally, to madness. The human being, then, in order to protect himself, closes his eyes, compulsively repeats his crimes, and enters a spiritual darkness which no one can describe."[15] This "spiritual darkness" is beginning to enshroud Jesse.

"Going to Meet the Man," in its bare outline, may be "an angry sermon and a pain-wracked lament ... which sings the blues for the white man's moral crisis as much as for the black man's frustration and agony"[16] just like *Blues for Mister Charlie*. But when Jesse turns to "the frail sanctuary of his wife" for ultimate comfort (regeneration), he becomes Nicodemus the Pharisee, who asked the Master: "How can a man be born when he is old?" Baldwin's answer is in accord with the Christian ethic—he must be reborn or purified in the fire of devastating experiences to forge a better self. This self is "the man" each one is going to meet the next morning and the next night, until he counts his days with "yesterday's seven thousand years."

NOTES

1. Two of these critics are Joseph Featherstone, "Blues for Mr. Baldwin," *The New Republic*, November 27, 1965, pp. 34–36; and Stanley Kauffman, "Another Baldwin," *New York Times Book Review*, December 12, 1965, p. 5.

2. Featherstone, "Blues for Mr. Baldwin," p. 35.

3. David Littlejohn, "Exemplary and Other Baldwins," *Nation*, December 13, 1965, p. 480.

4. James Balwin, "Going to Meet the Man," in *Going to Meet the Man* (New York: Dial Press, 1965), p. 243. Other references to the story will be entered by page number in the text.

5. Littlejohn, "Exemplary and Other Baldwins," p. 480.

6. James Baldwin, "Notes for Blues," in *Blues for Mr. Charlie* (New York: Dial Press, 1964), p. xiv.

7. *Ibid.*, xiv–xv.

8. *Ibid.*, p. xv.

9. James Baldwin, *No Name in the Street* (New York: Dial Press, 1972), p. 189.

10. James Baldwin, *The Fire Next Time* (New York: Dial Press, 1963), p. 102.

11. *Ibid.*, p. 57.

12. *Ibid.*, p. 117.

13. *Ibid.*, p. 56–57.

14. *Ibid.*, p. 57.

15. Baldwin, "Notes for Blues," p. xiv.

16. Stanley Kauffmann, review of *Going to Meet the Man* by James Baldwin, *New York Times Book Review*, December 12, 1965, p. 5.

MEL WATKINS

The Fire Next Time This Time

"If we ... do not falter in our duty now, we may be able ... to end the racial nightmare," James Baldwin said nine years ago in *The Fire Next Time*, warning that, if we did not, violent and vengeful racial clashes were inevitable. His caveat was clamorously hailed, but insufficiently heeded. Riots, assassinations, the emergence of black power and the intensification of white backlash have attested to Baldwin's powers of divination. Yet those same events may have rendered him an anachronism. Reading his latest book, *No Name in the Street*—a two-part, extended essay that is a memoir, a chronicle of and commentary on America's abortive civil-rights movement—that suspicion is nearly substantiated.

When Baldwin emerged as an essayist in 1955 the civil-rights movement was barely ambulatory. And in literature, Ralph Ellison's *Invisible Man* was still harmlessly ensconced in a cellar listening to Louis Armstrong wail "What did I do to be so black and blue," while Richard Wright's Bigger Thomas, whose pathological and decidedly unrevolutionary violence was so vividly portrayed in *Native Son*, was rare enough to be primarily a literary phenomenon. It was in this climate of superficial racial serenity that Baldwin published his first collection of essays, *Notes of a Native Son*, to instant acclaim. Alfred Kazin called it "one of the one or two best books written about the Negro in America," and said that Baldwin operated "with as much power in the essay

From *Critical Essays on James Baldwin*, Fred L. Standley and Nancy V. Burt, ed., pp. 232–238. Originally published in *The New York Times Book Review*, 28 May 1972, 17–18. © 1986 The New York Times Co.

form as I've ever seen." Baldwin's nest two essay-volumes (*Nobody Knows My Name* in 1961 and *The Fire Next Time* in 1963) elicited even more enthusiastic praise. Perhaps more important, Baldwin became the most widely read black author in American history.

Baldwin's passion, honesty and persuasiveness did much to free the impasse in racial discourse and helped create what now seems the fleeting illusion that non-black Americans could actually empathize with blacks and seriously confront the racial problem. Along with Martin Luther King Jr. he helped shape the idealism upon which the sixties civil-rights protest was based.

But Baldwin and King, while demonstrating that blacks were "the conscience of the nation," exposed the depth of American intransigence regarding the racial issue. They were instrumental in exhausting the dream of an effective moral appeal to Americans, and, in effect, set the stage for Malcolm X, and the emergence of Stokely Carmichael, "Rap" Brown, Huey Newton, Eldridge Cleaver and George Jackson—figures who reacted in a purely pragmatic (and therefore quintessentially American) manner to the blighted expectations of the sixties' failed idealism.

Since he was a political leader, King's influence on the events of the sixties is readily understandable. The source of Baldwin's influence as a writer is less apparent, particularly since the ideological content of his essays was rarely new—among others, Frederick Douglass, W. E. B. DuBois and Richard Wright had previously dealt with many of the ideas that he presented. Aside from the accident of timing, it was the uniquely personal perspective and style in which Baldwin couched his ideas that set him apart.

His essay style, in fact, set a literary precedent that would later develop into the "New Journalism"; *Notes*, for instance, predated and probably influenced the style of *Advertisements for Myself* and Norman Mailer's later forays into egocentric reportage—though Baldwin writes from the consciousness of an American victim, while Mailer enjoys the luxury and expansiveness of self-imposed alienation. Alfred Kazin's insights were again particularly incisive when he commented on the personal nature of Baldwin's essays: "More than any other Negro writer whom I, at least, have ever read [Baldwin] wants to describe the exact place where private chaos and social outrage meet ... the 'I,' the 'James Baldwin' who is so sassy and despairing and bright, manages, without losing his authority as the central speaker, to show us all the different people in him, all the voices for whom the 'I' alone can speak."

Moreover, as Kazin intimated, Baldwin did not write solely as a black advocate. In his essays, the multiple voices of the "I" spoke as passionately for the American heritage as they did for the Afro heritage. As a writer, then, he is part of the tradition of black-American polemical essayists that include David Walker, Henry Highland Garnet, Frederick Douglass, Booker T. Washington and W. E. B. DuBois. But he is just as much a part of the tradition of American romantic-moralists such as Ralph Waldo Emerson, Henry Thoreau and John Jay Chapman.

He became, as Albert Murray pointed out in *The Omni-Americans*, a hero of "the Negro revolution, a citizen spokesman, as eloquent ... as was citizen polemicist Tom Paine in the Revolution of '76," but he did not as Murray asserts, "write about the economic and social conditions of Harlem." Eldridge Cleaver was more accurate when, in his otherwise outrageous attack, *Notes on a Native Son*, he asserted that Baldwin's work "is void of a political, economic, or even a social reference." For Baldwin's technique was to write through events, focusing upon the enigma that plagued his own psyche. His influence and popularity depended upon the extent to which his psyche corresponded to the mass American psyche.

Reading Baldwin's latest work, one is initially struck by its familiar elements—his style, the recurring symbols that he favors (his father and family, the Manichean terminology that permeates his writing), and, of course, the cataclysmic social events of the past two decades. But early in the book, Baldwin shifts one's attention: "Since Martin's death ... something has altered me, something has gone away. Perhaps even more than the death itself, the manner of his death has forced me into a judgment concerning human life and human beings which I have always been reluctant to make." And perhaps because Baldwin and the civil-rights movement had demanded from Americans "a generosity, a clarity, and a nobility which they did not dream of demanding from themselves" or perhaps because of his promise of an apocalypse in *The Fire Next Time* or because of Mailer's admonition that Baldwin "seems incapable of saying—you," it is the explication of that presumably harsher "judgment" for which one looks throughout the remainder of the book.

Part One is primarily a series of personal anecdotes upon which are imposed summary political analyses. The Algerian War and the Parisians' reaction to it, Camus's equivocation on the question of liberty for Algerians, Franco, and McCarthyism are some of the subjects that Baldwin strings together in this rhetorical web of damnation of European and American politics. The moral rectitude that informs the exposition is unquestioned, yet for the most part the ideological discourse is either too abstract and facile or too obvious to impress.

The best sections of Part One are those in which he makes a brief excursion into his personal reaction to King's death and when he reports on his visit to the South in the mid-fifties. Here, as in previous essays, Baldwin invests his account with both historical resonance and a vivid sense of the people and feeling that shaped those events.

There are also passages that provide an implicit sense of his shift in perspective, the impending judgment that he has promised. He had said in an earlier book, speaking of the parents of black children involved in the school desegregation crisis: "They are doing it because they want the child to receive the education which will allow him to defeat, possibly escape, and not impossibly help one abolish the stifling environment in which they see, daily, so many children perish. But in this essay Baldwin states: "They [the children] were attempting to get an education, in a country in which education is a synonym for indoctrination, if you are white, and subjugation, if you are black. It was rather as though small Jewish boys and girls, in Hitler's Germany, insisted on getting a German education in order to overthrow the Third Reich.... They paid a dreadful price, those children, for their missionary work among the heathen."

After a rhetorical flurry in which Western humanism is damned as a lie, Part Two gives an account of Baldwin's experiences with and feelings about the prime movers of the civil-rights and black power movements of the past decade. Interspersed with this is the story of a personal friend and former bodyguard who was accused of murder. Baldwin comments on his relationships with King, Malcolm X, Huey Newton, Bobby Seale and Eldridge Cleaver, as well as the 1963 march on Washington, his abortive attempt to complete the screenplay for Malcolm's autobiography, Hollywood's coterie of civil-rights patrons and the "flower children."

This is the stronger section of the book, although it still does not provide any reasoned political assessment of the events and people discussed. There are references to politics and to America's domestic policies, but they function merely as lenses to better focus on the American psyche and the moral impasse with which Baldwin is ultimately concerned.

Baldwin's most vivid writing characterizes some of the black leaders that he has encountered. "Malcolm X," he says, "was not a racist, not even when he thought he was. His intelligence was more complex than that.... What made him unfamiliar and dangerous was not his hatred for white people but his love for blacks, his apprehension of the horror of the black condition, and the reasons for it, and his determination to work on their hearts and minds so that they would be enabled to see their condition and change it themselves."

On Cleaver and the inherent danger of the revolutionary's viewpoint, he says: "I think that it is just as well to remember that the people are one mystery and that the person is another. Though I know what a very bitter and delicate and dangerous conundrum this is, it yet seems to me that a failure to respect the person so dangerously limits one's perception of the people that one risks betraying them and oneself, either by sinking to apathy of cynical disappointment, or rising to the rage of knowing, better than the people do, what the people want."

But nowhere in the essay is the judgment that Baldwin indicated he was "forced into" defined. He finally evades this crucial question. Instead, Baldwin as "I" disappears and, as the omnipotent black, he concludes: "To be an Afro-American, or an American black, is to be in the situation, intolerably exaggerated, of all those who ever found themselves part of a civilization which they could in no way honorably defend—which they were compelled, indeed, endlessly to attack and condemn—and who yet spoke out of the most passionate love, hoping to make the kingdom new, to make it honorable and worthy of life."

The reader is left, then, precisely where he was at the conclusion of *The Fire Next Time*. Instead of the threat of a holocaust, we are told "it is terrible to watch people cling to their captivity and insist on their own destruction" and warned of "the shape of the wrath to come." Baldwin has taken us full circle: He initially exposes the "irreducible" error of the sixties idealism (for which his writing was partially responsible) and, after examining the political and sociological forces that rendered that idealism unworkable and the tragedy that ensued, he concludes by taking a moral stance that is not significantly different from the position he took in his previous essays.

For black political activists like Cleaver, his voice is, no doubt, the echo of a bygone time when black men could, as did Rufus in Another Country, go down singing "you took the best, why not take the rest."

But in an equally important sense Baldwin's is the timeless voice of a unique black-American tradition. Baldwin's essay style is a literary parallel of the black preacher's style. It is not just that his essays are sermonic or that *No Name in the Street*, like its predecessors, is filled with terms like "redemption," "damnation," "sinner," "soul" and "redeemed." Baldwin's experience as a Baptist minister in a storefront church is so vigorously applied to his prose style that it seems a demonstration of the "stylistic features" that Henry H. Mitchell enumerates in his book, *Black Preaching*. (As such, it should also serve as a partial source of objective standards for a black esthetic.)

Aside from oral intonation and physical gesture, according to Mitchell, rhythm, repetition for intensity, role playing, folk-storytelling techniques, personal involvement and rhetorical flair are the chief elements in the black preacher's style. Admittedly these features are general enough so that the presence of one or another of them may be seen in any writer's style; but in Baldwin's prose all of *them* are found in abundance.

Nearly every critic cites rhythm as an attribute of Baldwin's writing, and closely associated with this is his frequent use of repetition for emphasis—

"much, much, much has been blotted out" or "a terrible thing to happen to a man ... and I am always terribly humiliated for the man to whom it happens." Kazin's remarks concerning Baldwin's ability to "show us all the different people hidden in him" affirm his use of multiple voices, and almost every page of a Baldwin essay demonstrates his use of folk-storytelling techniques such as elaborate and melodramatic anecdotes.

If Baldwin's prose is a consummate literary adaptation of the stylistic features of black preaching, then that style imposes limitations on content. Black preaching adapts mythic scripture to the mimetic needs of black congregations—making the tenets of Christianity relevant to the reality of black experience. The style is contrary to rationalistic conception; instead, it seeks to communicate known religious truth through the emotions and senses. Baldwin uses the same style for secular purposes. Instead of redemption in the eyes of God, he is concerned with redemption in the eyes of man. God is replaced by morality and love. His message is finally as basic as it is undeniable: If we do not love one another, we will destroy one another.

When his essays are subjected to rigorous analysis, as by Marcus Klein in After Alienation, it is not surprising that the conclusion is that they are "evasive," lacking in "ideational development," and only accomplish a prophetic posture and an "indulgence of Edenic fantasies." But such conclusions are irrelevant since Baldwin's intent is not to explicate but to dramatize. What is important about Baldwin's essays is the style and eloquence with which he evokes the torment and human devastation of American racism and his ability to make us feel, if only momentarily, that redemption is possible.

In *No Name in the Street*, Baldwin's prose is often mesmerizing and, though they seem less shocking and disturbing now, there are passages that are as candid, insightful and moving as any in his previous essays. That the book may seem at this time less germane is not necessarily an indication of failure. It may very well be a more serious indictment against ourselves, a palpable indication of our own moral degeneration. Only if an eloquent appeal for morality is irrelevant in the seventies, is James Baldwin anachronistic.

LYNN ORILLA SCOTT

Excerpt from "The Celebrity's Return"

I t is also important to read *Train* in the context of Baldwin's own earlier texts and to understand its significance to his oeuvre. Several reviewers dismissed the novel as merely repetitive of Baldwin's earlier fiction.[77] However, it would be more accurate to view *Train* as a critical link between his first and third novels, *Go Tell It on the Mountain* and *Another Country*, and his last two novels, *If Beale Street Could Talk* and *Just Above My Head*. *Train* brings together the geographies of *Go Tell* (Harlem) and *Another Country* (the Village) in one novel, it continues the story of the young John Grimes in the story of the middle-aged Leo Proudhammer, and it is Baldwin's first rendering of sexual love between black men. Baldwin continues his exploration into the interrelationship between race and sex in American identity formation but pitches his representation to a new generation and a newly forming discourse of racial resistance. He is less concerned with delineating the processes of internalized racism, misogyny, and homophobia that dominate *Go Tell*, *Giovanni's Room*, and *Another Country* (although these remain givens) and is more concerned with representing the processes of conscious resistance to racial and sexual oppression in the lives of his three main characters, Leo Proudhammer, Barbara King, and Black Christopher.

In fact, *Tell Me How Long the Train's Been Gone* sharply revises several figures from Baldwin's earlier novels and stories, including the figure of the

From *James Baldwin's Later Fiction: Witness to the Journey*, pp. 48–61. © 2002 by Michigan State University Press.

black artist and the representation of interracial love in *Another Country*. As Baldwin told a French interviewer, Leo was "Rufus qui n'est pas un suicide."[78] In *Train* Baldwin recreates the black artist as a survivor and successful public figure in the character of Leo Proudhammer. Similarly, the Leo and Barbara relationship is a revised version of the relationship between Rufus and Leona (Barbara like Leona is a southern white girl, but unlike Leona, Barbara comes from a wealthy family). While Rufus and Leona have internalized their victimization so thoroughly that they destroy each other in an intensely sadomasochistic relationship (Rufus takes his revenge on the white world by abusing Leona, who goes mad, and then kills himself by jumping off the George Washington Bridge), Leo and Barbara resist the culturally scripted racial drama that punishes miscegenation. Their theatrical vocation is both the means and symbol by which they attempt to redefine their roles as a black man and a white woman. This redefinition is dramatized by the first scene they perform together for The Actors' Means Workshop. Leo "refused to consider doing anything from *All God's Chillun Got Wings*," Eugene O'Neill's play about a tragic interracial marriage destroyed by the couple's inability to resist internalizing racist definitions. Instead they choose to perform the concluding scene from Clifford Odets's *Waiting for Lefty* to "put the liberal San-Marquands to a crucial test."[79] While race is not a subject in Odets's play, Leo and Barbara can easily identify with the young lovers, Sid and Florrie, whose poverty during the Great Depression prevents them from marrying. The denial of domestic happiness is a radicalizing experience for Sid, who devotes himself to the struggle for economic and social justice.

The Leo–Barbara relationship represents the possibility of interracial love and the social barriers to its fulfillment in America. From the beginning Leo and Barbara recognize that the social inequalities of race and class, as well as their own ambitious natures (and, one might suppose, Leo's bisexuality) would be formidable obstacles to a happy marriage. As Barbara says,

> If we were different people, and very, very lucky, we might beat the first hurdle, the black–white thing. If we weren't who we are, we could always just leave this—unfriendly—country, and go somewhere else. But we're as we are. I knew, when I thought about it, that we couldn't beat the two of them together. I don't think you'd care much that your wife was white—but a wife who was both white and rich! It would be horrible. We'd soon stop loving each other.[80]

The terms of their relationship are severe they will focus on advancing their theatrical careers: "We must be great. That's all we'll have. That's the only way we won't lose each other."[81] Leo and Barbara, resilient and smart, represent—the possibility of interracial love. As Houston A. Baker Jr. has suggested, they are the fictional embodiment of Baldwin's call at the end of *The Fire Next Time* for "the relatively conscious whites and the relatively conscious blacks, who must, like lovers, insist on, or create the consciousness of the others."[82] But their relationship suggests the limits of such idealism as well. Paradoxically their love endures because it is based on their early renunciation of the dream of domestic happiness, which appeared totally out of reach (as it did to Sid and Florrie in Odets's play). The public success which enables their relationship to endure comes at the cost of their private lives. At the end of *Tell Me How Long the Train's Been Gone* the job of consciousness raising does not go to Barbara and Leo but to their symbolic "child," Christopher Hall, whose black nationalism suggests Leo and Barbara's failure to reproduce an interracial model of political resistance.

Tell Me How Long the Train's Been Gone also revisits and revises *Go Tell it on the Mountain*, initiating new directions that Baldwin will further explore in his later work as he looks to his familial, religious, and cultural heritage as resources of resistance and modes of expressing his wider vision. The rich intertextual relationship between *Tell Me How Long the Train's Been Gone* and *Go Tell It on the Mountain* offers readers important insight into Baldwin's development as an autobiographer, moral spokesman, and artist. The very title of Baldwin's fourth novel signals a revisionary relationship to his first. Both titles are from African American religious songs. "Go Tell It on the Mountain" is the first line of the spiritual announcing the "good news" that Jesus Christ is born.[83] The title points toward the culminating event of *Go Tell*, John's experience of salvation on the threshing floor in the Temple of the Fire Baptized, and is one of several allusions linking John Grimes to the biblical John of Revelation. "Tell Me How Long the Train's Been Gone" is the refrain of a gospel song which warns those who have fallen away from righteousness that judgment Day will come. The "train," God's followers, have left the temple and are living among the "unclean," oblivious that their days are numbered: "While everything you think is going on well / your poor soul is burning in hell / Tell me how long / the train's been gone."[84] The title of Baldwin's fourth novel points toward Leo's fearful speculations of a coming apocalypse suggested by Black Christopher's call for guns near the end of the novel. The titles mark the transition from innocence (John's salvation) to experience (Leo's fallen condition), from youth to maturity, signaling the autobiographical relationship between the novels.

The titles reflect the Manichean structure of a religious imagination suspended between the poles of salvation and damnation, but they also suggest the ambiguity characteristic of Baldwin's treatment of such dualism.

Neither John's salvation in the church nor Leo's regard for Black Christopher's political militancy should be read as uncomplicated acts or final solutions to the conflicts the novels depict. Both outsiders who want to be insiders, John and Leo remain in an ambiguous relationship to the religious and political frameworks of the communities they claim. While John Grimes is "saved," he continues to be in bondage not only to poverty and racism, but to his own lack of knowledge of his history: at the end of the novel, the truth of his origins remains in an undisclosed letter held by his aunt. Moreover, as Shirley Allen notes, the title, "Go Tell It on the Mountain," is ambiguous in its religious reference: "'Go tell it,' refers to the good news (gospel) that 'Jesus Christ is born' or to the message of Moses to the Pharaoh, 'Let my people go.' The ambiguity of the allusion in the title is intentional and also suggests the unity of Old Testament and New Testament faith that is characteristic of the Christian belief described in the novel."[85] The title of Baldwin's novel captures the paradox of John's condition as saved but still in bondage as a member of a group who continues to be oppressed.

Similarly Leo's complex situation is suggested in the mix of secular and religious associations in the title, *Tell Me How Long the Train's Been Gone*. As the main transportation north in the early twentieth century, the train came to represent escape, change, opportunity, and freedom. From the early blues, to Richard Wright's "Big Boy Leaves Home," to the movie *Clockers*, directed by Spike Lee (based on Richard Price's novel by the same name), the train carries a great deal of symbolic resonance in African American cultural expression. Indeed, the train plays a prominent role in Houston A. Baker Jr.'s blues theory of American literature, which he figures as the train at the crossroads.[86] The epigraph of *Tell Me How Long the Train's Been Gone*, which is the refrain of the spiritual, "Mary Had a Baby," also evokes the image of a departed train: "Never seen the like since I been born, / The people keep a-coming, / and the train's done gone." In its allusion to the story of Christ's birth, the subtitle signifies on the title of *Go Tell It on the Mountain*, suggesting the promise of "salvation" is yet to be fulfilled.[87] The title of *Tell Me how Long the Train's Been Gone* and the epigraph conflate secular and sacred meanings of train, as a vehicle of transportation and as a group of loyal disciples. Leo has clearly ridden the train of opportunity. He has been successful "against all the odds," but along the track he has lost his "train" (his followers); he is a prophet separated from the community. Success is a trap, as suggested by the title of book 1, "The House Nigger." As a spokesman for the Civil Rights movement, Leo has become superannuated by the younger, more militant generation, and he now finds himself under a double surveillance by the people and the police.[88] The title *Tell Me How Long the Train's Been*

Gone suggests Leo's difficult and divided relation to the black and white communities.

The two implied meanings of "train," as religious acolytes and as a vehicle for the pursuit of worldly opportunity, also represent a thematic movement from *Go Tell It on the Mountain* to *Tell Me How Long the Train's Been Gone* as Baldwin returns to an exploration of the black family and community in a more secular key. In many respects the story of the middle-aged Leo Proudhammer continues the story of the young John Grimes. From the innocence of youthful revelation to the experience of reaching maturity in a fallen world, John Grimes's dreams of the future become the reality of Leo Proudhammer's life. In part 1 of *Go Tell* John imagines himself to be a powerfully successful adult with a "Great Future." John's reflections are qualified by the narrator's quiet irony: "He might become a Great Leader of His People. John was not much interested in his people and still less in leading them anywhere, but the phrase so often repeated rose in his mind like a great brass gate, opening outward for him on a world where people did not live in the darkness of his father's house."[89] John imagines himself in various roles, as "a poet, or a college president, or a movie star,"[90] and later he climbs a hill in Central Park and imagines himself a "tyrant" conquering the city.[91] All of these images have intertextual referents in *Train*. Leo Proudhammer is fourteen, the same age as John Grimes, when he tells his older brother that he is going to be an actor.[92] Later in the day as the brothers walk along Broadway, Caleb asks if Leo will have his name on the great marquees:

> "Yes," I said. "I will. You wait and see."
> "Little Leo," said Caleb, "on the great white way."
> "It won't be so white," I said, "when I get through with it."[93]

About ten years later, Leo has his break in the experimental production of *The Corn Is Green* and is on his way to stardom: Leo becomes the movie star that John dreams of becoming. While Leo does not become a poet or a college president, he does become the combination of artist and public figure that John's fantasy suggests, and he does become a "leader of his people," albeit a reluctant and rather powerless one. The irony that one can somehow simultaneously "escape" and lead his people goes unrecognized by John Grimes, but not by Leo Proudhammer, who is acutely aware of the ways that success has distanced him from the people. Even as a young man Leo is a more politically astute version of John. Leo understands his family's problems as a result of racial and economic oppression, and, unlike John, he directs his anger outward at the landlords and the justice system.

The most striking intertextual moment linking Leo Proudhammer to John Grimes occurs near the end of *Tell Me How Long the Train's Been Gone*. Leo looks down at a panoramic view of San Francisco and reflects on his success in language that explicitly refigures John's vision of his future in part 1 of *Go Tell*. Standing on a hill in Central Park and looking down on opulent Fifth Avenue, John's vision of the city and his future role there is deeply divided. In his imagination the landscape takes on the shape of Christian myth. Is it the New Jerusalem beckoning or is it the City of Destruction?

> he felt like a long-awaited conqueror at whose feet flowers would be thrown, and before whom multitudes cried, Hosanna! He would be, of all, the mightiest, the most beloved, the Lord's anointed; and he would live in this shining city which his ancestors had seen with longing from far away. For it was his ...
>
> And still, on the summit of that hill he paused. He remembered the people he had seen in that city, whose eyes held no love for him.... Then he remembered his father and his mother, and all the arms stretched out to hold him back, to save him from this city where they said, his soul would find perdition.[94]

Midtown and Harlem: white and black; rich and poor; light and dark; broad and narrow; lost and saved; these are the boundaries of a physical and spiritual landscape that John must negotiate. For John the question is not will he conquer the city, but "what would his conquest of the city profit him on [judgment] day?"[95]

At the end of *Tell Me How Long the Train's Been Gone*, Leo Proudhammer, separated from John by a continent and a generation, answers the question:

> It was a beautiful, dark-blue, chilly night. We were on a height, and San Francisco unfurled beneath us, at our feet, like a many-colored scroll. I was leaving soon. I wished it were possible to stay. I had worked hard, hard, it certainly should have been possible by now for me to have a safe, quiet, comfortable life, a life I could devote to my work and to those I loved, without being bugged to death. But I knew it wasn't possible. There was a sense in which it certainly could be said that my endeavor had been for nothing. Indeed, I had conquered the city: but the city was stricken with the plague. Not in my lifetime would this plague end, and now, all that I most treasured, wine, talk, laughter, love, the embrace of a friend, the light in the eyes of a lover, the touch of a lover, that smell, that contest, that beautiful torment, and the mighty joy of

a good day's work, would have to be stolen, each moment lived as though it were the last, for my own mortality was not more certain than the storm that was rising to engulf us all.[96]

Leo at almost forty has conquered the city, but his conquest has profited him much less than he had hoped. Because the city is "stricken with the plague," he cannot enjoy the fruits of his labor, especially the domestic comforts of a stable private life that John Grimes imagined would result from worldly success. For Leo Proudhammer, who does not share (and explicitly rejects) John's evangelical tradition, the apocalyptic imagery is a metaphor for the escalating social and political turmoil resulting from the nation's continuing failure to address racism and its effects. Leo's apocalypse does not discriminate between the saved and the damned, but will "engulf us all." Leo may have "conquered" the city, but he is powerless to save it.

Just as Leo Proudhammer's story continues and revises the story of John Grimes, the Proudhammer family bears a revisionary relationship to the Grimes family. The initial description of the father, Mr. Proudhammer, in the opening pages of *Train* immediately reminds Baldwin's readers of Gabriel Grimes. Both men are characterized by a fierce pride at odds with their truly desperate and humiliating circumstances. Their pride, which isolates them from others in their community, is inherited as a burden and a challenge by their sons. Leo's father is "a ruined Barbados peasant, exiled in Harlem."

[He] brought with him from Barbados only black rum and a blacker pride, and magic incantations which neither healed nor saved. He did not understand the people among whom he found himself, for him they had no coherence, no stature and no pride. He came from a race which had been flourishing at the very dawn of the world—a race greater than Rome or Judea, mightier than Egypt—he came from a race of kings, kings who had never been taken in battle, kings who had never been slaves. He spoke to us of tribes and empires, battles, victories, and monarchs of whom we had never heard—they were not mentioned in our schoolbooks—and invested us with glories in which we felt more awkward than in the secondhand shoes we wore.... If our father was of royal blood and we were royal children, our father was certainly the only person in the world who knew it.[97]

Like Mr. Proudhammer, Gabriel Grimes also believed he was of "royal blood," although Gabriel received his authority from God. Gabriel believed that he was chosen, like Abraham, to father a line of royal descendants. It is

this conviction which causes him to reject his stepson, since John is not of his
seed, and to name his biological son "Royal." Mr. Proudhammer is clearly
a secular version of Gabriel Grimes; his pride and rage are based on a myth
of lost historical grandeur instead of the religious conviction that he is one
of God's elect. In fact, the Proudhammer family "had never gone to church,
for our father could not bear the sight of people on their knees."[98] While
John's illegitimate birth excludes him from his father's "royal" line, Leo is
biologically and, as his first name suggests, spiritually a Proudhammer. The
difference between the two fathers is important. By reconstructing Gabriel
as the secular Mr. Proudhammer, Baldwin writes a novel in which the son is
able to put the father's failures into perspective and finally bridge the chasm
that separates father and son.[99]

Throughout *Train* Mr. Proudhammer is never given a first name,
which suggests the diminished role he plays in Leo's life and in the text itself
compared to the role of Gabriel in John's life. In *Go Tell* the overwhelming
impact that Gabriel has on John is matched by the prominence of Gabriel's
story, which is the longest chapter, located in the center of the text. In contrast
Mr. Proudhammer is described briefly at a few key points in the novel. Often
drunk, angry, and emotionally absent, Proudhammer seems to have been
supplanted by his eldest son, Caleb, to whom Leo is fiercely attached. David
Leeming has argued that the Proudhammer family has autobiographical
significance, but, unlike the Grimes family, it is more "idealized than real."[100]
While it is true that the Proudhammers do have "rare joyful moments"
(one such moment occurs when Caleb and his mother waltz to a Calypso
tune),[101] Leeming's description of the Proudhammers as a "cohesive black
family" hardly seems supported by the text. Leo's memories of growing up
in Harlem are preoccupied by descriptions of separation and loss and the
disintegration of family life. Near the end of book 1, Leo recalls "our last
days as a family,"[102] days that precede Caleb's arrest. The father has been laid
off from work, they are evicted from their apartment, and Caleb quits school.
The mother, who holds the family together, brings home scraps from Miss
Anne's kitchen, which her proud husband refuses to eat. A shoe-shine box
and shopping bags become the "emblems of [Leo's] maturity" as he tries to
help his family out of desperate poverty.[103] Leo's family can neither protect
him nor provide models for his adult life: "I was very nearly lost because my
elders, through no fault of their own, had betrayed me. Perhaps I loved my
father, but I did not want to live his life. I did not want to become like him,
he was the living example of defeat."[104]

Some of the most poignant passages in the novel involve the
relationship between Leo and Caleb, which is developed through a series of
painful separations, reunions, and a reversal of roles in which Leo becomes

his older brother's protector and lover at one point. Leo loses Caleb three times: first when Caleb is arrested for a crime he didn't commit, second when he is drafted to serve in the World War II, and third when he converts to evangelical Christianity. The Leo–Caleb relationship is symbolic of Baldwin's critique of American racism, especially its assault on black men. It is not accidental that Leo loses Caleb to the three institutions that most frequently shape the lives of young black men, institutions which Baldwin believed continually perpetuated racism and denied black masculinity: the justice system, the army, and the church. Shattered by his experience in prison, and by his later experience in the army where he is betrayed by a white "friend," Caleb becomes afraid of his own rage and capacity for revenge. Burned twice and afraid of the fire, Caleb turns to the church for safety. While John Grimes's conversion to the Temple of the Fire Baptized is portrayed ambiguously, Caleb's conversion is not. John's conversion provides psychological and emotional advantages by joining him to his community and requiring the reluctant respect of his hostile father. But Caleb's conversion, viewed through his brother's eyes, is a psychological defeat. The old Caleb that Leo loved—warm, spontaneous, adventuresome—is gone for good. The new Caleb, like Gabriel in *Go Tell*, preaches a narrow, moralistic doctrine and judges others harshly. While prison and the army separated the brothers, Caleb's conversion to Christianity brings about an irreparable break in their relationship. In a reversal of *Go Tell*, Caleb's conversion also disappoints the father.

Caleb and Leo are foils; their lives evolve, suggesting different responses to poverty and racism. Both are actors—one in the pulpit and one on the stage. While Leo's life is the anomaly, Caleb's is more representative. Caleb, who doesn't think much of artists or their chaotic lifestyles, who refuses to attend Leo's first major performance, eventually becomes a respectable family man. Ironically, as Leo notes at the close of the novel, Caleb's family's respectability is underwritten by Leo's fame: "As we say in America, nothing succeeds like success—so much for the black or white, the related respectability."[105] But if Leo has lost a brother, he seems to have become his father's favorite son. The now-old Mr. Proudhammer resists his elder son's attempt to convert him: "in spite of the way Caleb went on at him about his soul, he never relented."[106] Mr. Proudhammer's black pride, his dream of ancient kingdoms, is redeemed by Christopher, Leo's militant young lover. The young man and the old man "spend hours together, reconstructing the black empires of the past, and plotting the demolition of the white empires of the present."[107] Baldwin brings the novel full circle by substituting Christopher for Caleb in a passage that repeats an earlier description of Caleb and his father: "They both looked very much like each other on those days—both big, both black, both laughing."[108]

In the last paragraph of the novel, Leo repeats this phrase; however, this time he is describing Christopher instead of Caleb: "Christopher and my father and I spent a day together, walking through Harlem. They looked very much like each other, both big, both black, both laughing."[109] By replacing Caleb, in Leo's affection and imagination, Christopher, as his Christian name implies, serves to restore Leo to a lost moment of familial harmony. Like Elisha in *Go Tell*, Christopher is a conduit for the protagonist's desire for a repaired relationship with the father and with an expressive black identity signified by the words, big, black, laughing.

The homoerotic subtext of John's attraction to Elisha in *Go Tell It on the Mountain* is made explicit in Leo's love for Caleb, and later for Christopher, in *Tell Me How Long the Train's Been Gone*. In *Train*, as in *Another Country*, homoerotic desire functions as a political intervention, occurring in contexts that demonstrate the ways in which American racial hierarchies have depended upon homophobic and misogynist discourses. In *Another Country*, Rufus's abuse of Leona is read as an effect of the pressures that a racist, sexist, and patriarchal culture have placed upon the black male body.[110] Rufus represses his homoerotic desires for fear of losing his already threatened manhood, but this repression causes him to reproduce the very cultural script of black masculinity that imprisons him. *Train* makes explicit the sexual dynamics of racism on the black male body in the story of Caleb on the southern prison farm, an episode that reads like a neoslave narrative, an iconography of American black male subjugation. Throughout his imprisonment Caleb is under the constant threat of rape by a white prison guard, Martin Howell, who verbally assaults Caleb, saying, "Nigger, if my balls was on your chin, where would my prick be."[111] Caleb responds by picking up a pitchfork to defend himself. Although he successfully resists Howell's sexual aggression, he is punished by being sent to the kitchen to do women's work. Howell again pursues Caleb, touching him on the behind in the kitchen and saying "something about my mama and my daddy."[112] Once again Caleb fights back and this time is banished to the cellar, where he again resists Howell's attempts to get him alone.[113] Caleb's long battle against sexual humiliation is figured as a battle for masculinity. Howell tries to turn Caleb into a woman: "I ain't my grandmother, I'm a man."[114] A debased feminine identity becomes the sign of the black male's subjugation by the white male. Although Caleb resists rape, he is still sent to the kitchen. Caleb's long struggle with Howell has left him beaten and hardened, alienating him from his family and from the possibility of intimacy with a woman. Leo says, "He was good to look at, good to dance with, probably good to sleep with; but he was no longer good for love. And certainly Caleb felt this, for in his dealings with the girls there was a note of brutality which I had never felt in him before."[115] Through

Caleb's story, Baldwin explicitly delineates the relationship between racial and sexual oppression, the white male's libidinal investment in the black male body, and the connection between the fear of homoerotic desire, the fear of a loss of masculinity, and the collapse of gender hierarchies.

While depictions of internalized homophobia and misogyny are not new to Baldwin's work, what is new and striking in *Tell Me How Long the Train's Been Gone* is Baldwin's willingness to posit intraracial, homoerotic love as a "solution" to the debasement of black masculinity and thereby directly challenge the homophobic discourse of black nationalism. Caleb's experience on a southern prison farm provides the historical ground for a black homophobia that identifies homosexuality as an act of white oppression and as a sign of black submission. When Caleb returns from prison, he is bitter, broken, and frightened. The once-admired older brother becomes, like the father, "an object lesson."[116] Leo, outraged at the way the white world has treated his brother, falls asleep dreaming of revenge and cursing an unjust God. But, less expectedly, Leo wakes struggling with sexual desire for his brother, and the dream of revenge dissolves into a passionate embrace as Leo and Caleb sexually consummate their brotherhood. The sexual episode between Leo and Caleb occurs in the very center of the text and marks Leo's transition to manhood; no longer the little brother, Leo wishes to care for Caleb. He remembers this experience as the first time he tried to give love and the first time he felt himself "to be present in the body of another person."[117] Leo, like other Baldwin protagonists, experiences self-recognition (or identity) as an intersubjective, loving act. When Leo comforts and then makes love to his brother, he is rescuing Caleb from the effects of racism. Caleb's masculinity and his family ties are restored (at least temporarily) through an act of brotherly intimacy. The restorative effects of this intimacy are revealed the following day in one of the rare happy family scenes and by the fact that Caleb tells his prison story later, as if his intimate relationship with Leo made it possible to confess his humiliation. By figuring an incestuous homosexual act as repairing the damage of white homosexual rape (or threatened rape), Baldwin is challenging the homophobia in the Black Nationalist movement that equated all homosexuality with signs of white oppression and internalized self-hatred.

By symbolizing Leo's transition to manhood with an incestuous and homosexual act, Baldwin challenges Freudian psychology (which dominated cultural understandings of homosexuality throughout the fifties and early sixties) that read homosexuality as evidence of an unresolved Oedipus complex, a sign of arrested development, and a failure of maturity.[118] Indeed, *Tell Me How Long the Train's Been Gone* makes a very bold intervention not only in the political discourses of its time, but in psychological and literary ones as well. Following the Freudian script, Leslie Fiedler reads the "boy" stories of classical American literature as homoerotic, which he interprets as an evasion of heterosexual love and a sign of cultural immaturity.[119] On the other hand, Baldwin suggests that the true sign of American immaturity is not to be found in its homosexual stories (coded or otherwise), but in the denial or—worse—the debasement of homoerotic desire. Unlike Rufus, Leo returns home, and unlike Rufus, opens "the unusual door,"[120] risks love, embraces his bisexuality, and finds his maturity, his manhood, in a troubled world.

NOTES

77. For example, the reviewer for *Time* stated that *Tell Me How Long the Train's Been Gone* "rambles like a milk train over the same run that Baldwin covered in *Another Country*, creaks over the same hard ground, sounds the same blast about the Negro's condition, rattles the same rationale for homosexuality" See "Milk Run," review of *Tell Me How Long the Train's Been Gone*, by James Baldwin, *Time*, 7 June 1968, 104. Also see Calvin C. Hermon's description of *Train* as "nothing but a reshuffling of the same old cards on the same old games" ("A Fiery Baptism," in *James Baldwin*, 119).

78. Campbell, *Talking at the Gates*, 228.

79. Baldwin, *Tell Me How Long the Train's Been Gone*, 108.

80. Ibid., 213.

81. Ibid., 209

82. Baker, "Embattled Craftsman," 40; James Baldwin, *The Fire Next Time* (New York: Dial, 1963), 141.

83. Following are the lyrics to "Go Tell It on de Mountains," in *Spirituals and Gospels*, 19. Originally copyrighted in 1975 by Dorsey Brothers Music Limited.

When I was a learner, I sought both night and day,
I ask the Lord to help me, An' He show me the way.
Go tell it on de mountains, O-ver de hills an' ev'ry where.
Go tell it on de mountains, Our Je-sus Christ is born.

* * *

He made me a watch-man, Up on the city wall,
An if I am a Christian, I am the least of all.
[Repeat: Go tell ...

* * *

While shepherds kept their watching, O'er wand'ring flock by night;
Behold! from out the heavens, There shone a holy light.
[Repeat: Go tell ...]

* * *

And lo! when they had seen it, They all bowed down and prayed;
Then travel'd on together, To where the babe was laid.
[Repeat: Go tell ...]

84. George D. Kelsey, "George D. Kelsey preaches and leads congregation in gospel music in Washington, D.C.," recorded 22 August 1948, Voice Library, M579 bd.2, Michigan State University, East Lansing, Mich.

85. Shirley Allen, "Religious Symbolism and Psychic Reality in Baldwin's *Go Tell It on the Mountain*," *CLAJ* 19 (December 1975): 175.

86. Houston A. Baker Jr., *Blues, Ideology, and Afro-American Literature: A Vernacular Theory* (Chicago: University of Chicago Press, 1984), 1–14.

87. Following are the lyrics to "Mary Had a Baby, Yes Lord," in Erskine Peters, ed., *Lyrics of the Afro-American Spiritual: A Documentary Collection* (Westport, Conn.: Greenwood, 1993), 28.

Yes, Lord!
Mary had a baby,
Yes, Lord!
Mary had a baby,
Yes, Lord!
The *people keep* a-coming
And the train done gone.

* * *

Mary had a baby,
Yes, Lord!
What did she name him?
She named him King Jesus,
She named him Mighty Counselor.
Where was he born?
Born in a manger
Yes, Lord.

* * *

Mary had a baby,
Yes, Lord!
The *people keep* a-coming
And the train done gone.

88. Baldwin, *Tell Me How Long the Train's Been Gone*, 368.

89. James Baldwin, *Go Tell It on the Mountain* (New York: Dial, 1953; New York: Laurel-Dell, 1985), 19.

90. Ibid.

91. Ibid, 33.

92. Baldwin, *Tell Me How Long the Train's Been Gone*, 171.

93. Ibid., 174

94. Baldwin, *Go Tell It on the Mountain*, 33.

95. Ibid., 34.

96. Baldwin, *Tell Me How Long the Train's Been Gone*, 366.

97. Ibid., 11–12.

98. Ibid, 170.

99. Calvin Hernton completely missed the revision of the father–son relationship in *Train*, claiming that "the obsession with the father comes across as nothing less than Patricidal Mania." See Hernton, "A Fiery Baptism," 188.

100. Leeming, *James Baldwin*, 280.

101. Baldwin, *Tell Me How Long the Train's Been Gone*, 165.

102. Ibid., 90

103. Ibid.

104. Ibid., 157.

105. Ibid., 370

106. Ibid., 335.

107. Ibid.

108. Ibid., 19.

109. Ibid., 370.

110. For an excellent analysis of Baldwin's depiction of the connection between racism and homophobia in *Another Country*, see Susan Feldman's "Another Look at *Another Country*: Reconciling Baldwin's Racial and Sexual Politics," in *Reviewing James Baldwin: Things Not Seen*, ed. D. Quentin Miller (Philadelphia: Temple University Press, 2000), 88–104.

111. Baldwin, *Tell Me How Long the Train's Been Gone*, 179.

112. Ibid., 182.

113. Ibid., 185–86.

114. Ibid., 180.

115. Ibid., 159.

116. Ibid., 157.

117. Ibid., 163.

118. For a critique of Freud's construction of homosexuality as immaturity, see Jonathan Ned Katz, *The Invention of Heterosexuality* (New York: Plume-Penguin, 1996), 73–79.

119. See especially Leslie Fiedler's "The Failure of Sentiment and the Evasion of Love," chapter 11 of *Love and Death in the American Novel*, rev. ed. (1966; New York: Third Scarborough Books Edition, 1982), 337–90.

120. The "unusual door" is Baldwin's metaphor for homoerotic love. In the introduction to *The Price of the Ticket: Collected Nonfiction, 1948–1985* (New York: St. Martin's and Marek, 1985) Baldwin describes the importance of his friendship with the black, homosexual artist Beauford Delaney: "*Lord, I was to hear Beauford sing, later, and for many years, open the unusual door*. My running buddy had sent me to the right one, and not a moment too soon" (x; italics in the original). Near the beginning of *Tell Me How Long the Train's Been Gone*, Leo imagines "how Christopher must have sometimes felt" and goes on discuss love as the doorway to the self: "And yet—one would prefer, after all, not to be locked out. One would prefer, merely, that the key unlocked a less stunningly unusual door" (7).

MARIO PUZO

His Cardboard Lovers

T ragedy calls out for a great artist, revolution for a true prophet. Six years ago James Baldwin predicted the black revolution that is now changing our society. His new novel, "Tell Me How Long the Train's Been Gone" is his attempt to recreate, as an artist this time, the tragic condition of the Negro in America. He has not been successful; this is a simpleminded, one-dimensional novel with mostly cardboard characters, a polemical rather than narrative tone, weak invention, and poor selection of incident. Individual scenes have people talking too much for what the author has to say and crucial events are "told" by one character to another rather than created. The construction of the novel is theatrical, tidily nailed into a predictable form.

It becomes clearer with each book he publishes that Baldwin's reputation is justified by his essays rather than his fiction. It may be that he is not a true or "born" novelist. But it must be said that his essays are as well written as any in our language; in them his thought and its utterance are nothing less than majestical. He has, also, the virtues of passion, serious intelligence and compassionate understanding of his fellow man. Yet it would seem that such gifts, enough for critics and moralists and other saintly figures, are not enough to insure the writing of good fiction. Novelists are born sinners and their salvation does not come so easily, and certainly the last role the artist should play is that of the prosecutor, the creator of a propaganda novel. A

From *The New York Times Book Review* June 23, 1968, p. 5. © 1968 by The New York Times Co.

propaganda novel may be socially valuable ("Grapes of Wrath," "Gentlemen's Agreement"), but it is not art.

"Tell Me How Long the Train's Been Gone" is written in the first-person singular, the "I" person, perhaps the most misused, most misunderstood technique today, from its irrelevance in Mailer's "The Deer Park" to its crippling effect on Styron's thought and style in "The Confessions of Nat Turner." It doesn't do Baldwin any good here because the "I" person should never be used in a novel of social protest, which this is. Why? Because it doesn't work.

To be specific, the "I" person should be used in either of two ways (geniuses are excused): either to narrow the focus, to let the main character telling the story filter everything through his own particular vision of the world and of himself; and to get away with it he has to be someone with a special vision—nutty or eccentric, not balanced. (Donleavy's "The Ginger Man" is a good example.) Or the "I" person should be a minor character telling us about a main character who is basically unexplainable and perhaps would be unbelievable if presented in the third person ("The Great Gatsby"). The best use of the "I" person is in Céline's "Death on the Installment Plan," where you get the wild "I" person observing a great romantic character in the balloonist-inventor-charlatan, Courtial des Pereires. Both are nutty and both are a treat.

What the "I" person cannot be is a bore, or a moralist in a straight-out polemical way. In Baldwin's book the "I" person hero is both. His name is Leo Proudhammer; he has risen from the slums of Harlem to become the most famous Negro actor in America and the opening chapter has him suffering a massive heart attack on stage. We get flashbacks covering his life while he is being given emergency first aid and then while he is recovering in the hospital. The flashbacks are done in thin theatrical fashion rather than novelistic technique, and this doesn't help.

The flashbacks showing Leo Proudhammer as a child growing up in Harlem are the most successful sections of the book. His alienated, bitterly religious father (who appears often with slight variations in Baldwin's fiction) and Leo's brother Caleb are the only characters who come alive. Leo loves Caleb, and when the white society humiliates Caleb, arrests and beats him before the younger brother's eyes, Leo is traumatized. When Caleb is released from prison and runs away to California, Leo feels deserted and the effect on him is disastrous. He succumbs to all the seductions of the ghetto streets and finally becomes the kept boy of a pimp-gangster. Fascinating material but Baldwin just tells us what happened to Leo in a few lines; he doesn't show us, doesn't create it. And this is exactly where the use of the "I" person technique could have been effective.

Still, the relationship between the two brothers is always moving and sometimes heartbreaking. The family life is honestly portrayed. Here in the streets of Harlem, in the dark bedrooms, the dangerous hallways, the chanting churches, Baldwin is at his best. Leo as a child is an interesting and alive character. Unfortunately, the novel next moves into the phony milieu of the theatrical world, and we get Leo as an important actor who muses that the kiss he plants on a nurse's forehead will probably keep her from washing. The theater as background for a serious novel so earnest in tone is simply not right. Not here anyway.

Leo is 19 years old when he escapes Harlem and moves to Greenwich Village, sharing living space with a young, white, unmarried couple. Barbara is a pretty girl, Kentucky bred; Jerry is an amiable fellow of Italian parentage. By this time Leo is bisexual, but his relationship with the young couple is completely innocent. All three of them are concerned only with becoming actors and they finagle their way into the strawhat dramatic workshop of a famous theater guru, whose characterization is done with deadly wit.

Inevitably, Barbara and Leo become lovers. Jerry is terribly hurt but understands. Barbara and Leo have their troubles with the natives of the strawhat village, and finally this and other pressures make them split up. They remain close friends as they climb the ladder of success. In fact, Barbara is on stage with Leo when he suffers his heart attack 20 years later, and she helps nurse him back to health.

Leo finally finds happiness with a young black militant named Christopher. Barbara seduces Christopher because she wants to recapture the young Leo (I think), Leo forgives them both (Christopher has an equally, classy excuse), and everybody remains friends and lovers. Christopher takes Leo to some black-power meetings and Leo agrees that the blacks must get guns. Finally Leo, completely recovered from his heart attack, is again in the wings waiting for his cue, ready for work he loves. Ready for life!

If this makes the book sound like soap opera, that's exactly right. White Barbara, white as snow, is right out of a slick magazine, flat as cardboard. At the end of the book Barbara tells Leo she has always loved him and will always continue to love him. Her lines are extravagant, theatrical; she will always come to him when he calls. Barbara gives this speech at the age of 39; she is rich, she is famous, she has been presented as a reasonably intelligent woman. She has known Leo for 20 years. And yet we are asked to believe that the only man in the whole world she can love forever is a Negro homosexual actor. This is a romantic condescension equal to anything in "Gone With the Wind," in that Baldwin does not recognize a parallel revolution, the feminine against the masculine world. In the conception of Barbara's character, in the undying-devotion speech, Baldwin glorifies a sexual Uncle Tom.

Baldwin's greatest weakness as a novelist is his selection or creation of incident. Time and again his conclusions are not justified by narrative action. Too many of his characters are mere cardboard. There are scenes that are simply echoes of the literature of the thirties, and they were cornball even then.

It is possible that Baldwin believes this is not tactically the time for art, that polemical fiction can help the Negro cause more, that art is too strong, too gamy a dish for a prophet to offer now. And so he gives us propagandistic fiction, a readable book with a positive social value. If this is what he wants, he has been successful. But perhaps it is now time for Baldwin to forget the black revolution and start worrying about himself as an artist, who is the ultimate revolutionary.

Chronology

1924	Born James Arthur Baldwin to Emma Berdis Jones on August 2 in Harlem, New York City.
1927	Emma Jones marries David Baldwin, a Pentecostal minister.
1936–1938	Baldwin attends Frederick Douglas Junior High School where he meets and is mentored by poet Countee Cullen.
1938–1942	Attends De Witt Clinton High School in the Bronx. There he edits the school literary magazine with Richard Avedon and Emile Capouya.
1938	Baldwin begins preaching in storefront churches.
1940	Meets artist and mentor Beauford Delaney, Greenwich Village.
1942	After high school Baldwin stops preaching and becomes a railroad worker.
1943	David Baldwin dies on August 1.
1943–1944	Baldwin enters a period of drifting and begins writing a novel, which becomes *Go Tell It on the Mountain*. He works odd jobs to help support his mother and siblings.
1944	Meets novelist Richard Wright.
1945	Wright helps Baldwin win a grant for his writing; Baldwin travels to upstate New York to write.
1947	Baldwin's first piece of professional writing is published in *The Nation*.

1948	Receives a fellowship and publishes "The Harlem Ghetto" in *Commentary*; moves to Paris in November.
1949	Publishes "Everybody's Protest Novel," effectively ending his relationship with Richard Wright.
1953	Publishes *Go Tell It on the Mountain*, to wide acclaim. The novel is nominated for the National Book Award. Travels around Europe.
1954	Part of *The Amen Corner* is published; receives Guggenheim Fellowship. Baldwin returns to America where he spends time in New York and Washington.
1955	*The Amen Corner* is produced and staged at Howard University. *Notes of A Native Son* is published. Baldwin returns to Europe.
1956	*Giovanni's Room* is published. Baldwin wins support from the *Partisan Review* and the National Institute of Arts and Letters; writes "Sonny's Blues;" meets Norman Mailer.
1957	Returns to United States and lives in New York; travels through the American South for the first time; meets many writers including Ashberry, Kerouac, and Styron.
1959	With Ford Foundation support, Baldwin returns to Paris.
1961	Publishes *Nobody Knows My Name* and meets Elijah Mohammed in Chicago. Baldwin finishes writing *Another Country* in Istanbul where he lives with friends.
1962	Publishes *Another Country*; travels to Africa. Baldwin becomes increasingly activity involved with Civil Rights movement.
1963	Publishes *The Fire Next Time* which becomes a best-seller.
1964	Publishes *Blues for Mister Charlie* and *Nothing Personal*.
1965	Publishes *Going to Meet the Man*; debates William F. Buckley at Cambridge University.
1966	Baldwin returns to Istanbul.
1968	Publishes *Tell Me How Long the Train's Been Gone*; moves to Hollywood to work on screenplay for *Autobiography of Malcolm X*.
1970s	Throughout the seventies, Baldwin takes lecture engagements, debates, and short-term teaching positions at universities. Appears on television several times.
1971	Publishes *A Rap on Race* with anthropologist Margaret Mead; returns to Paris.

1973	Publishes *A Dialogue* (with poet Nikki Giovanni).
1974	Publishes *If Beale Street Could Talk*.
1976	Publishes *The Devil Finds Work*.
1979	Publishes *Just Above My Head*.
1983	Suffers first of what will be several heart attacks.
1985	Publishes *Evidence of Things Unseen, The Price of the Ticket: Collected Nonfiction 1948-1985*, and *Jimmy's Blues: Selected Poems. Go Tell It on the Mountain* is adapted for television and broadcast on PBS.
1987	James Baldwin dies on December 1 while living in southern France.

Contributors

HAROLD BLOOM is Sterling Professor of the Humanities at Yale University. He is the author of 30 books, including *Shelley's Mythmaking*, *The Visionary Company*, *Blake's Apocalypse*, *Yeats*, *A Map of Misreading*, *Kabbalah and Criticism*, *Agon: Toward a Theory of Revisionism*, *The American Religion*, *The Western Canon*, and *Omens of Millennium: The Gnosis of Angels, Dreams, and Resurrection*. *The Anxiety of Influence* sets forth Professor Bloom's provocative theory of the literary relationships between the great writers and their predecessors. His most recent books include *Shakespeare: The Invention of the Human*, a 1998 National Book Award finalist, *How to Read and Why*, *Genius: A Mosaic of One Hundred Exemplary Creative Minds*, *Hamlet: Poem Unlimited*, *Where Shall Wisdom Be Found?*, and *Jesus and Yahweh: The Names Divine*. In 1999, Professor Bloom received the prestigious American Academy of Arts and Letters Gold Medal for Criticism. He has also received the International Prize of Catalonia, the Alfonso Reyes Prize of Mexico, and the Hans Christian Andersen Bicentennial Prize of Denmark.

HENRY LOUIS GATES, JR. is W.E.B. Du Bois Professor of the Humanities, Chair of African and African American Studies, and Director of the W.E.B. Du Bois Institute for Afro-American Research at Harvard University. He is the author of several works of literary criticism, including *Figures in Black: Words, Signs and the 'Racial' Self*; *The Signifying Monkey: A Theory of Afro-American Literary Criticism*; and *Loose Canons: Notes on the Culture Wars*.

NICK AARON FORD was a professor of English for many years at Morgan State College in Baltimore. He is considered a pioneer scholar and critic of African American letters. His books include *The Contemporary Negro Novel: A Study in Race Re*lations and *Black Insights*.

SHIRLEY S. ALLEN has written on James Baldwin as well as the role of women in the *Decameron*.

HORACE PORTER is the author of *Stealing Fire: The Art and Protest of James Baldwin and one of the editors of Call and Response: The Riverside Anthology of the African American Literary Tradition*. His most recent book is *Jazz Country: Ralph Ellison in America* published by the University of Iowa Press in 2001.

CAROLYN WEDIN SYLVANDER is the author of *Jessie Redmon Fauset, Black American Writer* and *James Baldwin*.

TRUDIER HARRIS is J. Carlyle Sitterson Professor of English at the University of North Carolina at Chapel Hill. Her books include *From Mammies to Militants: Domestics in Black American Literature, Exorcising Blackness: Historical and Literary Lynching and Burning Rituals, Black Women in the Fiction of James Baldwin, Fiction and Folklore: The Novels of Toni Morrison, The Power of the Porch: The Storyteller's Craft in Zora Neale Hurston, Gloria Naylor, and Randall Kenan, Saints, Sinners, Saviors: Strong Black Women in African American Literature*, and *South of Tradition: Essays on African American Literature*.

IRVING HOWE was a socialist political leader in the 1940s, founding editor of *Dissent* magazine, and co-founder of the Democratic Socialists of America. He was Distinguished Professor of Literature, City University of New York (CUNY) and a noted editor of Yiddish literature. His books include *A Margin of Hope, World of Our Fathers*, and *Socialism and America*.

JULIUS LESTER is Professor of Judaic Studies, English, and History at the University of Massachusetts. He has published 34 books, more than two hundred essays and reviews, recorded two albums of original songs, hosted and produced a radio show on WBAI-FM in New York City for eight years, and hosted a live television show on WNET in New York for two years.

DAVID LEEMING is the author of *James Baldwin: A Biography*, and *Amazing Grace: A Life of Beauford Delaney*. His many books on mythology focus on the role of myth in shaping the vision and identity of cultures and communities. From early 1963 until mid-1967, Leeming worked for James Baldwin as his secretary/assistant. Leeming is Professor Emeritus of English at the University of Connecticut.

JOHN M. REILLY has published criticism on the works of James Baldwin, Richard Wright, Ralph Ellison, and others.

RICHARD N. ALBERT is Associate Professor Emeritus of English at Illinois State University.

ARTHENIA BATES MILLICAN is the author of *Seeds Beneath the Snow: Vignettes from the South*, as well as numerous articles on African American literature.

MEL WATKINS, a former editor and writer for *The New York Times Book Review*, is the author of *Dancing with Strangers*, a Literary Guild Selection, and of the highly acclaimed *On the Real Side: A History of African American Comedy*.

LYNN ORILLA SCOTT is author of *James Baldwin's Later Fiction*, and editor, with Lovalerie King, of *New Essays on James Baldwin and Toni Morrison*.

MARIO PUZO is the author of eleven novels, the most famous of which is *The Godfather*, as well as two books of nonfiction.

Bibliography

Auger, Philip. *Native Sons in No Man's Land: Rewriting Afro-American Manhood in the Novels of Baldwin, Walker, Wideman, and Gaines.* New York: Garland Publishers, 2000.

Balfour, Katharine Lawrence. *The Evidence of Things Not Said: James Baldwin and the Promise of American Democracy.* Ithaca: Cornell University Press, 2001.

Bawer, Bruce. "Race and Art: The Career of James Baldwin." *New Criterion* 10:3 (1991):16–26.

Beavers, Herman. "Finding Common Ground: Ralph Ellison and James Baldwin." In *The Cambridge Companion to the African American Novel,* edited by Maryemma Graham, 189–202. Cambridge: Cambridge University Press, 2004.

Bell, George E. "The Dilemma of Love in *Go Tell It on the Mountain* and *Giovanni's Room,*" *CLA Journal* 17: 397–406.

Bloom, Harold, ed. *James Baldwin.* New York: Chelsea House, 1986.

Campbell, James. *Exiled in Paris: Richard Wright, James Baldwin, Samuel Beckett and Others on the Left Bank.* New York: Scribner, 1995.

Champion, Ernest A. *Mr. Baldwin, I Presume: James Baldwin—Chinua Achebe, A Meeting of the Minds.* Lanham: University Press of America, 1995.

Clark, Keith. *Black Manhood in James Baldwin, Ernest J. Gaines, and August Wilson.* Urbana: University of Illinois Press, 2002.

Cohen, William A. "Liberalism, Libido, Liberation: Baldwin's *Another Country.*" *Genders* 12 (1991): 1–21.

Cooper, Grace C. "Baldwin's Language: Reflection of African Roots." *MAWA Review* 5:2 (December 1990): 40–45.

Courage, Richard A. "James Baldwin's *Go Tell It on the Mountain*: Voices of a People." *CLA Journal* 32:4 (1989): 410–425.

Crawford, Margo. "The Reclamation of the Homoerotic as Spiritual in *Go Tell It on the Mountain*." *MAWA Review* 19:1 (June 2004): 26–38.

Csapó, Csaba. "Race, Religion and Sexuality in *Go Tell It on the Mountain*." *MAWA Review* 19:1 (June 2004): 71–89.

Cunningham, James. "Public and Private Rhetorical Modes in the Essays of James Baldwin." In *Essays on the Essay: Redefining the Genre*, edited by Alexander J. Butrym, 192–204. Athens: University of Georgia Press, 1989.

Davis, Nicholas K. "Go Tell It on the Stage: *Blues for Mister Charlie* as Dialectical Drama." *Journal of American Drama and Theatre*, 17:2 (Spring 2005): 30–42.

DeGout, Yasmin Y. "Dividing the Mind: Contradictory Portraits of Homoerotic Love in *Giovanni's Room*." *African American Review* 26:3 (Fall 1992): 425–435.

Eckman, Fern Marja. *The Furious Passage of James Baldwin*. New York: M. Evans, 1966.

Elman, Richard. "A Rap on Race." *The New York Times*, June 27, 1971.

Field, Douglas "Looking for Jimmy Baldwin: Sex, Piracy and Black Nationalist Fervor." *Callaloo: A Journal of African-American and African Arts and Letters* 27:2 (Spring 2004): 457–480.

Flemming, John. "In Short: Nonfiction." *The New York Times*, November 24, 1985.

Hardy, Clarence E. *James Baldwin's God: Sex, Hope, and Crisis in Black Holiness Culture*. Knoxville: University of Tennessee Press, 2003.

Harris, Trudier, ed. *New Essays on* Go Tell It on the Mountain. New York: Cambridge University Press, 1996.

———. *Black Women in the Fiction of James Baldwin*. Knoxville: University of Tennessee Press, 1985.

Henderson, Carol. "Reconciling the Spirit of the Father: James Baldwin's *Go Tell It on the Mountain*–50 Years Later." *MAWA Review* 19:1 (June 2004): 3–10.

Holmes, Carolyn L. "Reassessing African-American Literature through an Afrocentric Paradigm: Zora N. Hurston and James Baldwin." In *Language and Literature in the African-American Imagination* edited by Carol Aisha Blackshire-Belay, 37–51. Westport: Greenwood Press, 1992.

Jothiprakash, R. *Commitment as a Theme in African American Literature: A Study of James Baldwin and Ralph Ellison*. Bristol: Wyndham Hall Press, 1994.

Junker, Dave. "Gospel Memory and Afro-Modernism in *Go Tell It on the Mountain*." *MAWA Review* 19:1 (June 2004): 11–25.

Kinnamon, Kenneth. *James Baldwin: A Collection of Critical Essays*. New York: Prentice Hall, 1974.

Köllhofer, Jacob. *James Baldwin: His Place in American Literary History and His Reception in Europe*. Frankfurt am Main: Peter Lang Publishing, 1991.

Lee, Susanna. "The Jazz Harmonies of Connection and Disconnection in 'Sonny's Blues.'" *Genre: Forms of Discourse and Culture* 37:2 (Summer 2004): 285–300.

Leeming, David. *James Baldwin*. New York: Knopf, 1989.

Macebuh, Stanley. *James Baldwin: A Critical Study*. New York: The Third Press, 1973.

M'Baye, Babacar. "African Retentions in *Go Tell It on the Mountain*." *MAWA Review* 19:1 (June 2004): 90–104.

McBride, Dwight A., ed. *James Baldwin Now*. New York: New York University Press, 1999.

Miller, D. Quentin, ed. *Re-Viewing James Baldwin*. Philadelphia: Temple University Press, 2000.

Nagpal, B. R. "Baldwin's Black Vision: The Beyond." *Panjab University Research Bulletin* 20:1 (1989): 75–79.

Nash, Julie. "'A Terrifying Sacrament': James Baldwin's Use of Music in *Just Above My Head*." *MAWA Review* 7:2 (December 1992): 107–111.

Nelson, Emmanuel. "Critical Deviance: Homophobia and the Reception of James Baldwin's Fiction." *Journal of American Culture* 14:3 (Fall 1991): 91–96.

Newsome, Virginia. "Gabriel's Spaces in Baldwin's *Go Tell It on the Mountain*." *MAWA Review* 5:2 (December 1990): 35–39.

Norman, Brian. "Reading a 'Closet Screenplay': Hollywood, James Baldwin's Malcolms, and the Threat of Historical Irrelevance." *African American Review* 39:1/2 (2005): 103–118.

O'Daniel, Therman B. *James Baldwin: A Critical Evaluation*. Washington, D.C.: Howard University Press, 1977.

Onyeberechi, Sydney. "Satiric Candor in *The Fire Next Time*." *MAWA Review* 5:2 (December 1990): 46–50.

Porter, Horace. *Stealing the Fire: The Art and Protest of James Baldwin*. Middletown: Wesleyan University Press, 1989.

Pratt, Louis H. *James Baldwin*. Boston: Twayne Publishing, 1978.

Puzo, Mario. "Tell Me How Long the Train's Been Gone." *The New York Times*, June 23, 1968.

Robertson, Patricia R. "Baldwin's 'Sonny's Blues': The Scapegoat Metaphor." *University of Mississippi Studies in English* 9 (1991): 189–198.

Rusk, Lauren. *The Life Writing of Otherness: Woolf, Baldwin, Kingston, and Winterson*. New York: Routledge, 2002.

Savery, Pancho. "Baldwin, Bebop, and 'Sonny's Blues.'" In *Understanding Others: Cultural and Cross-Cultural Studies and the Teaching of Literature*, edited by Joseph Trimmer and Tilly Warnock, 165–176. Urbana: National Council of Teachers of English, 1992.

Scott, Linda Jo. "James Baldwin and The Moveable Feast." *Michigan Academician* 24:2 (1992): 401–408.

Scott, Lynn Orilla. *Witness to the Journey: Jams Baldwin's Later Fiction*. East Lansing: Michigan State University Press, 2002.

Standley, Fred L. and Louis H, Pratt, ed. *Conversations with James Baldwin*. Jackson: University Press of Mississippi, 1989.

Standley, Fred L., and Nancy V. Burt. *Critical Essays on James Baldwin*. Boston: G. K. Hall & Co., 1988.

Sylvander, Carolyn Wedin. *James Baldwin*. New York: Ungar, 1980.

Troupe, Quincy. *James Baldwin: The Legacy*. New York: Simon and Schuster, 1989.

Washington, Bryan R. *The Politics of Exile: Ideology in Henry James, F. Scott Fitzgerald, and James Baldwin*. Boston: Northeastern University Press, 1995.

Warren, Nagueyalti. "The Substance of Things Hoped For: Faith in *Go Tell It on the Mountain* and *Just above My Head*." *Obsidian* 7:1/2 (1992): 19–32.

Watkins, Mel. "An Appreciation." In *James Baldwin: The Legacy*, edited by Quincy Troupe, 107–123. New York: Simon and Schuster, 1989.

Acknowledgments

"The Fire Last Time" by Henry Louis Gates, Jr. From *The New Republic*, Vol. 206, No. 22, June 1, 1992, pp. 37–43. © 1992 by *The New Republic*. Reprinted with permission.

Nick Aaron Ford, "The Evolution of James Baldwin as Essayist" from *James Baldwin: A Critical Evaluation*, edited by Therman B. O'Daniel. Copyright © 1977 by Howard University Press. Reprinted with the permission of the publishers, c/o The Permissions Company, www.permissionscompany.com.

Shirley S. Allen, "The Ironic Voice in Baldwin's 'Go Tell It on the Mountain'" from *James Baldwin: A Critical Evaluation*, edited by Therman B. O'Daniel. Copyright © 1977 by Howard University Press. Reprinted with the permission of the publishers, c/o The Permissions Company, www.permissionscompany.com.

"The South in *Go Tell It on the Mountain*: Baldwin's Personal Confrontation" by Horace Porter. From *New Essays on Go Tell It on the Mountain*, Trudier Harris, ed., pp. 59–75. © 1996 by Cambridge University Press. Reprinted with permission of the Cambridge University Press.

Porter, Horace (pp. 23–37) from *Stealing the Fire: The Art and Protest of James Baldwin* (Wesleyan University Press, 1989). © 1989 by Horace Porter and reprinted by permission of Wesleyan University Press.

"'Making Love in the Midst of Mirrors': *Giovanni's Room* and *Another Country*" by Carolyn Wedin Sylvander. From *James Baldwin*, pp. 45–66. © 1980 by Frederick Ungar Publishing Co., Inc. Reprinted by permission of The Continuum International Publishing Group.

Chapter Three, "The Exorcising Medium: *Another Country*" reprinted from *Black Women in the Fiction of James Baldwin* by Trudier Harris. Copyright © 1985 by the University of Tennessee Press. Reprinted with permission.

"A Protest of His Own" by Irving Howe. From *The New York Times*, July 2, 1961. © 1961 by The New York Times Co. Reprinted with permission.

"Some Tickets Are Better: The Mixed Achievement of James Baldwin" by Julius Lester. From *Critical Essays on James Baldwin*, Fred L. Standley and Nancy V. Burt, ed., pp. 244–250. Originally published in *Dissent* 33 (1986):189–192. © 1986 Julius Lester. Reprinted with permission.

"Africa and *The Fire Next Time*" by David Leeming. From *James Baldwin: A Biography*, pp. 207–215. © 1994 by David Leeming. Reprinted with permission.

John M. Reilly, "'Sonny's Blues': James Baldwin's Image of Black Community" from James Baldwin: A Critical Evaluation, edited by Therman B. O'Daniel. Copyright © 1977 by Howard University Press. Reprinted with the permission of the publishers, c/o The Permissions Company, www.permissionscompany.com.

"The Jazz-Blues Motif in James Baldwin's 'Sonny's Blues'" by Richard N. Albert. From *College Literature* Vol. XI, No. 2 (1984), pp. 178–185. © 1984 by West Chester University. Reprinted with permission.

Arthenia Bates Millican, "Fire as the Symbol of a Leadening Existence in 'Going to Meet the Man'" from James Baldwin: A Critical Evaluation, edited by Therman B. O'Daniel. Copyright © 1977 by Howard University Press. Reprinted with the permission of the publishers, c/o The Permissions Company, www.permissionscompany.com.

"The Fire Next Time This Time" by Mel Watkins. From *Critical Essays on James Baldwin*, Fred L. Standley and Nancy V. Burt, ed., pp. 232–238.

Originally published in *The New York Times Book Review*, 28 May 1972, 17–18. © 1986 The New York Times Co. Reprinted with permission.

Excerpt from "The Celebrity's Return," by Lynn Orilla Scott. From *James Baldwin's Later Fiction: Witness to the Journey*, pp. 48–61. © 2002 by Michigan State University Press. Reprinted with permission.

"His Cardboard Lovers" by Mario Puzo. From *The New York Times Book Review* June 23, 1968, p. 5. © 1968 by The New York Times Co. Reprinted with permission.

Index

Characters in literary works are indexed by first name (if any), followed by the name of the work in parentheses